W9-AUF-281

Teacher's Book

A RESOURCE FOR PLANNING AND TEACHING

Level 1.2

Senior Authors   J. David Cooper, John J. Pikulski

Authors   Kathryn H. Au, Margarita Calderón, Jacqueline C. Comas, Marjorie Y. Lipson, J. Sabrina Mims, Susan E. Page, Sheila W. Valencia, MaryEllen Vogt

Consultants   Dolores Malcom, Tina Saldivar, Shane Templeton

INVITATIONS TO LITERACY

Houghton Mifflin Company • Boston

Atlanta • Dallas • Geneva, Illinois • Palo Alto • Princeton

Literature Reviewers

Librarians: **Consuelo Harris,** Public Library of Cincinnati, Cincinnati, Ohio; **Sarah Jones,** Elko County Library, Elko, Nevada; **Maeve Visser Knoth,** Cambridge Public Library, Cambridge, Massachusetts; **Valerie Lennox,** Highlands Branch Library, Jacksonville, Florida; **Margaret Miles,** Central Library, Sacramento, California; **Danilta Nichols,** Fordham Library, New York, New York; **Patricia O'Malley,** Hartford Public Library, Hartford, Connecticut; **Rob Reid,** L.E. Phillips Memorial Public Library, Eau Claire, Wisconsin; **Mary Calletto Rife,** Kalamazoo Public Library, Kalamazoo, Michigan

Teachers: **Marilynn Bracelin,** Stewart School, Pinole, California; **Carmen del Hierro,** Lorenzo Loya Primary School, El Paso, Texas; **Carol Miles,** Cottonwood Creek Elementary School, Wasilla, Alaska; **Joanne Nicodemus,** Judd Elementary School, North Brunswick, New Jersey; **Karen B. Stuart,** Ashley Park Magnet School, Charlotte, North Carolina

Program Reviewers

Susan Bleecker, Mt. Jumbo School, Missoula, Montana; **Leslie Edwards,** Roy Clark Elementary School, Tulsa, Oklahoma; **Sue Mowery,** Butcher Elementary School, Lancaster, Pennsylvania; **Joanne Nicodemus,** Judd Elementary School, North Brunswick, New Jersey; **Mary Lauren Smidansky,** Fowler Elementary School, Atlanta, Georgia; **Mary Smith,** Tremont Elementary School, Upper Arlington, Ohio

Be a Writer Feature

Special thanks to the following teachers whose students' compositions appear in the Be a Writer features in this level:

Sabreen Akbar, William Blackstone Elementary School, Boston, Massachusetts; **Leslie Edwards,** Ray Clark Elementary School, Tulsa, Oklahoma; **Linda Vaile,** John F. Kennedy Elementary School, Green Bay, Wisconsin; **Ramona Wright,** Navy Point Elementary School, Pensacola, Florida.

Credits

Cover photography by Tracey Wheeler (t); Tony Scarpetta (b)

Photography: Tracey Wheeler Studio pp.T49, T73, T86, T133, T145, T197, T199

Banta Digital Group p. T199

Illustration: Piotr Kazmeric p. T49

Rick Rizzotto pp. T140, 141, T194, T195

Acknowledgments

"A Hippo Yawned," from *A Rumbudgin of Nonsense,* by Arnold Spilka. Copyright © 1970 by Arnold Spilka. Reprinted by permission of the author.

"The Hokey-Pokey," traditional.

"Miss Lucy Had a Baby," from *The Fun-to-Sing Songbook,* by Esther L. Nelson. Copyright © 1986 by Esther L. Nelson. Reprinted by permission of the author.

"Spaghetti! Spaghetti!" from *Rainy Rainy Saturday,* by Jack Prelutsky. Copyright © 1980 by Jack Prelutsky. Reprinted by permission of Greenwillow Books, a division of William Morrow & Company, Inc.

Special thanks to David E. Freeman and Yvonne S. Freeman for their contribution to the development of the instructional support for students acquiring English.

Printed in U.S.A.

ISBN: 0-395-79551-6

23456789-B-99 98 97

Bugs!

GETTING STARTED

INVITATIONS
TO LITERACY

ANTHOLOGY

SELECTION: Bugs!

by Patricia and Fredrick McKissack

A ROOKIE READER®

$2.95

BUGS!

By Patricia and Fredrick McKissack

Award-winning authors
- **Jane Addams Book Award**
- **Coretta Scott King Award**

Selection Summary

Have you ever seen a bug? Two children search for bugs. Where? They find bugs in trees, under rocks, and on leaves. They find big, fat, red bugs, and long, skinny, yellow bugs. Soon they learn that bugs are everywhere!

Lesson Planning Guide

	Skill/Strategy Instruction	Meeting Individual Needs	Lesson Resources
1 Introduce *the* Literature *Pacing: 1 day*	**Preparing to Read and Write** Warm-up, T4 Prior Knowledge/Background, T4 **Selection Vocabulary,** T5 • bugs • where • under • everywhere	**Other Choices for Building Background,** T5 **Students Acquiring English,** T5 **Extra Support,** T5	*Literacy Activity Book* Selection Vocabulary, p. 3 *Transparency* Selection Vocabulary, GS-1
2 Interact *with* Literature *Pacing: 1–3 days*	**Reading Strategies,** T8 Self-Question, T8, T9 Monitor, T8, T11 Predict/Infer, T8, T17 Think About Words, T8, T19 Evaluate, T8, T31 Summarize, T8, T33	**Choices for Reading,** T8 **Extra Support,** T25 **Students Acquiring English,** T27 **Challenge,** T32 **Minilessons** Self-Question, T9 Monitor, T11 Predict/Infer, T17 Think About Words, T19 Evaluate, T31 Summarize, T33	*Literacy Activity Book* Comprehension Check, p. 4 The Learning Company's new elementary writing center software

See page T47 for assessment options.

Getting Started kicks off Level 1.2 by giving children the chance to enjoy a good story and to practice reading for fluency. It also provides teachers an opportunity for informal observations of reading and writing and a chance to provide for any special needs.

Formal instruction begins with the first selection of The World Outside My Door. See page T51.

Introduce *the* Literature

Preparing to Read and Write

INTERACTIVE LEARNING

Warm-up

Creating a Word Web

Encourage children to talk about bugs they have seen. Ask them to tell about how the bugs moved and what size, color, and shape they were. Use children's responses to make a word web for *bugs*.

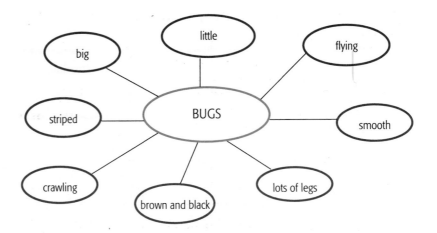

Prior Knowledge/Building Background

Key Concept
Bugs are everywhere

Continue the discussion of bugs by having children discuss places where they might look for bugs. Elicit from children that bugs are everywhere.

Invite children to draw pictures of bugs they have seen and the places where they have seen them. Encourage them to label their drawings. Post the drawings on a bulletin board titled *Bugs Everywhere*.

Managing Instruction

Reading Strategies

- At the beginning of and throughout each selection, children will be directed in thinking about various reading strategies.

- In this selection, minilessons are provided to give practice with each strategy. Use these as needed to help children learn the strategies.

Choices for Building Background

Selection Vocabulary

Key Words: *bugs, where, under, everywhere*

- Tell children that they are going to practice reading some words that appear in *Bugs!*

- Display Transparency GS–1 and read the sentences aloud, pointing out the underlined words.

- Discuss the meanings of the words with children, then have them practice identifying the words.

- Invite children to complete the last two sentences.

Vocabulary Practice Have children complete *Literacy Activity Book* page 3.

Count Out Loud

Students Acquiring English Help children review the numbers one through ten. Ask volunteers to count out loud as you write the number words on a chart or on the board. Then point to a number word and ask children to find that many objects in the classroom. For example, point to the number word *three* and ask a child to find and count out that many of something. The child may respond: "I see three chairs. One, two, three."

Bug Concentration

Extra Support Make a set of bug flash cards with two cards for each kind and number of bug. Invite children to play Bug Concentration by turning all the cards face down and then turning them over two at a time to find the matching cards.

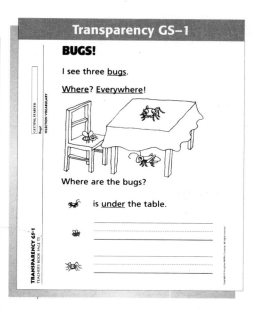

Interact
with
Literature

More About the Authors

Patricia and Fredrick McKissack were both born in Nashville, Tennessee, and grew up in the same small town. They had known each other for years, but it was not until they graduated from Tennessee State University that they married. Before writing children's books, they had both worked in other occupations. Fredrick McKissack had been in the Marines for three years and had owned a general contracting company. Patricia had been an English teacher and a book editor. They both found writing enjoyable and rewarding.

The McKissacks lived in the South during the 1960s, one of the most turbulent yet promising eras in United States history. They use their experiences during this decade as a foundation for their writings. Their goal is to make the past come alive for young readers. "The reason that we write for children," Fred said, "is to tell them about these things and to get them to internalize the information, to feel just a little of the hurt, the tremendous amount of hurt and sadness that racism and discrimination cause—for all people, regardless of race."

Patricia and Fredrick have collaborated on over one hundred books for children, including *Look What You've Done Now; Country Mouse and City Mouse; The Little Red Hen;* and *Abram, Abram, Where Are We Going?* The McKissacks currently live in Saint Louis, Missouri, with their children Fredrick Lemuel and twins Robert and John.

Meet Patricia and Fredrick McKissack

Patricia and Fredrick McKissack have worked together on almost one hundred books. Most of their books are about people. Mr. and Mrs. McKissack also like to work in their garden. That might be where they got the idea to write about bugs!

10

Bugs.

11

Interact *with* Literature

Reading Strategies

▶ **Predict/Infer**
Monitor
Think About Words
Self-Question
Evaluate
Summarize

Teacher Modeling Model how good readers use strategies before, during, and after reading.

Think Aloud

Before I read, I'll look at the pictures and make predictions about the selection. I'll also ask myself questions about it. As I read, I'll stop once in a while to check my predictions and to make new ones. I'll also look for answers to my questions and I'll think about whether I have new questions.

If I don't understand something I read, I'll read parts again and look at the pictures. I can also ask for help when I need to. I'll also try to figure out new words by thinking about what makes sense and by using what I know about word parts and the sounds for letters. I'll look at the pictures for clues, too.

As I read and when I'm finished, I'll think about the important parts to remember. I'll also think about how I feel about the selection.

Predicting/Purpose Setting

Ask children to look at the cover, title, and first two pages of the selection. Have them predict what the selection is about and what they will find out as they read it.

Choices for Reading

Give students a choice or assign them a way to read the selection:

Cooperative Reading   **Independent Reading**

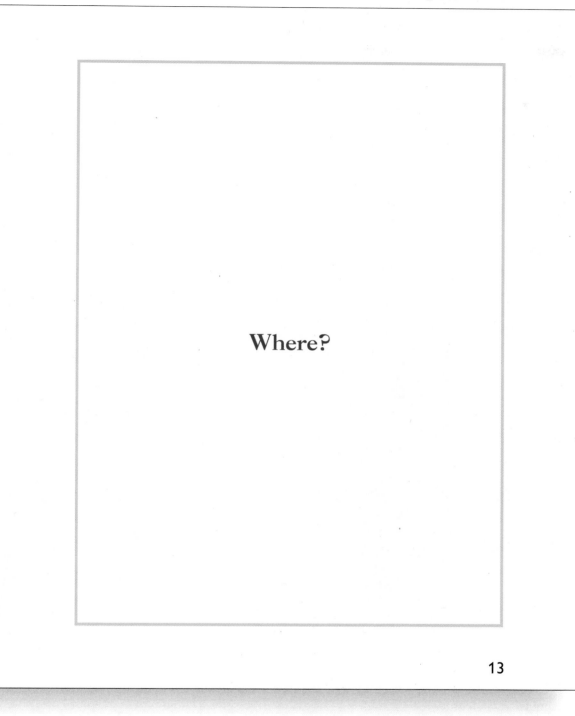

Where?

13

Self-Question

Teach/Model

Explain that sometimes readers have questions that they want to find the answers to as they read. Have children look at pages 12–13. As you model how to use the Self-Question strategy, record your questions on chart paper.

Think Aloud

I see a boy and a girl climbing on a fence. I ask myself, Where are they going? Are they looking for something? and What will they see? When I read these pages and the next pages I'll look for answers to my questions.

Read pages 12–19 with children. Ask volunteers to give answers to the questions you asked. Record the answers on chart paper.

Practice/Apply

Have children look at the rest of the pictures in the selection and pose questions. Read together to the end of the selection to find answers. Discuss which questions were answered and which were not.

Interact
with
Literature

Up here.

14

One fat red bug.

15

Monitor

Teach/Model

Explain that even good readers get confused once in a while. Discuss how rereading, looking at pictures, and asking for help can help children understand what they read. Then direct them to look at pages 14–15, and model for them how to use the Monitor strategy as they read.

Think Aloud

At first, I wondered what the boy and girl were doing. Then I noticed the bug on the apple and read the words and looked at the pictures again. I remembered that the boy and girl were trying to find out where bugs are. They are looking up at the fat red bug on the apple.

Practice/Apply

Read pages 18–19 and 26–27 with the children. Ask volunteers to tell what is happening in each scene. Discuss how rereading and looking at the pictures can help children understand what they read.

Interact
with
Literature

Bugs. Bugs.

Where?

17

Interact
with
Literature

Under here.

18

Two long, skinny, yellow bugs.

19

Interact
with
Literature

Bugs. Bugs. Bugs.

Where?

21

MINILESSON

Predict/Infer

Teach/Model

Read pages 11–21 aloud and model for children how to use the pattern of the story to predict that next the children will find three bugs.

Think Aloud

First I read the word *Bugs.* Then the children found one fat red bug. Then I read *Bugs. Bugs.* The children found two long, skinny, yellow bugs. I see that the children are finding more bugs on each page. On page 20, I read *Bugs. Bugs. Bugs.* I can predict that next the children will find three bugs. I can also predict that I will learn what color the bugs are.

Practice/Apply

Discuss with children how they can use the patterns of the selection and what they know about counting to predict what they will read on pages 24–27 and 28–31.

 Multicultural Link

Invite children to tell the class the words for *bugs, fat,* and *skinny,* as well as the words for various colors in their primary languages. Discuss any similarities between the words in English and other languages.

Interact
with
Literature

Over there.

22

Three fat, green bugs with two big eyes.

23

Think About Words

Teach/Model

Model for children how they could figure out the word *green* if they didn't know it already.

Think Aloud

What makes sense The sentence says *Three fat, _____ bugs with two big eyes.* The word tells something about the bugs. I think it names their color because so far the selection has always named the colors of the bugs.

Sounds for letters The word begins with *g.* What word begins with *g* and names a color?

Picture clues When I look at the picture, I see three green bugs. The word must be *green.*

Have children read the sentence aloud to see if *green* makes sense.

Practice/Apply

Have children find another word in the story and tell how they can use clues to figure it out.

Interact
with
Literature

Bugs. Bugs. Bugs. Bugs.

Where?

25

Interact
with
Literature

In here.

26

Four bugs with four hundred feet.

27

Interact *with* Literature

Bugs. Bugs. Bugs. Bugs. Bugs.

Informal Assessment

If you notice that children reading independently are having difficulty, suggest that they complete their reading cooperatively. Have partners take turns reading pages aloud.

Where?

29

QuickREFERENCE

Extra Support

MEETING INDIVIDUAL NEEDS

Ask children how many times the word *bugs* appears on page 28. Have them count the number aloud. Then have children turn to page 31. Ask them how many bugs they see.

Interact *with* Literature

Out there.

30

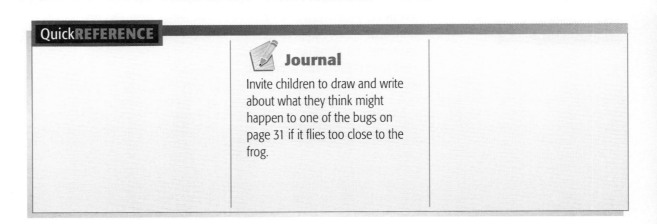

QuickREFERENCE

Journal

Invite children to draw and write about what they think might happen to one of the bugs on page 31 if it flies too close to the frog.

Five little bugs that fly here and there.

31

 Students Acquiring English

Have children demonstrate how to fly, hop, crawl, or scurry to various places around the classroom. Adapt the locations to fit your situation. Direct children to

- hop over there (designate the science center)

- fly up here (designate the top of a low table)

- scurry under here (designate a low table)

- crawl in here (designate a small area)

Interact
with
Literature

Bugs. Bugs.

32

Lots of bugs.

Interact
with
Literature

Where?
Where?

Evaluate

Teach/Model

Ask children whether they like the selection so far. Explain that thinking about what they like or don't like about a selection is an important part of reading. Have them turn to pages 34–35. Model the Evaluate strategy.

Think Aloud

I like this part of the story because it shows some interesting bugs. The boy and girl are having fun looking at all the bugs.

Practice/Apply

Ask volunteers to tell what they like or don't like about the selection. What parts of the selection do they think are interesting?

QuickREFERENCE

Visual Literacy

Have children page through the story and find the word *where* on pages 13, 17, 21, 25, 29, and 35. Ask how the word changes and why the authors might have chosen to have the word printed in bigger and bigger letters.

Interact
with
Literature

36

Self-Assessment

To encourage children to think about their reading, have them ask themselves these questions.

- Did I ask myself questions about the selection? Did I look for answers as I read?

- Were there any words I did not recognize? What did I do to figure them out?

- What else did I do as a good reader?

Quick REFERENCE

Challenge

Challenge children to name as many of the bugs pictured on page 36 as they can. Write the names on the board and help children to pronounce them.

MEETING INDIVIDUAL NEEDS

Everywhere!

37

Summarize

Teach/Model

Explain that children can help themselves remember the most important parts of a selection by telling what they learned from it. Model this with a Think Aloud.

Think Aloud

I learned that there are all kinds of bugs. There are red bugs, fat bugs, green bugs, yellow bugs, and skinny bugs. There are bugs in lots of places, too. The selection *Bugs!* is about finding lots of bugs everywhere you look.

Practice/Apply

Invite children to tell in their own words what they learned from the selection.

Background: FYI

Bugs really are everywhere. Bugs have been found in all environments, from frozen Antarctica to totally dark subterranean caverns.

2

Interact *with* Literature

More About the Illustrator

Fred Willingham

Fred Willingham was born and raised in Youngstown, Ohio. He graduated from the Art Institute of Pittsburgh, where he received an associates degree in Visual Communications. Mr. Willingham has been a freelance illustrator since 1987. His favorite media are pastels and air-brush. He is the illustrator of several children's books, including *Mae Jemison, A Hole in Harry's Pocket,* and *The Magic Quilt.* Mr. Willingham currently lives in Cleveland with his wife and their two daughters.

Meet Fred Willingham

Guess who helped Fred Willingham make the pictures for *Bugs!* It was Desirée, his seven-year-old daughter! She had fun modeling for her dad's drawings.

Mr. Willingham ▶ working on a pastel drawing for *Bugs!*

◀ Mr. Willingham with his daughter

38

Bug-a-Boo!

Make a mask, and pretend you're a bug. You can play hide-and-seek with your friends.

RESPONDING

39

Responding Activities

Personal Response

Ask children to draw or write about the part of the story they liked best or the bug they liked best.

Anthology Activity

Recall with children the different bugs in the story. Then invite them to create bug masks. Encourage children to use their imaginations to think of other bugs: blue bugs, spotted bugs, orange bugs, and so on.

QuickREFERENCE

MEETING INDIVIDUAL NEEDS **Challenge**

Take interested children outside to find live bugs. Put the bugs temporarily in a terrarium or large jar. Ask children to draw or write about their observations.

Home Connection

Invite children to draw a picture of a bug family to take home and share.

Informal Assessment

Use the Comprehension Check, the Literature Discussion, or the Guided Reading questions to assess children's general understanding of the story.

Additional Support:

• Reread any confusing sections aloud to help children understand the story.

Interact *with* Literature

Responding

Comprehension Check

To determine children's understanding of the story, use these questions and/or *Literacy Activity Book* page 4.

1. Can you tell me, using only one word, where bugs can be found? (everywhere)

2. Where are some places the children in the story found bugs? (on an apple, on top of a tree stump, on leaves, flying over a pond)

3. What kinds of bugs were in the story? (butterflies, ladybugs, centipedes, spiders, beetles, grasshoppers, caterpillars)

Literacy Activity Book, p. 4

Bugs. Bugs. Bugs.

Draw one place where the children saw bugs.

Write about it.

Getting Started

More Responding Activities

Bugs Crossing

Review with children where the bugs in the story were seen. Then have them create a mural to show the different places. Have some children paint on butcher paper large pictures of grass, leaves, rocks, tree stumps, and other places where bugs were seen. Then ask others to draw and cut out bugs to post on the mural. Display the mural on a bulletin board.

Bugs Crossing

Materials
- butcher paper
- paints
- construction paper
- scissors

Literature Discussion
Cooperative Learning

Divide the class into small groups to discuss the following questions:

- How were the bugs alike? How were they different?
- Which part of the story did you enjoy most? Explain why.
- What are some things you learned about bugs?

Shared Writing: *A Class Description*

- Ask children to look back at page 31 of the selection. Then ask what number comes after five. Brainstorm with children what a group of six bugs might look like. Together make a word web that describes the bugs.

- Ask volunteers to contribute sentences to a class description using the words from the web. Record their sentences on chart paper.

- Have volunteers draw and label pictures of the six bugs on the chart paper.

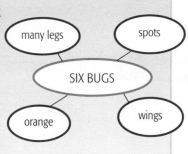

many legs · spots · SIX BUGS · orange · wings

More Responding Activities

Bugs Bugs

Invite pairs to play this game. One child holds up a number of fingers and the other child says "Bugs" to match the number. For example, if a child holds up three fingers, the other player would say "Bugs Bugs Bugs." Have pairs switch roles.

Bug Moves

Reread the story and invite volunteers to pretend to move like the bugs described. For example, when you read the words *Two long, skinny, yellow bugs,* have two volunteers act out how the two long, skinny bugs might move.

Clothespin Bugs

Take a picture walk through the story to review the many different types of bugs shown. Then invite children to follow these steps to make their own bugs.

- From construction paper, cut out eyes, multicolored wings, or other bug-body parts, such as an orange back for a ladybug.

- Glue the parts to the wood.

- Add legs made from pipe cleaners by inserting them through the middle of the clothespin.

Materials
- squeeze-type wooden clothes-pins
- construction paper
- pipe cleaners
- scissors
- glue

Portfolio Opportunity

- As a record of selection comprehension, save *Literacy Activity Book* page 4.

- As a writing sample, save children's Personal Response.

Selection Wrap-Up

ASSESSMENT

Reflecting/Self-Assessment

Make copies of the chart below to distribute to children. Then discuss what was easy for them and what was more difficult as they read the selection and completed the activities. Have children put a check mark under either *Easy* or *Hard*.

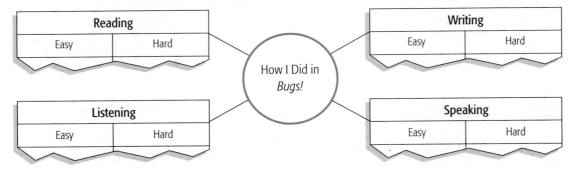

Reading	
Easy	Hard

Writing	
Easy	Hard

How I Did in *Bugs!*

Listening	
Easy	Hard

Speaking	
Easy	Hard

Monitoring Literacy Development

During the year, there will be many opportunities to observe and evaluate children's increasing literacy development. As children participate in literacy activities, note whether each child has a beginning understanding, a developing understanding, or a proficient understanding of the following concepts and knowledge. The Observation Checklist is included in the *Teacher's Assessment Handbook*.

Concepts of Print
- Understands that spoken language can be written
- Knows that print is read from top to bottom and left to right
- Understands the concept of a letter
- Understands the concept of a word
- Understands the concept of a sentence
- Matches spoken words to print

Book Knowledge
- Turns pages in sequence
- Moves from front to back of book

Decoding Behaviors
- Names letters
- Associates sounds with letters
- Uses context to anticipate missing words
- Uses letter-knowledge to decode
- Recognizes high-frequency words

Writing Behaviors
- Scribbling
- Drawings and scribblelike writing
- Letters and letterlike characters appearing
- Letters relating to speech; not matching sounds but syllables
- Letters matching with sounds in left-to-right order

Portfolio Opportunity

Tell children that they will be saving samples of their work throughout the year. Invite them to save one piece of work they did during *Bugs!* You may want to talk to children about creating collection folders and portfolios to hold their work.

The World Outside My Door

Table of Contents

THEME: The World Outside My Door

WATCH ME READ Books *PRACTICE FOR HIGH-FREQUENCY WORDS AND PHONICS SKILLS*

Our Plants
by Jeannie W. Berger

A Fish Trip
Margo Lemieux

A Walk in the City
by Tanner Ottley Gay

Each title is also available in black and white. This version includes a home activity.

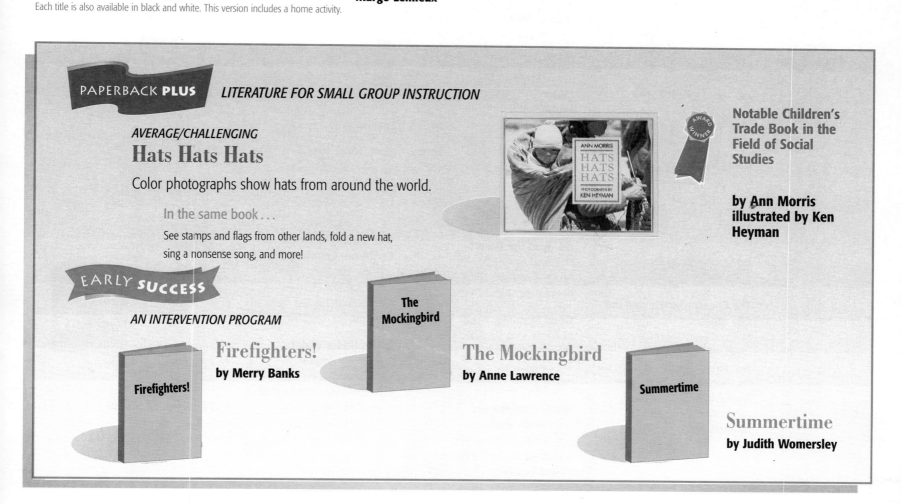

PAPERBACK PLUS *LITERATURE FOR SMALL GROUP INSTRUCTION*

AVERAGE/CHALLENGING

Hats Hats Hats

Color photographs show hats from around the world.

In the same book . . .

See stamps and flags from other lands, fold a new hat,
sing a nonsense song, and more!

Notable Children's
Trade Book in the
Field of Social
Studies

by **Ann Morris**
illustrated by **Ken Heyman**

EARLY SUCCESS

AN INTERVENTION PROGRAM

Firefighters!
by **Merry Banks**

The Mockingbird
by **Anne Lawrence**

Summertime
by **Judith Womersley**

Bibliography
Books for Independent Reading

 Multicultural

 Science/Health

 Math

 Social Studies

 Music

 Art

VERY EASY

Dots, Spots, Speckles, and Stripes
by Tana Hoban
Greenwillow 1987 (32p)
Readers discover patterns in unexpected places.

Truck
by Donald Crews
Greenwillow 1980 (32p)
Puffin 1985 paper
A truckload of tricycles journeys across the country.

Shadows and Reflections
by Tana Hoban
Greenwillow 1990 (32p)
Intriguing patterns encourage visual exploration.

At the Zoo
 by Douglas Florian
Greenwillow 1992 (32p)
An outing at the zoo is described in simple verse.

Going for a Walk
by Beatrice Schenk de Regniers
Harper 1993 (24p)
A little girl goes for a walk and finds a friend.

EASY

The Country Mouse and the City Mouse
by Patricia and Fred McKissack
Childrens 1985 (32p)
Two mice decide they like their own homes best in this classic story.
Available in Spanish as *El ratoncito del campo y el ratoncito de la ciudad.*

The Snowy Day
 by Ezra Jack Keats
Viking 1962 (32p) Puffin paper
An African American boy named Peter plays outside in the snow.
Available in Spanish as *Un dia de nieve.*

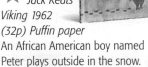

I Read Signs
by Tana Hoban
Greenwillow 1983 (32p)
Mulberry paper
Words identify familiar scenes.

Nature Walk
 by Douglas Florian
Greenwillow 1989 (32p)
A walk in the woods offers unexpected sights and sounds.

Like Me and You
by Raffi
Crown 1994 (32p)
This song about children all over the world emphasizes their similarities.

AVERAGE

A Day in the Desert
Willowisp 1994 (22p)
First-grade authors and illustrators describe the Mojave Desert.

Good Morning, Pond
by Alyssa Satin Capucilli
Hyperion 1994 (32p)
The creatures of a pond greet the morning.

Houses and Homes
by Ann Morris
Lothrop 1992 (28p)
A photographic look at houses around the world.

City Street
by Douglas Florian
Greenwillow 1990 (32p)
The city bustles with people and activity.

Bus Stops
by Taro Gomi
Chronicle 1988 (32p)
A bus follows its daily route through town, picking up and letting off passengers.

Elephants Aloft
by Kathi Appelt
Harcourt 1993 (40p)
Two elephants are off on a delightful balloon adventure.

The Trek
by Ann Jonas
Greenwillow 1985 (32p)
Mulberry paper
On a walk to school, a girl's imagination transforms the ordinary into the extraordinary. **Available in Spanish as *El trayecto.***

Hoot, Howl, Hiss
 by Michelle Koch
Greenwillow 1991 (24p)
Woods, farm, jungle, and mountains are alive with animal sounds.

One Smiling Grandma: A Caribbean Counting Book
by Ann Marie Linden
Dial 1992 (32p)
A girl explores the lush sights and sounds of her island home.

Otters Under Water
by Jim Arnosky
Putnam 1991 (32p)
Two otters play in the pond while their mother watches.

Sing a Song of People
by Lois Lenski
Little 1987 (32p)
A tremendous variety of people are busy in the city.

The Earth and I
by Frank Asch
Gulliver 1994 (32p)
A boy details his respect for the world around him.

Tools
by Ann Morris
Lothrop 1992 (32p)
This photo essay shows people around the world using tools in many ways.

Traffic: A Book of Opposites
by Betsy and Giulio Maestro
Crown 1991 (32p)
A little car makes a long journey home.

The Wild Woods
by Simon James
Candlewick 1993 (26p)
Jess and her grandfather follow a squirrel into the woods.

CHALLENGING

Have You Seen Trees?
by Joanne Oppenheim
Scholastic 1995 (32p)
A celebration of trees throughout the seasons.

I Am Eyes/Ni Macho
by Lelia Ward
Greenwillow 1978 (32p)
Scholastic 1987 paper
Waking in the morning, a girl in Kenya names things she sees.

Squish! A Wetland Walk
by Nancy Luenn
Atheneum 1994 (32p)
A child exuberantly explores the plant and animal life of a wetland.

Mr. Gumpy's Motorcar
by John Burningham
Crowell 1976 (32p)
Mr. Gumpy and a group of friends go out for a drive and run into trouble.

Our Yard Is Full of Birds
by Anne Rockwell
Macmillan 1992 (32p)
A boy observes the different birds in his yard through the changing seasons.

It Could Still Be Water
by Allan Fowler
Childrens 1992 (32p)
An exploration of the many forms and uses of water. **Available in Spanish as *Y aún podría ser agua.***

The Acorn's Story
by Valerie Greeley
Macmillan 1994 (32p)
In this circular story, an acorn grows into a mighty oak tree.

Away from Home
by Anita Lobel
Greenwillow 1994 (32p)
Take a grand journey in this round-the-world alphabet adventure.

Max Found Two Sticks
by Brian Pinkney
Simon 1994 (32p)
Max taps out the rhythms he hears around him.

Taking a Walk: A Book in Two Languages/Caminando: Un libro en dos lenguas
by Rebecca Emberley
Little 1990 (32p) 1994 paper
A walk through the neighborhood. **In English and Spanish.**

Wake Up, City
by Alvin Tresselt
Lothrop 1990 (32p)
Across the city, the morning sky brightens as the day begins.

Books for Teacher Read Aloud

This House Is Made of Mud
by Ken Buchanan
Northland 1994 (32p) paper
A poem celebrates a house and its surroundings. **In English and Spanish.**

All Eyes on the Pond
by Michael J. Rosen
Hyperion 1994 (32p)
Readers see a pond through the eyes of the creatures that live there.

The Little House
by Virginia Lee Burton
Houghton 1978 paper
A city moves closer and closer to a little house that was once in the country.

Where Are You Going, Manyoni?
by Catherine Stock
Morrow 1993 (32p)
Crossing the African veld on her way to school, Manyoni sees many interesting animals.

Country Fair
by Gail Gibbons
Little 1994 (32p)
A chronicle of the sights, sounds, and tastes of a country fair.

Books for Shared Reading

Polar Bear, Polar Bear, What Do You Hear?
by Bill Martin, Jr.
Holt 1991 (24p)
Zoo animals playfully tell about the other animal sounds they hear.

Who Is Tapping at My Window?
by A. G. Deming
Puffin 1994 (24p) paper
In this poem, Rain asks a variety of animals a question.

Does a Mouse Have a House?
by Anne Miranda
Bradbury 1994 (32p)

Rhyming verse tells where different animals make their homes.

Technology Resources

Software

C.D.'s Story Time Macintosh CD-ROM software. Houghton Mifflin Company.

"Friends Near and Far" CD: Consonant Clusters with *l* and *r*
"Animal Friends" CD: Noting Details

Writing Software The Learning Company's new elementary writing center. Macintosh or Windows software. The Learning Company®.

Internet See the Houghton Mifflin Internet resources for additional bibliographic entries and theme-related activities.

Teacher's Resource Disk Macintosh or Windows software. Houghton Mifflin Company.

Video Cassettes

Animals That Live in the City *Nat'l Geo*
Rain *by Peter Spier. Spoken Arts*
Where Animals Live *Nat'l Geo*
Your Town, Series 1 *Nat'l Geo*
Over in the Meadow *by John Langstaff. Weston Woods*

Audio Cassettes

Animals in the Desert *Nat'l Geo*
The Little House *by Virginia Lee Burton. Weston Woods*
On Market Street *by Anita Lobel. Am. Sch. Pub.*
Audio Tapes for The World Outside My Door. *Houghton Mifflin Company.*

Filmstrips

Mr. Gumpy's Motorcar *by John Burningham. Weston Woods*
The Snowy Day *by Ezra Jack Keats. Weston Woods*
Henry, the Explorer *by Mark Taylor. Weston Woods. Available in Spanish.*
A Tree Is Nice *by Janice May Udry. Weston Woods*

AV addresses are on pages H13–H14.

Theme at a Glance

| Selections | Reading | | | Writing and Language Arts |
	Comprehension Skills and Strategies	Vocabulary	Phonics	Writing
My River	✓ Text organization and summarizing, T61, T69, T74–T75 ✓ Making generalizations, T71 Reading strategies, T58, T62, T66, T72; **Responding, T73**	✓ High-frequency words, T80 ✓ Contractions with 's, T81 Bodies of water, T81	✓ Consonant clusters with r, T65, T76, T77 ✓ Clusters with l, s, T67 ✓ Think about words, T78–T79	Class story, T54 Names for places, T82–T83
The Blue Boat				
River Life				
Whose River Is This?				
Citybook	✓ Noting details, T125, T134–T135 Text organization and summarizing, T109; Reading strategies, T102, T108, T112, T114, T120, T126, T130 **Responding, T131–T133**	✓ High-frequency words, T99, T138 Word family: shop, T139 City words, T139	✓ Consonant clusters with l and s, T123, T136, T137 Clusters with r, T107 Base words and endings -s, -es, -ing, T127	More names for places, T140–T141
Reading-Writing Workshop **Be a Writer: My Neighborhood**				The world outside your door, T146–T147
Find the Signs				
Sunrise				
My Street Begins at My House				Letter, T157
Listen to the Desert/ Oye al desierto	✓ Making generalizations, T177, T188–T189; Noting details, T175; Reading strategies, T164, T168, T170, T172, T178, T184 **Responding, T186–T187**	✓ High-frequency words, T161, T192 Sense words, T193 Onomatopoeia, T193	✓ Consonant clusters review, T190, T191 Clusters with r, l, s, T181	Describing places, T194–T195
Desert Critter Fun Facts				
Sand Paintings				
Sleeping Outdoors, I Love the World				Letter to the world, T205 Poem, T205

✓ *Indicates Tested Skills.* See page T47 for assessment options.

Theme Concepts	Pacing	Multi-Age Classroom
People and animals live in many different environments.	This theme is designed to take 2 1/2 to 4 weeks, depending on your students' needs and interests.	This theme can be used in conjunction with themes found in other grade levels. Kindergarten: Going Places Grade 2: That's Incredible!

Cross-Curricular

Spelling	Grammar, Usage, and Mechanics	Listening and Speaking	Viewing	Content Areas and Study Skills
✔ Consonant clusters with *r*, T76, T77	Travel posters, T83	Persuasive speaking, T84 Sounds of the river, T84	Photographs and illustrations, T84	**Math:** making a Venn diagram, T86 **Art:** making a river scene, T86 **Social Studies:** planning a trip down the river, T87; locating rivers, T87 **Science:** how and why rivers flow, T88 **Creative Movement:** river dance, T88
				Art: experimenting with watercolor, T89
				Science: learning about river animals, T92
				Social Studies: recycling ideas, T94; stopping pollution, T95 **Art:** creating recipes for river animals, T95
✔ Consonant clusters with *l, s*, T136, T137	Business cards, T141	Giving a talk, T142 Sounds of the city, T142	Looking for signs, T142	**Social Studies:** making a photo or picture essay, T144; modes of transportation, T144 **Science:** using the five senses, T145 **Music:** singing traveling songs, T145
				Social Studies: making signs, T149; international road signs, T149
				Social Studies: comparing environments, T150
		Song rhythm, T154	Snapshots, T155	**Social Studies:** creating a neighborhood picture essay, T157
✔ Consonant clusters review, T190, T191	Adding *s* to *say*, T195	Echo-reading, T196 Demonstrate animal noises, T196	Desert colors, T196	**Science:** growing cactus plants from seeds, T198 **Math:** weighing sand, T199 **Art:** making colored sand bottles, T199 **Social Studies:** creating a desert relief map, T200 **Drama:** acting out *Listen to the Desert*, T200
				Art: making a desert display, T201
				✔ **Study Skill:** following directions, T203, H2
		Choral reading, T204		

Theme at a Glance **T45**

Meeting Individual Needs

Key to Meeting Individual Needs

Students Acquiring English

Activities and notes throughout the lesson plans offer strategies to help children understand the selections and lessons.

Challenge

Challenge activities and notes throughout the lesson plans suggest additional activities to stimulate critical and creative thinking.

Extra Support

Activities and notes throughout the lesson plans offer additional strategies to help children experience success.

Managing Instruction

Flexible Groups and Independent Work

When meeting with small flexible groups, simplify classroom management by keeping the meeting time short; a focused, well-paced lesson of fifteen minutes is often the optimum time frame. The rest of the students should be using this time for self-selected reading or self-selected writing.

For further information on this and other Managing Instruction topics, see the *Professional Development Handbook.*

PERFORMANCE STANDARDS

During this theme, children will

- *recognize that people and animals live in many different environments*
- *make predictions and evaluate them as they read*
- *apply comprehension skills: Text Organization and Summarizing, Noting Details, Making Generalizations*
- *decode and spell words having clusters with l, s, r*
- *build dioramas*
- *create silly characters together for a class story*

Students Acquiring English	Challenge	Extra Support
Develop Key Concepts Children focus on Key Concepts through picture comparisons and descriptions.	**Apply Critical Thinking Skills** Children engage in problem-solving activities as they read and make use of map keys, investigate the growth of cactus plants, and compare and contrast cities.	**Receive Increased Instructional Time** Background-building suggestions give children time to explore concepts related to the literature. Minilessons provide individualized instruction.
Expand Vocabulary Opportunities for expanding vocabulary include using context clues, discussing meanings, and modeling definitions. Children also use word webs, graphic organizers, and other tools.	**Explore Topics of Interest** The literature in this theme serves as a springboard for independent research on cities, deserts, and geography.	**Increase Independent Reading** Easy and engaging theme-related books in the classroom motivate children to self-select independent reading. (See Launch, T48–T49; Bibliography, T42–T43.) Children may also take home the black-and-white versions of the WATCH ME READ titles to read.
Negotiate Meaning in Conversation Opportunities for checking understanding and personalizing conversation arise as children prepare class presentations and join in group discussions.	**Engage in Creative Thinking** Opportunities for creative expression include writing rhyming couplets and imagining unusual animals.	

Additional Resources

Invitaciones
Develop bi-literacy with this integrated reading/language arts program in Spanish. Provides authentic literature and real-world resources from Spanish-speaking cultures.

Language Support
Translations of Big Books in Chinese, Hmong, Khmer, and Vietnamese. *Teacher's Booklet* provides instructional support in English.

Students Acquiring English Handbook
Guidelines, strategies, and additional instruction for students acquiring English.

Extra Support Handbook
Additional theme, skill, and language support.

Early Success: An Intervention Program
Additional instructional support for at-risk students in a small-group setting. Includes little books and daily lesson plans, plus a consumable book of take-home story summaries.

Writing Software
The Learning Company's new elementary writing center software.

Planning for Assessment

Informal Assessment

Informal Assessment Checklist

- Reading and Responding
- Text Organization and Summarizing; Noting Details; Making Generalizations
- Writing Skills
- Phonics and Spelling
- Phonics/Decoding
- Listening and Speaking
- Attitudes and Habits

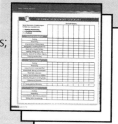

Literacy Activity Book

- Comprehension Check, pp. 17, 29
- Comprehension Skills, pp. 5, 18, 30
- Language and Writing, pp. 14, 25, 37
- Phonics and Spelling, pp. 7–10, 19–22, 31–34

Performance Assessment

- Many Homes, p. T206
- Scoring Rubric, p. T206

Retellings—Oral/Written

- *Teacher's Assessment Handbook*

Formal Assessment

Integrated Theme Test

This test may be given after completing the themes The World Outside My Door and Get the Giggles. The combined test applies the following theme skills to a new reading selection:

- Reading Strategies
- Comprehension Skills
- Clusters with *r, l,* and *s*
- Writing Fluency
- Self-Assessment

Integrated Theme Test

Theme Skills Test

- Text Organization and Summarizing; Noting Details; Making Generalizations
- Clusters with *r, l,* and *s*
- High-Frequency Words
- Study Skills

Theme Skills Test

Managing Assessment

Work Samples

Question: How can I manage all the work samples I gather to assess my class?

Answer: Try these management tips:

- Don't try to save everything. Determine what areas are most important to assess, and gather materials that show children's progress toward those goals.

- Be flexible. For some children a few samples may be all you need. For others, you may want to gather more information.

- Have children make theme collection folders to collect their work during the theme. Every two or three weeks, review the folders with children to make portfolio selections. Remaining work can be sent home.

For more information on this and other topics, see the *Teacher's Assessment Handbook*.

Portfolio Assessment

The portfolio icon signals portfolio opportunities throughout the theme.

Additional Portfolio Tips:

- Conferencing with Children, p. T207
- Sending Work Home, p. T207

Launching the Theme

INTERACTIVE LEARNING

See the Houghton Mifflin **Internet** resources for additional activities.

See the **Teacher's Resource Disk** for theme-related support material.

See the *Home/Community Connections Booklet* for theme-related materials.

Launching Activity

Where Am I Going?

Bring in three travel bags packed with items you might use when visiting the desert, a river, or the city. (Desert: hat, canteen, sunscreen; City: museum tickets, subway tokens; River: boots, net, snorkel)

- Introduce the theme title, The World Outside My Door. Tell children they will be learning about three kinds of places: rivers, cities, deserts.

- Tell children you packed for these places. Have them look in the travel bags and guess where you might be going with each one.

- Have children suggest questions about these three places. Record their questions on chart paper. Return to them throughout the theme to see if any have been answered.

Interactive Bulletin Board

Outside My Door

River   City   Desert

Outside My Door Help children create a display of the river, the city, and the desert.

- Have children leaf through the theme selections to gather information about the three settings.

- Then ask them to cut pictures from old magazines that tell about each setting.

- Divide a bulletin board into three sections and ask children to add their pictures accordingly.

Ongoing Project

Dioramas

Invite children to create dioramas of the settings they will learn about in this theme. Have each child choose a setting and begin to recreate that environment in a small shoebox. Children can use materials such as construction paper for backdrops and pop-up buildings; toy animals and paper cutouts for wildlife; and twigs, rocks, and sand for outdoor features. Children can add details to their dioramas throughout the theme.

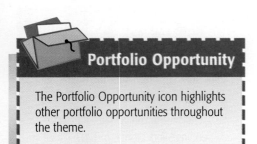

Portfolio Opportunity

The Portfolio Opportunity icon highlights other portfolio opportunities throughout the theme.

Choices for Centers

Creating Centers

Use these activities and materials to create learning centers in the classroom.

Phonics and Word Study

- Rhyming, T77
- Rhyme Time, T137
- Wisdom from Mother Goose, T191

Writing and Computer

- Habitat Books, T82
- Shared Writing: A Class Poem, T187
- Writing Post Cards, T194

Social Studies

Materials: map of the United States, construction paper, felt-tip markers, camera and film (optional), oak tag, crayons, scissors, stapler, string or yarn

- Locating Rivers, T87
- Getting from Here to There, T144
- Cities and Towns in Pictures, T144

Art

Materials: construction paper, paintbrushes, paste, tissue paper, liquid starch, clear plastic soda bottles, colored sand, funnels, plastic or paper cups

- A River Scene, T86
- Colored Sand Bottles, T199

BIG BOOK

SELECTION:
My River

Little Big Book Plus

Big Book Plus

- **Outstanding Science Trade Book for Children**
- **Child Study Children's Books of the Year**
- **Science Books and Films Best Children's Science Book**

by Shari Halpern

Other Books by the Author

Moving from One to Ten

Little Robin Redbreast: A Mother Goose Rhyme

What Shall We Do When We All Go Out?

Selection Summary

Whose river is this? The turtle, frog, fish, and eel each claim it is their river. But ducks, dragonflies, and many other animals live there, too. Vegetation needs the river to grow. Even people depend on the river. So whose river is it? It's everybody's river! We all need the river to live.

Lesson Planning Guide

	Skill/Strategy Instruction	Meeting Individual Needs	Lesson Resources
1 **Introduce** *the* **Literature** *Pacing: 1 day*	**Preparing to Read and Write** Warm-up, T52 Prior Knowledge/Background, T52 **High-Frequency Words,** T80 • do • here • it's • need • so • this • was • where	**Other Choices for Building Background,** T53	**Poster** Building Background, 3A
2 **Interact** *with* **Literature** *Pacing: 1–3 days*	**Shared Reading and Writing,** T54 **Reading Strategies** Monitor, T58, T66 Summarize, T58, T62, T72 Think About Words, T66 **Minilessons** ✓ Text Organization and Summarizing, T61, T69 ✓ Clusters with *r,* T65 Clusters with *l* and *s,* T67 Making Generalizations, T71	**Choices for Rereadings,** T55 **Choices for Reading,** T58 **Guided Reading,** T58, T60, T64, T68, T70 **Students Acquiring English,** T61, T72 **Extra Support,** T71 **Responding Choices,** T73	**Reading-Writing Workshop** The World Outside Your Door, T146–T147 **Sentence Strips,** 1–15 **Audio Tape** for The World Outside My Door: *My River* The Learning Company's new elementary writing center software
3 **Instruct** *and* **Integrate** *Pacing: 1–3 days*	**Comprehension** ✓ Text Organization and Summarizing, T74–T75 **Phonics and Spelling** ✓ Consonant Clusters with *r,* T76, T77 ✓ Think About Words, T78 Using Context, T79 **Vocabulary** ✓ High-Frequency Words, T80 Contractions with *'s,* T81 Bodies of Water, T81 **Language and Writing** Writing Names for Places, T82–T83 **Communication Activities,** T84 **Independent Reading & Writing,** T85 **Cross-Curricular Activities,** T86–T88	**Activity Choices/Reteaching** Text Organization and Summarizing, T75 **Activity Choices** Consonant Clusters, T76, T77 **Activity Choices** High-Frequency Words, T80 **Activity Choices** Language and Writing, T82–T83	**Reading-Writing Workshop** The World Outside Your Door, T146–T147 **Poster** Comprehension, 3B *Literacy Activity Book* Comprehension Skill, p. 5 Phonics and Spelling, pp. 7–10 High-Frequency Words, p. 11 Vocabulary Skill, p. 13 Language and Writing, p. 14 **Sentence Strips,** 1–15 **Audio Tape** for The World Outside My Door: *My River* The Learning Company's new elementary writing center software

✓ *Indicates Tested Skills. See page T47 for assessment options.*

1

Introduce *the* Literature

Preparing to Read and Write

This is the way we wash our clothes
Wash our clothes, wash our clothes.

This is the way we wash our clothes
So early in the morning.

... wash our face

... clean our hands

... bathe our dog

... brush our teeth

... mop the floor

... scrub the stairs

Warm-up

Sharing a Song　Invite children to make up verses for activities that involve using water and sing them to the tune of "The Mulberry Bush."

- Ask children what was necessary to do each of the activities they acted out. (water)

- Invite them to name other ways they use water every day.

- Ask if children know where the water they use at home comes from. Explain that it usually comes from rivers, wells, and lakes and not the salty oceans.

- Tell them that water is also very important to the plants and animals that live in and around rivers, lakes, ponds, and streams.

Prior Knowledge/Building Background

Key Concept
What a river is and what lives there

Show children the picture of the river on Poster 3A, and have them describe it. Also, encourage children who have seen rivers, lakes, ponds, and streams to share their experiences.

Have children draw things they see in and around the river on Poster 3A. Prompt them to think about

- what they see in the water

- what they see on the land around the water

- what they see in the air around the water

Help them label the things they draw. Tell children that they should look for things to add to their drawings as they read *My River*.

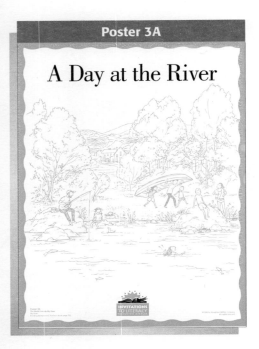

Poster 3A

A Day at the River

Other Choices for Building Background

Down by the River

Concept Development Invite children to look through books and magazines for pictures of rivers or river scenes. Encourage them to discuss the things they see in each picture. Have volunteers choose a picture they like and describe some of the sights, sounds, and smells they might find if they stepped inside the picture.

Quick-Write

Have children quick-draw a water scene and label all the things they might see there. Invite them to create oral or written stories based on their scenes.

Pronouns and Referents

Help children focus on the meaning of pronouns by holding up a book and asking:

> **Whose book is this?**

Help children rephrase, if necessary: Who does this book belong to? Be sure they know that *this* refers to the book at hand, as opposed to that book some distance away. Give the book to a child and help him or her form these sentences:

> I am (name).
> This is my book.
> It is mine.

Follow a similar procedure to help children understand the first-person plural pronouns, using these sentences:

> We are children.
> This is our book.
> It is ours.

Science

Teacher FactFile

More About Our Rivers

Share these facts about rivers with children:

- The Nile River in Africa is the longest river in the world (4,145 miles long).
- Rivers start as narrow streams called *rills*. Rills come together in wider brooks, which in turn meet to become deeper streams that flow into the river.
- The *mouth* of a river is where the river empties into a larger body of water.

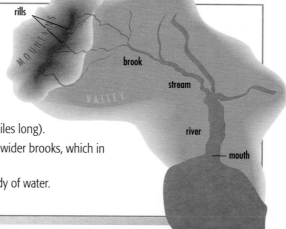

Interact *with* Literature

Shared Reading and Writing

BIG BOOK PLUS

Use the Big Book Plus for Shared Reading and Writing activities.

INTERACTIVE LEARNING

Shared Reading

Preview
- Show children *My River,* and read the title aloud. Explain that this selection gives factual information about things found around a river.

Predict/Infer
- Read aloud pages 4–11. Ask children to describe what they see.

Think Aloud

The story title tells me that the book is going to be about a river. The first page asks, *Whose river is this?* The next three pages show different animals that say the river belongs to them. I know from my own experiences that many other plants and animals need the water from rivers to live. I think we're going to find out what some of those other animals and plants are.

- Ask children what other animals and plants they might find in the book.

Read Together
Have children read with you to see which of their predictions match the story. Point to the words as you read and invite children to chime in. Allow time for questions and a brief discussion.

Personal Response
Have children think about all the things they saw in and around the river. Ask if they were surprised by any of those things. Encourage them to write and draw about how the story made them feel.

Shared Writing: *A Class Story*

duck's feet
turtle's shell
frog's legs
duck's tail
fish's eyes
dragonfly's wings

Prewriting
Invite children to invent silly river creatures by combining parts of several different river animals, such as a duck's feet, a frog's legs, and a dragonfly's wings. Record their ideas on chart paper. Have children choose their favorite ideas to combine into one creature.

Drafting
Have children name their creature. Have volunteers contribute oral sentences about what the creature looks like, what it eats, what sound it makes, and why it needs the river. Record children's sentences on chart paper.

Publishing
Have children create pictures of the silly creature to go with the sentences. Combine the pictures and the text into a booklet. Invite a volunteer to take the class on a picture walk through the book.

Listen and Read

 Audio Tape for The World Outside My Door: *My River*

 Extra Support Invite small groups of children to follow the words in the book *My River* as they listen to the Audio Tape. Encourage them to chime in with familiar words.

Cloze Reading

Cover the last word on each page of the story with a self-stick note. Read each page, pausing to let children supply the covered words. Children can check their responses by lifting the notes and reading the words underneath.

Choral Rereading

Invite children to do a choral rereading of the story. Have them read with you as they follow the words in the book. You may want to have volunteers make the sound or movement of each animal as it appears in the story.

Sentence Strips

Distribute Sentence Strips to children. Then, as you reread the selection aloud, have them re-create the story using the pocket chart. Children can rebuild the story sentence by sentence or page by page.

> **Whose river is this?**
>
> **It's my river.**
>
> **We *all* need the river!**
>
> **This river is mine.**

Exploring Language Patterns

- Help children recall the repeated pattern in the story.

  > It's _____ river.

- Have them use picture and word clues from pages 7, 8, 11, and 30 to find words that will fill in the blank. Each time children supply a word, write the complete sentence on the chalkboard.

- You may also want to work with the pattern found on pages 13 and 18.

  > This is _____.

 More Choices for Shared Writing

- Write a class song about the river.

- Write sentences about what the river might say if it could talk.

- Write a story about the sky. Use the pattern *It's my_____.*

Interact *with* **Literature**

More About the Author-Illustrator

Shari Halpern

Shari Halpern became a published author as a result of winning a contest when she was a student at Rhode Island School of Design. The contest was an assigned project about the importance of our rivers. Shari Halpern decided to write and illustrate a children's book about the issue. She was thrilled to find out not only that she was one of the winners but also that a publisher was interested in her book. She continued working on it, and eventually *My River* was published.

Since then, Shari Halpern has also written and illustrated *Moving from One to Ten, Little Robin Redbreast,* and *I Have a Pet.* She lives in Boston, Massachusetts, and says that her two cats, Fern and Ruby, sometimes appear in her books.

Meet Shari Halpern

Shari Halpern wrote *My River* when she was in art school. To get writing and drawing ideas, she visited the nearby Hudson River.

Shari Halpern, Age 7

"The river belongs to everyone, so I made that the theme of my book," says Ms. Halpern.

MY RIVER

by Shari Halpern

LITTLE BIG BOOK
PLUS

In the same book...
Learn more about river life from
a watercolor, photographs,
and a cleanup project!

Interact *with* Literature

Reading Strategies

▶ **Monitor**
Summarize

Teacher Modeling Talk with children about how good readers look for important information and stop once in a while to think about what they have read so far. If they can't remember important facts, or if they are confused about something, they can go back and reread or look at the illustrations. They can also ask others for help.

Think Aloud

I know from the title that *My River* is a book about a river. The first page asks a question: *Whose river is this?* As I read, I'll notice how the author answers this question. I'll also stop now and then to think about what I've learned about the river. If something doesn't make sense, I'll reread and look at the pictures.

Predicting/Purpose Setting

Invite children to reread the selection, looking for important information about the river. Tell them that they will be retelling the selection and ask them to think about ways to list the facts so they will be able to remember them.

Choices for Reading

Guided Reading

Have children read pages 4–11 to notice three different answers to the question *Whose river is this?* Follow up with the questions under Guided Reading on page T60.

Cooperative Reading

Have partners take turns reading sentences aloud. Remind them to stop now and then to discuss what they have learned so far about the river and to be sure they understand what they're reading.

Independent Reading

Help children preview pages 4–11 to establish the pattern and set some purposes for reading. Then have them read silently to the end to meet their purposes. Remind children to stop periodically to summarize what they've learned and to ask questions.

Whose river is <u>this</u>?

5

<u>It's</u> my river.

7

High-Frequency Words
this, it's

Have children find and read the word *this* and use it in oral sentences. Then have them find and read the word that is a shorter way to say *it is.* *(it's)* Ask what *it* refers to. (the river)

Concepts of Print

Punctuation Help children note the question mark at the end of the asking sentence on page 5 and the period at the end of the telling sentence on page 7. Remind them to use these marks in their own writing.

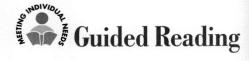

It's our river.

8

Comprehension/Critical Thinking

Ask children what they learned about the river from the words and the pictures in this part of the selection. Then ask the following questions:

1. Which animals said the river belonged to them? (the turtle and the frogs)

2. Which animals said the river belongs to everyone? (the fish)

3. Whose river do you think it is? Why?

Predicting/Purpose Setting

Remind children that they will be retelling the selection. Ask them to read pages 12–19 to notice what important information the words and pictures give on these pages. Use the questions on page T64 for discussion.

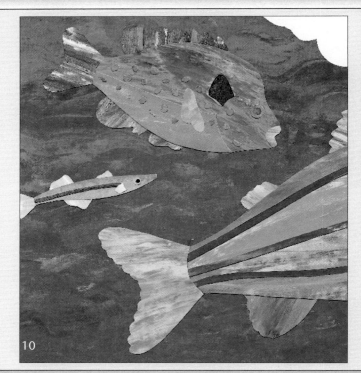

10

Informal Assessment

If children's responses indicate that they understand the selection, you may wish to have them finish reading it cooperatively or independently.

QuickREFERENCE

Concepts of Print

Exclamation Point Point to and name this punctuation mark on page 11. Explain that it means to read the sentence with a strong feeling of excitement. Mention to Spanish-speakers that they might see an inverted mark like this at the beginning of this sentence in Spanish.

Social Studies Link

Frogs live on every continent except Antarctica, but they are most numerous in tropical areas. Help children find these areas on a map or globe.

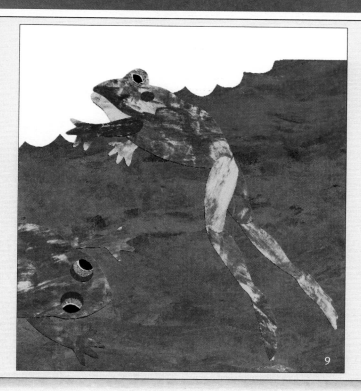

It's everyone's river!

Science Link

Discuss with children how frogs and fish are alike and different. Both are born in the water. Frogs, however, gradually develop lungs, which allow them to live on land and in the water. Fish must remain in the water.

MEETING INDIVIDUAL NEEDS
Students Acquiring English

Possessives Help children rephrase the sentence on page 11: *The river belongs to everyone!* Have children name things that belong to them. Give a sentence, using the possessive form of the child's name.

MINILESSON

Comprehension

Text Organization and Summarizing

Teach/Model

TESTED SKILL

Explain that book titles often tell us what books are about. Display the cover of *Pumpkin Pumpkin*. Ask what the title tells readers about this story. (It's about a pumpkin.) Repeat this with *When This Box Is Full*.

Then ask children what they think *My River* is about. Write the words *The River* at the top of a piece of chart paper; explain that the river is the *topic* of the selection, or what it is about.

Next, have children reread the text up to page 11. Ask what the author wants us to know about the river. (It belongs to everyone.) Write children's suggestions on the chart. Then ask them how the author explained to us who needs the river. (She used pictures and had the plants and animals speak to us.)

> **The River**
> It belongs to everyone.

Practice/Apply

As you turn the pages of the book, have children suggest words for you to write on the chart that name the plants, animals, and people that need the river.

SKILL FINDER
Full lesson/Reteaching, pp. T74–T75; Themes 7, 10

Minilessons, pp. T69, T109

Interact *with* Literature

Reading Strategies

▶ **Summarize**

Model for children how to summarize the selection so far by identifying important information.

Think Aloud

I notice that different animals are answering the question, *Whose river is this?* So far, a turtle, some frogs, some fish, an eel, and two salamanders have answered. Each type of animal lives in or by the river.

12

14

QuickREFERENCE

Journal

Remind children to use their journals to write down any words they don't know or want to remember as they read or listen to the selection.

Background: FYI

Most fish live in either fresh water or salt water. The common eels of North America and Europe, however, leave their rivers and streams and migrate to the Sargasso Sea, where they breed, lay eggs, and die. Their larvae return to fresh water.

This is my home.

13

We live 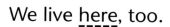here, too.

15

 Home Connection

Suggest that children watch nature specials on television with family members to find out more about animals and the habitats in which they live. Encourage children to work with a family member to draw or write about what they learned.

Phonics/Decoding Review

Hold up these letter cards one at a time: *h (here)*, *t (too)*, *l (live)*, *w (we)*. Have children find and read the word on page 15 that begins with each letter.

wa-1

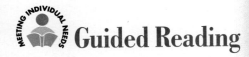

Interact *with* Literature

Guided Reading

Comprehension/Critical Thinking

Have children tell what important information they found on the pages they just read. Then ask the following questions:

1. Which animal said it was born here? (the dragonfly)

2. How are the living things on pages 18 and 19 different from the other ones you've read about so far? (They are plants. The others are all animals.)

Predicting /Purpose Setting

Have children read pages 20–27 to identify more important information they will need to remember to retell the selection. Use the questions on page T68 for discussion.

16

This is <u>where</u> we grow.

18

Self-Assessment

Ask children to think about their reading by asking themselves these questions:

- Was there anything so far that I didn't understand? What did I do to help myself?

- Have I been using the pictures to help myself understand what the words mean?

QuickREFERENCE

Science Link

Ask if children know the name of the insect shown on page 16. Explain that a dragonfly is an insect that eats other insects. A dragonfly has four gauzelike wings and six legs. It folds its legs together to form a basket in which to capture insects. Dragonflies are fast, flying up to eighty miles an hour. They lay their eggs in the water or on a water plant.

Math Link

Have children count the wings on each side of the dragonfly's body and write a number sentence about how many wings it has in all. (2 + 2 = 4)

I <u>was</u> born here.

17

19

Phonics/Decoding Review

_wA-1_

Say the following words. Have children identify the beginning letter and find the word on page 17 that begins with the same sound and letter: _boy_ (born), _will_ (was), _he_ (here).

High-Frequency Words
was, where

Have children find the words _was_ and _where,_ and discuss their meanings in this selection.

Phonics/Decoding
Clusters with _r_

Teach/Model

Write the word _dragonfly_ on the board and underline the cluster _dr._

Explain that when the letters _d_ and _r_ come together in a word, their sounds are so close together that they almost seem like one sound. Have children say _dragonfly_ and listen for the beginning sounds.

Tell children that _r_ is often paired with consonants. Begin a chart like the one shown below. Then, as you say some words that begin with _r_ clusters, have children repeat them and tell what two letters together stand for the beginning sounds. Enter the words on the chart. (Examples: _fruit, brown, draw, treat, grape, friend, grass, brook, draw, trial, branch, frog, drive_)

br	dr	fr	gr	tr

Practice/Apply

Print the sentences below on the board. Read them aloud, saying _blank_ for the underlined words and having children identify them.

> We went to the river and sat on the <u>bridge</u>. A <u>frog</u> jumped in the water. A deer came to <u>drink</u>.

Invite children to copy the sentences and complete the story, using words from the chart.

SKILL FINDER

Phonics and Spelling, pp. T76, T77, T190, T191

Minilessons, pp. T107, T181

Interact
with
Literature

LITTLE BIG BOOK
PLUS

Reading Strategies

 Monitor

Model for children what they can do if something they are reading doesn't make sense.

Think Aloud

The sentence on page 22 just says *So do we*. If I don't understand what that means, I can reread. Right before that, the muskrat says *I need the river*. When I read both sentences—*I need the river,* and *So do we*—I see that the water beetles are saying they need the river, too.

▶ **Think About Words**

Model how children could figure out the word *need* if they did not recognize it.

Think Aloud

- **What makes sense** So far, each new animal says something about the river. This sentence tells what the muskrat says about it: *I _____ the river*.

- **Sounds for letters** I see that the word begins with the sound for *n* and ends with the sound for *d*. What word has those sounds and makes sense?

- **Picture clues** The picture shows that the muskrat lives by the river. I think the muskrat needs the river. The word is probably *need*.

Have volunteers read the sentence aloud and discuss its meaning.

So do we.

22

Quick**REFERENCE**

Background: FYI

Muskrats are well adapted to living around ponds, streams, and rivers. They use their flattened tails to swim and steer through the water; their hind feet have stiff, weblike hairs on them. Muskrats eat mostly vegetation but may also eat shellfish.

Some water beetles spend their whole lives in the water while others stay only during their larval stage.

I <u>need</u> the river.

21

23

Technology Link

Talk with children about how they could find out more about rivers and what lives around them. Discuss computer sources, such as CD encyclopedias and on-line services. If either is available to you, show children how to research topics.

High-Frequency Words
need, so, do

Have children find and read the word on page 21 that means "must have." Call on volunteers to name things they need. Direct their attention to *so* and *do.* Help children note that they end with the same letter but not the same sound.

MINILESSON

Phonics/Decoding
Clusters with ₩A-1
l and *s*

Teach/Model

- Have children put their fingers on the stem of the cattail on page 18.

- Write *stem* on the board, underlining the letters *st.* Say *stem,* stressing the initial sounds.

- Point out that when two letters are side by side at the beginning of a word, such as *st* in *stem,* we say the sounds so close together that they almost seem to be one sound.

- Have children say *stem* with you several times and listen for the beginning sounds.

- Repeat the procedure with the word *plant.*

Practice/Apply

Have children name other words that begin with *pl.* List the words on chart paper and display the list on the Word Wall. Invite children to add illustrations.

pl
plant
play
please
plug
plow

SKILL FINDER

Phonics and Spelling, pp. T136, T137, T190, T191

Minilessons, pp. T123, T181

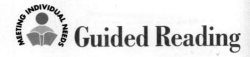

Interact *with* Literature

LITTLE BIG BOOK PLUS

24

This river is mine.

Comprehension/Critical Thinking

Discuss what important information children learned from the pages they just read. Then discuss these questions:

1. What did the creatures say about the river? (The muskrat and the water beetles said they need the river. The duck said they all need the river. The crayfish said the river belonged to it.)

2. Why do you think the river is so important to the plants and animals you've met so far?

Predicting/Purpose Setting

Have children read to the end of the story on page 31 to notice what other living things need the river. Use the questions on page T70 for discussion.

Informal Assessment

Oral Reading Use pages 20–27 to informally assess children's oral reading fluency. See the Oral Reading Checklist in the *Teacher's Assessment Handbook* for criteria.

QuickREFERENCE

Background: FYI

Crayfish are crustaceans. Their soft bodies are covered with hard shells like a suit of armor. They have ten legs—two with claws for grabbing and eight for walking.

Science Link

Have children compare and contrast the crayfish on this page with the bony fish on pages 10–11 and the eel on pages 12–13. What other kinds of bony fish and shellfish do children know about?

We *all* need the river!

25

27

Phonics/Decoding Review

WA-1

Have children look at pages 24–25, name the animal they see, and tell what letter that name begins with. (*duck, d*) Have children suggest other words that begin with the sound for *d*. Then review the sounds for initial *c, f, g, p,* and *r* by having children suggest animal names that begin with those letters. Discuss where each animal lives.

Comprehension

Text Organization and Summarizing

TESTED SKILL

Teach/Model

Look through the story together and have children review all the animals and plants that they read about. Then ask children how they would tell a friend about this story. Begin a chart with their ideas.

Think Aloud

I would want my friend to know that this book is about a river— that's the topic. I'll write that on the chart. I would also want to tell my friend that animals and plants and people need the river.

Ask children if they can think of a sentence that would tell about this story. If necessary, write a sentence frame such as the one shown on the chart next to *Main Idea*.

My River	
Topic	the river
Main Idea	*My River* is a book about a river that belongs to _____.

Help children use the information to summarize the selection.

Practice/Apply

Have children compose sentences for other stories they have heard or read. Have them choose one sentence to illustrate.

SKILL FINDER

Full lesson/Reteaching, pp. T74–T75; Themes 7, 10

Minilessons, pp. T61, T109

Interact *with* Literature

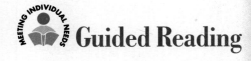

Guided Reading

Comprehension/Critical Thinking

Ask what two new living things children met on these pages. Then discuss the following questions:

1. What did the boy and girl say about the river? *(It's everyone's river!)*

2. What kinds of living things need the river? (people, animals, plants)

3. What might happen to these plants and animals if people don't take care of the river?

28

It's *everyone's* river!

30

Self-Assessment

Ask children where in the story they stopped to summarize what they read. Discuss what they did if they were confused or couldn't remember something important:

- Did they have to go back and reread something? What was it?

- How did the pictures help them?

QuickREFERENCE

Visual Literacy

Help children note that all the animals in the picture on pages 28–29 are ones they met before. Point to different plants and animals, and call on volunteers to name them and find the page on which they first met each.

Concepts of Print

Italic Type Ask children to find the words on pages 29 and 30 printed in slanted type. Remind them that words in this type should be said with more feeling. Call on volunteers to read aloud the sentences, stressing the words in italics.

Whose river is it?

Visual Literacy

Invite children to imitate the body and facial expressions of the children in the picture. Ask how they feel when they look like this. Talk about how to "read" different postures and facial expressions. Ask children to demonstrate examples.

MEETING INDIVIDUAL NEEDS
Extra Support

Oral Reading Model how to read the question on page 29 and the exclamation on page 30. Have children practice reading these sentences aloud, then team up with partners and take turns rereading the selection aloud.

Multi-Age Classrooms Pair an older child with a younger one. The older child can read a page and the younger one reread it. On another rereading, the younger child can read first, and the older one can help with word recognition.

Comprehension
Making Generalizations

Teach/Model

Ask children what they learned about rivers that they didn't know before they read this book. Then ask them: Whose job do you think the author would say it is to take care of the river? (everyone's)

Explain that taking care of rivers often means being sure that trash is not put in the water, because it might harm the animals that live there. Point out that the author didn't say everyone should keep the river clean, but we know from what she wrote that many living things use the river. That helps us know that she probably would tell everyone to take care of it.

Practice/Apply

Ask children what other rivers they know about. Then ask them: Whose job do you think the author would say it is to take care of those rivers? (everyone's)

SKILL FINDER

Full lesson/Reteaching, pp. T188–T189; Theme 8

Minilessons, p. T177

Interact *with* Literature

Reading Strategies

▶ **Summarize**

Have children recall the important information they have been noticing as they read the selection. Then explain that they don't need to remember everything shown on page 32 to retell the story; they can group similar objects. They can remember that the river is important to people, plants, and animals and then recall the specific ones they want to tell about.

 LITTLE BIG BOOK PLUS

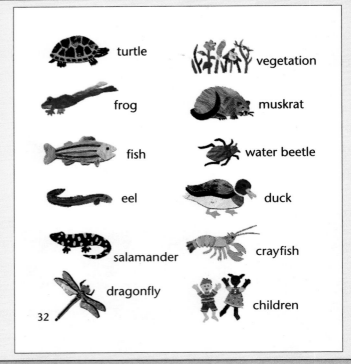

turtle

vegetation

frog

muskrat

fish

water beetle

eel

duck

salamander

crayfish

dragonfly

children

32

 Informal Assessment

Use the Guided Reading questions, the Literature Discussion, or the mural activity to assess children's general understanding of the selection.

Additional Support:

- Have children track the words, supplying any they know, as they listen to the Audio Tape for The World Outside My Door: *My River.*

- Reread aloud any sections children found confusing.

 Quick**REFERENCE**

 Students Acquiring English

Vocabulary Read the names of the labeled items on this page and let children name any they know in their first language. Encourage children to describe any experiences they may have had with the items.

Responding

Materials
- mural paper
- construction paper
- scissors
- paste

Environmental Mural

Divide the class into three groups. Invite one group to make cutouts of the people, plants, and animals shown in the story. Have another group of children create the background for the river scene. Ask the third group to write sentences about the river and cut them out. Have children add the cutouts to the background. Children can take a "river walk" along the completed mural, retelling the story as they go along.

It's everyone's river!

My Favorite Things

Invite children to create individual books about their own belongings. Have them draw pictures of their favorite things and write sentences about their choices. You might wish to provide a model from the story for children to copy and expand on: *This is my* _____.

Encourage children to share their books with the class.

Animal Acts

Extra Support Whisper the name of an animal, plant, or person from *My River* to a volunteer. Have the child use a combination of visual and oral clues to help classmates guess which river creature it is. For example, a child acting out the turtle might crawl slowly on all fours and say, "I carry my home on my back."

Literature Discussion

Cooperative Learning

Divide the class into small groups to discuss the following questions:

- What creatures depend on the river? Why?

- What are some things we can do to help take care of our rivers?

Portfolio Opportunity

For a writing sample, save children's work from the My Favorite Things activity.

Instruct and Integrate

Comprehension

Literacy Activity Book, p. 5

Name That Scene

✂ Cut and paste the picture that goes with each story. Write a name for each story. Then write a sentence to tell about it.

I plant seeds here.
The seeds grow.
The plants will grow big.

I run here.
I jump here.
I have a nice time here.

The World Outside My Door 5

Poster 3B

Story Title:

Topic:

Main Idea:

Details:

Informal Assessment

Listen to children talk as they work on the story structure activities. Observe which ones see the overall picture quickly and which ones have difficulty seeing through the details.

Additional Support:

Reteaching, p. T75

Text Organization and Summarizing

TESTED SKILL

LAB, p. 5

Teach/Model

Assign the roles of the animals, the plants, and the children in the selection, and have the class dramatize *My River* as you turn the pages. When the story ends, ask the players if their characters all felt important and why.

Display Poster 3B. On the chalkboard, write the words shown:

water   river   fish

Read the words with children, and ask which word best tells what the whole selection is about. *(river)* Explain that even though water and fish are important in the selection, they tell only about parts of it; the river is the *topic* of the whole selection, or what it is about. Write *The River* on the Poster in the Topic section.

Next, ask children to say some sentences that tell about the river in the story. Write them on the chalkboard and, with children, see if there is one sentence that best tells about the river in the story. (Sample answer: *It's everyone's river.*) Explain that this sentence tells the *main idea* of the whole selection. Record the sentence on the Poster in the Main Idea section.

Look through the book with children, helping them to recall all the characters and what they said about the river. Record these details in the last section on the Poster.

Practice/Apply

- Have children work in small groups. Give each group a copy of the graphic organizer on the Poster. Children can work together to review the selection *Bugs!* and identify the topic, main idea, and important details.

- Have children complete *Literacy Activity Book* page 5.

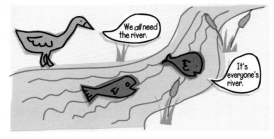

SKILL FINDER   Minilessons pp. T61, T69, T109

More Practice Activities

Name This Scene

Help children to find magazine or newspaper photos of scenes that show something happening. Have them cut out the scenes and paste them to sheets of art paper. Then have children brainstorm names for each scene. Write the names on the board and have the class choose the one that best tells about the scene. Write that title on a sentence strip for a volunteer to paste below the picture.

Materials
- old magazines or newspapers
- scissors
- paste
- art paper
- paper for sentence strip

A Famous Egg

Write the rhyme shown on the chalkboard. Show an illustration of Humpty Dumpty and read the rhyme with children.

Use questions such as these to help children understand the topic and main idea:

- What is the rhyme about? (an egg)

- What happened to the egg? (it broke)

- What does the author of that rhyme want us to know?
  (that you can't put a broken egg back together)

Humpty Dumpty sat on a wall
Humpty Dumpty had a great fall.
All the king's horses
And all the king's men
Couldn't put Humpty together again.

Reteaching

Text Organization and Summarizing

Read aloud the paragraph shown, asking children to listen for the main idea and the smaller ideas that go with it. Then discuss the topic (dragonflies and water beetles) and the main idea of the whole paragraph (how those insects are alike and different).

Dragonflies and water beetles are both insects. They both have six legs. And they both have feelers on their heads that help them hear and smell things. But only one of them can fly. That's the dragonfly.

Portfolio Opportunity

For a record of children's understanding of text organization and summarizing, save *Literacy Activity Book* page 5.

3

Instruct *and* Integrate

Phonics and Spelling

WA-1

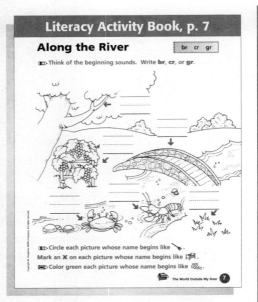

Informal Assessment

As children read new texts or work on these activities, listen for the ease with which they can decode words with beginning clusters.

Portfolio Opportunity Save *Literacy Activity Book* pp. 7–10 as a record.

I N T E R A C T I V E   L E A R N I N G

 TESTED SKILL

Consonant Clusters with *r*

LAB, pp. 7, 8

Reread page 18 in *My River* with children. Point to *grow,* and have children read it again and listen for the sounds for *g* and *r* together at the beginning.

Write the following on the board: crayfish, brown. Read *crayfish* for children. Ask them if they can explain why you've underlined two letters at the beginning of that word. (When we say *crayfish*, we say the letters *c* and *r* together so they are almost like one sound.) Repeat with the cluster *br* in *brown.* Remind children that *r* often appears together with other consonants in words.

Read the following riddles and ask children to think of answers that begin with sounds for *br, cr,* or *gr.* Then have children make up similar riddles.

- What color name rhymes with *seen?* (green)
- I'm thinking of a big black bird whose name rhymes with *grow.* (crow)
- What will a glass do if you drop it on the floor? (break)

Write the words *green, break,* and *crow* on the board and ask volunteers to use them in sentences.

Have children complete *Literacy Activity Book* pages 7, 8.

SKILL FINDER | Minilessons, pp. T65, T107, T181

More Practice Activities

Clusters for the Word Wall

Write the words *group, brother, crayon,* and *crowd* on the board and read them with children. Invite them to choose one word to write and illustrate.

Add an *r*

Display these puzzles. Explain that each word is missing the letter *r* from the letters that stand for its beginning sounds. Ask volunteers to fill in the missing *r* and read each word.

b_ush   b_oom
c_ib   c_ied
g_ay   g_eat

INTERACTIVE LEARNING

More Consonant Clusters with *r*

LAB, pp. 9, 10

Reread page 32 in *My River* with children. Using a self-stick note, cover the *fr* in *frog.* Then ask children to say the word and tell what's missing.

Write the following words on the board, underlining the beginning sounds: *dragonfly, trail.* Read *dragonfly* for children. Ask them to tell how the first two letters sound when they read them together at the beginning of the word; you may want to pronounce /dr/ yourself as a model. Repeat the procedure with the cluster *tr* in *tree.*

Remind children that *r* often appears together with other consonants in words. Read aloud each of the following sentences and have children complete it with two words that begin with the sounds for *fr, dr,* or *tr.*

- I like to eat hamburgers and _____. (French fries)

- Squirrels make their homes in _____. (tree trunks)

- Words for the sound of water leaking are _____. (drip drop)

Write the word pairs *French fries, tree trunks,* and *drip drop* on the chalkboard and ask volunteers to use them in sentences.

Have children complete *Literacy Activity Book* pages 9, 10.

SKILL FINDER Minilessons, pp. T65, T107, T181

Our Plants

Our Plants
by Jeannie W. Berger

This story includes words with *r* clusters for decoding practice.

Literacy Activity Book, p. 9

To the River We Go! dr tr fr

Think of the beginning sounds. Write **dr**, **fr**, or **tr**.

Color green the pictures that begin like □.
Color brown the pictures that begin like 🐸.

The World Outside My Door 9

Literacy Activity Book, p. 10

Down by the River dr tr fr

Read the story. Write each word below the picture it names.

Help me open this **trunk**.
I see a **dress**.
I see a red **truck**.
A **frog** just jumped out.

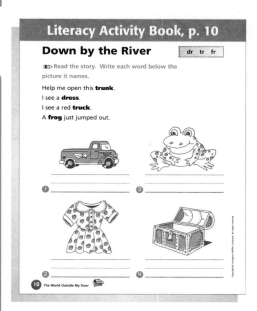

10 The World Outside My Door

More Practice Activities

Rhyming
Cooperative Learning

Give pairs of children cards for the clusters *tr, dr, fr,* and *cr* and the letter card *y.* Ask partners to combine their cards and make as many words as they can that rhyme with *my.*

Challenge Children can use the words to write rhyming couplets.

Clusters for the Word Wall

Write the words *drizzle, drench, frozen, frilly, traffic,* and *triangle* on the chalkboard and read them with children. Invite them to choose one word to write and illustrate for the Word Wall.

Instruct *and* Integrate

Phonics/Decoding

INTERACTIVE LEARNING

TESTED SKILL ✓

Think About Words

Teach/Model   Using a self-stick note or card, cover the word *river* on page 7 of *My River.* Read the sentence with children, substituting the word *blank* for *river.* Then uncover the word and ask children how they could figure it out if it didn't look familiar to them right away.

Think Aloud

What Makes Sense First, I'll read the sentence. … The word names something that belongs to the turtle.

Sounds for Letters Next I'll think about letter sounds. This word begins with the sound for *r* and ends with the sound for *r.*

Picture Clues The turtle is on a log in some water. Rivers are places with water, and *river* begins and ends with the sound for *r.* The word must be *river.*

Cover the words *need* and *mine* on Sentence Strips 10 and 13, and then display them. Read the sentences, saying *blank* for the hidden words. Then ask volunteers to uncover the words, read the text, and identify the clues they used to figure out *need* and *mine.*

Practice/Apply   Distribute Sentence Strips to small groups of children. Have them take turns reading aloud different sentences from the story and explaining how they figured out any words they didn't know at first. Encourage listeners to point out other clues that could be used to figure out the word.

Informal Assessment

As children read aloud from *Our Plants,* note their ability to combine clues such as these to decode words:

- meaning (context)
- phonics
- comparison with familiar words that have a corresponding spelling pattern (phonograms)
- word structure clues

MINILESSON

Using Context for Decoding

Teach/Model

Help children to recall that one important clue in figuring out words is the meaning of the text, or what makes sense in the sentence. Display pages 12–13 of *My River*. Read the sentence, having children supply the word *home.* Model how to use context to figure out the word.

Think Aloud

I know from the sentence that this word tells where the eel lives. It lives in the river so the river is its home. *Home* makes sense, and *home* begins with the sound for *h*. The word must be *home*.

Have children tell how they know the word isn't *house.* (*House* begins with the sound for *h* but it doesn't make as much sense.)

Practice/Apply

Ask children to read page 18 and tell how the meaning of the sentence and the picture clues could help them figure out the word *grow.* Ask how they know the word isn't *groan.*

turtle

muskrat

MINILESSON

Word Meaning from Context

Teach/Model

Help children reread page 32. Ask why it wasn't important to know all these animal names in order to read the story. (We could tell from the pictures which animal was speaking.)

Practice/Apply

Ask each child to choose an animal name from the story and write a sentence about it.

Encourage children to write on cards any new words they learn as they read other stories during this theme. The words can be added to the Word Wall or to children's individual word banks.

Instruct and Integrate

Vocabulary

Our Plants

Our Plants
by Jeannie W. Berger

This story provides practice and application for the following skills:

- **High-Frequency Words:** *do, here, it's, need, so, this, was, where*
- **Phonics/Decoding Skills:** Clusters with *r*
- **Cumulative Review:** Previously taught decoding skills and High-Frequency Words

Literacy Activity Book, p. 11

Make a Book

✂ Cut and paste the strips on art paper. Add your own pictures. On strip 5, use **need** in a sentence about the river. Staple the pages to make a book.

> **It's Our River**
> 1
>
> Here is a river.
> It's so big.
> 2
>
> This is where the 🐟 is.
> Do you see the 🐟 ?
> 3
>
> A 🐟 was in the river.
> Then it went up.
> 4
>
> 5

Informal Assessment

As children read aloud the WATCH ME READ Book or complete other activities on this page, observe their ability to recognize the High-Frequency Words in different contexts.

High-Frequency Words

High-Frequency Words: *do, here, it's, need, so, this, was, where*

Mystery Words

Display the Sentence Strips and cover the High-Frequency Words with self-stick notes. Distribute word cards for the High-Frequency Words to children.

Have children read each sentence chorally, omitting the hidden word. Have the child holding the word card for the missing word read it and uncover the mystery word to see if it matches the one on his or her card.

| Whose river is | ? |

| | my river. |

| We live | , too. |

| I | born here. |

| This is | we grow. |

| | I | the river. |

| we. |

Materials
- Sentence Strips 2, 3, 7, 8, 9, 10, 11
- word cards
- self-stick notes
- pocket chart

Make a Book

LAB, p. 11

Review the High-Frequency Words with children. Together, read the directions on *Literacy Activity Book* page 11. Have children complete the book and share their work with a partner.

Sentence Completion

On the chalkboard, write these sentences, which contain the High-Frequency Words.

Have children copy the sentences and complete them with words or pictures of their choice. Display the completed sentences for reading and discussion.

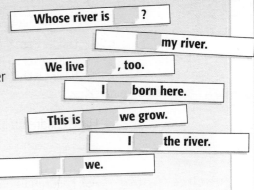

It's a _____.
Here is _____.
This was _____.
This is so _____.
We need _____.
This is where we _____.
Do we need this _____?

MINILESSON

Vocabulary Skill
Contractions with 's

LAB, p. 13

Teach/Model Write the word *it's* on the chalkboard. Circle the apostrophe and explain that sometimes an apostrophe takes the place of a letter. Ask whether anyone knows what letter this one takes the place of. Elicit that it is taking the place of an *i* and that *it's* is a shorter way of saying *it is*.

Practice/Apply
- Ask children to name a shorter way of saying these words using an apostrophe:

  she is (she's)

  he is (he's)

- Ask for volunteers to use *it's, she's,* and *he's* in sentences and write them on the chalkboard.

- Have children complete *Literacy Activity Book* page 13.

Literacy Activity Book, p. 13

Contraction Action

Use a contraction. Write each sentence.

❶ It is our river.

❷ She is hot.

❸ He is cold.

Write another sentence using **she's, he's,** or **it's.**

The World Outside My Door 13

MINILESSON

Vocabulary Expansion
Bodies of Water

Teach/Model Ask children what body of water the story tells about. (a river) Have them name other bodies of water. Write their suggestions on the chalkboard.

Ask children to consider what makes a river different from these other bodies of water. Explain that a river is a large stream of fresh water that flows into a lake, bay, or ocean.

pond	bay
lake	lagoon
stream	sea
creek	ocean

Practice/Apply Show children a map of your state or region. Ask volunteers to identify some of the bodies of water on the map. Invite children to look through old magazines for pictures of different bodies of water to share with the class.

Portfolio Opportunity

- Since children must read the High-Frequency Words to complete *Literacy Activity Book* page 11, you might want to save the page as a record.

- Save *Literacy Activity Book* page 13 as a record of children's familiarity with contractions with 's.

Instruct *and* Integrate

Language and Writing

Literacy Activity Book, p. 14

Take a Walk

➡ Draw a line along the path.

woods   river   hill   lake

➡ Write about the places you went. Use words from the box.

⓮ The World Outside My Door

Writing Names for Places

LAB, p. 14

- Tell children that you are going on a bear hunt and that you will see many wonderful sights, including a river, along the way. Perform the traditional bear hunt song shown, using hand gestures. Repeat the second verse, with children suggesting places, such as *river* or *mountains,* for the first line and actions, such as *jump over,* for the second line.

- After you have finished the song, ask children to remind you of all the places you went. On the board, draw a map of the imaginary route you took. Write the names of the places, such as *river, mountains,* and *cave,* on the map.

- Have children complete *Literacy Activity Book* page 14 for practice in writing names of places.

A Bear Hunt

Going on a bear hunt,
I'm not afraid.
I have my trusty dog,
And all my friends are by my side.

Look, there's a _____ .
We'll have to _____ it.

Look, there's a cave. A deep dark cave.
We'll have to go through it.
Tip-toe, tip-toe, tip-toe.
Ah! There's a bear! Run!
Phew! We're home again.

Practice Activities

Find the Answers
Cooperative Learning

Have children work in small groups and choose a place, such as a river, island, rain forest, or desert, that they would like to visit. Suggest they write a list of questions they have about that place. Then invite children to try to find the answers to their questions. Provide resource materials, such as nonfiction books and geography magazines.

Habitat Books
Cooperative Learning

Have children work in groups to make books about a natural habitat, such as a field, woods, or desert. Invite groups to choose a habitat and brainstorm a list of animals that live there. Remind children that *My River* begins and ends with the question *Whose river is this?* Have them follow this format, with animals answering the question in different ways.

Informal Assessment

Check children's ability to write the names of places.

More Practice Activities

Travel Posters

Grammar Connection Ask children the names of beaches, mountains, parks, or other places they have visited. Write the places on the board. Point out the capital letters that begin any special names of places.

Invite children to create a travel poster of a special place they have been. Explain that travel posters try to make other people want to visit a place too. Have children write the name of the place and any words that they think will entice people.

Students Acquiring English Have children make posters of a special place in their country of origin. Ask them to teach the other children in the class how to say the name of the place.

Children can use The Learning Company's new elementary writing center to write, illustrate, and publish their work to share with others.

Whose Is It?

Oral Language Development Work with a small group of children. Ask each child a question such as *Whose shirt is this?* while pointing to an object. Have children answer with words that show ownership:

- Whose belt is this? (That belt is mine. That belt is yours. That belt is hers/his.)

- Whose room is this? (This room is ours.)

After a few rounds, have the children answer questions with this word pattern: *That desk is my desk. That desk is your desk. That desk is her/his desk. Those desks are our desks.*

Making Maps

Have children make maps of the routes taken by familiar fairy tale characters, such as Little Red Riding Hood or Goldilocks. Guide children to create picture symbols for rivers, mountains, and roads and to make a legend. Invite children to make up names for places characters pass through, such as "Bat Woods" or "Lonesome River." Remind them to capitalize the names of special places.

Legend:
Robin Wood
Smith Meadow
house
Winding River
route of Goldilocks

Portfolio Opportunity

- Save *Literacy Activity Book* page 14 as a sample of children's ability to write names for places.

- Save children's written responses to activities on these pages as samples of their writing development.

Instruct *and* **Integrate**

Communication Activities

Audio Tape for The World Outside My Door: *My River*

Have children listen for the question that comes at the beginning and at the end of the story.

Listening and Speaking

Persuasive Speaking

- Ask children to think about why rivers are important to them.

- Have children draw pictures of how people can save water and take care of their rivers so that everyone has clean water.

- Invite children to hold up their pictures and talk to the class about what they show. Encourage them to convince classmates of the importance of saving water.

Sounds of the River
Cooperative Learning

Invite children to think of sounds they might hear if they took a trip down a river. Have them demonstrate each sound and explain what makes it. Then have children perform the sounds of a trip down a river, incorporating all the sounds they have brainstormed. If necessary, remind children to include sounds of the water splashing and the wind rustling the grass.

Viewing

Photographs and Illustrations

- Tell children that the animal pictures they saw in *My River* were illustrations, that is, pictures that were drawn by someone. Then have them look through old magazines for pictures of animals. Ask children to hold up the pictures they find and tell whether the picture is a photograph or an illustration.

- If possible, take photographs of children or have them bring photographs of themselves from home. Invite children to look at their photographs and create illustrations of themselves.

- Put their illustrations and photographs side by side on a bulletin board display titled *Photographs and Illustrations*.

Materials
- paper
- crayons or markers
- camera and film (optional)

Independent Reading & Writing

Student-Selected Reading

Book Bags

Create thematic book bags for children to take home for a week at a time. Include the following items:

- several books about a particular theme, such as weather or friendship
- activities for children to do with their families
- an inventory list so children can keep track of the bag's contents

Reading Poster

You might want to emphasize the importance of reading by creating a reading poster to display in the classroom. Encourage children to decorate the poster with reasons why they think reading is an important and fun activity.

Books for Independent Reading

Encourage children to choose their own books. They might choose one of the following titles.

Hats, Hats, Hats
by Ann Morris
illustrated by Ken Heyman

Our Plants
by Jeannie W. Berger

My River
by Shari Halpern

Have children reread this selection silently or aloud to a partner.

See the Bibliography on pages T42–T43 for more theme-related books for independent reading.

Ideas for Independent Writing

Encourage children to write on self-selected topics. For those who need help getting started, suggest one of the following activities:

- a **report** about a river animal or plant
- a **poster** reminding people to take care of rivers
- a **drawing with captions** of a local river

Student-Selected Writing

Setting Purposes

Encourage children to begin writing conferences by stating the kind of help they need. Would they like a response to their draft? Do they need help with planning, revising, or editing? Do they need assistance with a particular problem? Determining the purpose of a conference helps keep children focused.

Writing Process

Introduce the steps of the writing process to children. Help them to understand that writers go through a series of stages: planning, drafting, revising, editing, and publishing. You may want to choose one step of the process to discuss each day for a week. For example, you might model different ways of planning, such as drawing, talking to a friend, having a conference with the teacher, or making a web.

Portfolio Opportunity

Save examples of the writing children do independently on self-selected topics.

Cross-Curricular Activities

Math

Venn Diagrams

Draw a Venn diagram on the chalkboard. Ask children to name the land and water animals in *My River*. Then help them name animals that can live on land and in the water. Write the names in the appropriate spaces.

Land Animals

muskrat

frog
turtle
salamander
dragonfly

Water Animals

fish
eel

- Invite pairs or small groups to create their own diagrams using desert animals.

- Help children decide on the categories. The categories may include animals with shells, animals that fly, animals that swim, animals that crawl or walk, two- (four-, six-) legged animals, animals with scales, animals with fur, animals with feathers.

Art

A River Scene

Invite children to create an underwater river scene, using the steps shown below.

Materials
- construction paper
- paintbrushes
- paste
- tissue paper (light blue, dark blue, green)
- liquid starch

1 Draw shapes of river animals on colored construction paper and cut them out. With a paintbrush, cover a section of white construction paper with a coat of liquid starch.

2 Tear tissue paper into small pieces. Lay the tissue on the starch, light blue tissue at the top, dark blue and green at the bottom. Cover with more starch and let dry.

3 Paste the animals onto the paper.

Choices for Social Studies

Down the River

Divide the class into small groups. Have them plan a trip down a river. Ask children to write sentences telling how they will get down the river, what things they will need for the trip, and what they hope to see along the way. Invite groups to present their plans to the class.

Locating Rivers

MEETING INDIVIDUAL NEEDS

Challenge Explain to children that rivers are streams of water flowing toward other bodies of water such as oceans or lakes.

- Display the map and call children's attention to the map key.

- Have children identify the symbol mapmakers use to represent rivers. Ask them if they think the symbol is a good one for rivers and why.

- Ask volunteers to locate rivers on the map. Challenge them to follow the flow of different rivers to see where they end on the map.

- Some children may want to draw their own map.

Materials
- map of the United States with a map key and symbol for rivers

Book List

Social Studies

First Look at Rivers
by Susan Baker

All Along the River
by Allan Fowler

Three Days on a River in a Red Canoe
by Vera Williams

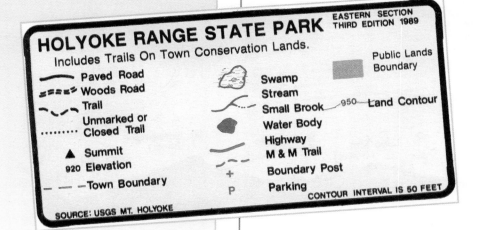

HOLYOKE RANGE STATE PARK   EASTERN SECTION THIRD EDITION 1989
Includes Trails On Town Conservation Lands.

— Paved Road
≈≈≈ Woods Road
∿ Trail
········ Unmarked or Closed Trail
▲ Summit
920 Elevation
— — —Town Boundary

🪨 Swamp
Stream
∿ Small Brook
⬛ Water Body
Highway
∿ M & M Trail
+ Boundary Post
P Parking

Public Lands Boundary
—950— Land Contour
CONTOUR INTERVAL IS 50 FEET

SOURCE: USGS MT. HOLYOKE

Instruct *and* **Integrate**

Cross-Curricular Activities *(continued)*

Science

Materials
- blue food coloring
- newspaper
- large aluminum roasting pan
- plastic wrap
- spray bottle
- water

How and Why Rivers Flow

Ask volunteers who have been to a river to describe how the water moved. Tell children that they will be doing an experiment to show how and why a river moves or flows.

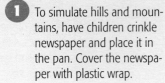

1 To simulate hills and mountains, have children crinkle newspaper and place it in the pan. Cover the newspaper with plastic wrap.

2 Fill a spray bottle with water and add a few drops of food coloring.

3 Ask a volunteer to spray water on the plastic wrap. Have children observe and describe how the water flows down "hills" and "mountains," forming tributaries, lakes, and ponds on its route.

Creative Movement

River Dance

Extra Support Have a group of volunteers act like a river, mimicking the movement and sound of the water. Have other volunteers act like a river, animals, plants, and trees. You might want to ask volunteers to act like the wind or rain. Encourage children to switch roles to give everyone a chance to act like a river.

LITTLE BIG BOOK
PLUS

The Blue Boat
by Winslow Homer

Winslow Homer loved to spend time outdoors. He painted what he saw and liked best. Look at this watercolor painting and tell what he saw.

33

Introduce the Literature

Building Background

Invite children to share what they know about boats, especially small craft such as sailboats or rowboats. If any of them have ever been on a boat, ask them to tell about their experiences. Then ask children to name bodies of water where they might see boats: rivers, oceans, lakes, ponds. Tell them that they are going to learn about a painting by Winslow Homer, a famous artist who loved to paint pictures of boats and water.

Interact with Literature

Looking at a Painting

As children look at *The Blue Boat,* tell them that this type of painting is called watercolor, which is done by using special paints and adding water to them. Read the page with children, and have them tell what they think Winslow Homer saw as he painted this picture. Ask children these questions about the painting:

- What are the people in the painting doing? (fishing)

- Do you think the weather in the painting is calm or stormy? Why do you think so?

Instruct and Integrate

Fine Art

Experiment with Watercolor Distribute these materials to children: white paper, brushes with soft bristles, small jars of water for dipping, and watercolor paints. Help them discover how to make a color lighter (add more water) or darker (add more paint). Since watercolors dry much faster than other paints, children can paint strokes of different colors over their dried strokes to create new colors.

LITTLE BIG BOOK
PLUS

Introduce
the
Literature

Building Background

Ask children to tell what they know about rivers. Discuss any local rivers that they might know. If children have been to rivers, have them share their experiences, describing animals and plants that they have seen there. Tell children that they are going to find out about some other rivers in the world and about animals or plants that live in or near those rivers.

River Life

Pelicans
Ewaso Ng'Iro River, Kenya

Elephant
Zambezi River,
Zimbabwe

Bear
Toklat River, Alaska

34

Hippopotamuses
Victoria Nile, Uganda

Manatee
Homosassa River, Florida

Dragonfly
Santa Clara River, California

35

Interact with Literature

Discussion

Help children locate the United States and Africa on a globe or world map. Read the captions on Anthology pages 34–36 and help children locate some of the rivers on the map. Discuss these questions with children:

- If you could travel to one of these rivers, which one would you choose? Why?

- Have you ever seen any of the animals on these pages? Where did you see them? What were they like?

- Why do you think these animals live near rivers?

Interact with Literature

Background: FYI

Remind children that every river starts out small and gets bigger as more water flows through it. Most rivers end by flowing into an ocean. Here are two ways that rivers can get started:

- An underground spring of water bubbles up out of the ground and begins to flow.

- Snow melts in the mountains and water from the snow flows into streams.

LITTLE BIG BOOK
PLUS

Science

Find Out More Have children use junior encyclopedias or animal books to find out more about the animals shown on page 35, such as the hippopotamus and the manatee. Encourage them to write a sentence about their favorite fact and illustrate it.

Reeds
Rio Grande River, New Mexico

Lupine
Merrimack River, Massachusetts

36

Background: FYI

Share these facts about two river animals with children.

- The manatee's upper lip is divided into halves, which work like pliers to grab plants.

- The hippopotamus is the world's largest river animal. It is found in nature only in Africa. In spite of its huge body and short legs, the hippopotamus is a good swimmer and can also run fast, especially for short distances.

Whose River Is This?

What do you think happened to this river?

37

Building Background

Ask children how they feel when they see a place that is full of trash. Have children suggest ways such as recycling to deal with the problem of too much trash. Review the recycling procedures in your community, and encourage children to share their own recycling experiences.

Interact with Literature

Discussion

Read pages 37–38 with children. Encourage them to answer and discuss the questions on these pages. Use these questions as additional prompts:

• What kinds of trash do you see in the picture on page 37?

• Which of these things could be recycled?

• Why do you think it's especially important to keep our rivers and other waterways clean and free of trash?

Interact with Literature

Background: FYI

When children point out the tire, explain that tires are one of the biggest trash problems. Encourage children to suggest imaginative ways in which old tires might be reused.

LITTLE BIG BOOK PLUS

Whose Earth Is It?

Remind children that rivers are not the only part of their environment in danger of pollution. Have them suggest other parts that people should keep clean. (air, land, sea, lakes, streams) Record their ideas on chart paper. Encourage children to discuss how they can help keep their environment clean.

It's Everybody's River!

What are these people doing?
What could you do to help a river?

38

Social Studies

Trash Treasures! Have children think of things they throw away every day, such as paper, plastic bottles, and aluminum cans. Ask them to think of a new product from something they usually just throw away. For instance, two soda cans could become a play telephone when attached with string, or old newspapers could be made into hats for a play. Have children draw their ideas and present them to the class.

Whose River Is This?

Art

River Recipes Invite children to create recipes for foods that river animals might like.

> **Materials**
> • construction paper
> • crayons
> • old magazines
> • scissors
> • paste

- Brainstorm with children things that river animals might eat. (for example: plants, bugs, fish)

- Encourage them to pick two or three items to include in their recipes.

- Have children draw or cut pictures from old magazines that show the recipe ingredients.

- Have them paste the pictures on construction paper and help them write labels.

- Display their recipes in the classroom.

Social Studies

Let's Stop Pollution Have children create their own antipollution publicity campaign.

> **Materials**
> • construction paper
> • crayons, markers, or paints
> • old magazines
> • scissors
> • paste

Help children create antipollution slogans and then make posters of them. Children may do their own illustrations or cut appropriate pictures out of magazines. If possible, put up the posters on school or community bulletin boards to remind everyone of these important issues.

ANTHOLOGY

SELECTION:
Citybook

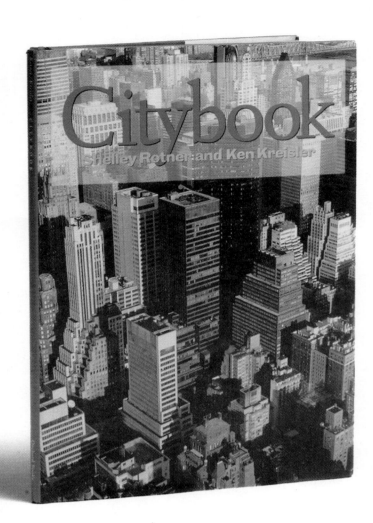

by Shelley Rotner and
Ken Kreisler

Other Books by the Authors

Faces
Nature Spy
Ocean Day

Selection Summary

Kevin loves going to the city because there is so much to see. There are
people on the go—riding trains, taxis, buses, and even in-line skates. It's fun
to look at the lights and neon signs, the bridges and buildings. There are so
many interesting things to do. In this selection, explore the city with Kevin
and you'll see that it's a fun place to be!

Lesson Planning Guide

	Skill/Strategy Instruction	Meeting Individual Needs	Lesson Resources
1 ⭐ **Introduce** *the* **Literature** *Pacing: 1 day*	**Preparing to Read and Write** Warm-up, T98 Prior Knowledge/Background, T98 **Key Words**, T99 • city • sights **High-Frequency Words**, T99 • go • long • many • of • on • people • walk	**Other Choices for Building Background**, T99 **Students Acquiring English**, T99	**Poster** Warm-up, 3C **Transparency** Selection Vocabulary, 3–1 *Literacy Activity Book* Selection Vocabulary, p. 15
2 ⭐ **Interact** *with* **Literature** *Pacing: 1–3 days*	**Reading Strategies** Self-Question, T102, T112, T130 Summarize, T102, T108, T114, T120, T130 Think About Words, T126 **Minilessons** Clusters with *r*, T107 Text Organization and Summarizing, T109 ✓ Clusters with *l* and *s*, T123 ✓ Noting Details, T125 Base Words and Endings *-s, -es, -ing*, T127 **Responding**, T131	**Choices for Reading**, T102 **Guided Reading**, T102, T108, T114, T120, T130 **Students Acquiring English**, T104, T108 **Extra Support**, T106, T107, T110, T130 **Responding Choices**, T132–T133	**Reading-Writing Workshop** The World Outside Your Door, T146–T147 *Literacy Activity Book* Comprehension Check, p. 17 The Learning Company's new elementary writing center software
3 ⭐ **Instruct** *and* **Integrate** *Pacing: 1–3 days*	✓ **Comprehension** Noting Details, T134–T135 ✓ **Phonics and Spelling** Consonant Clusters with *l*, T136 Consonant Clusters with *s*, T137 ✓ **Vocabulary** High-Frequency Words, T138 Word Family: *shop*, T139 City Words, T139 **Language and Writing** Writing More Names for Places, T140–T141 **Communication Activities**, T142 **Independent Reading & Writing**, T143 **Cross-Curricular Activities**, T144–T145	**Activity Choices/Reteaching** Noting Details, T135 **Activity Choices** Consonant Clusters with *l*, T136 Consonant Clusters with *s*, T137 **Activity Choices** High-Frequency Words, T138 **Activity Choices** Language and Writing, T140–T141	**Reading-Writing Workshop** The World Outside Your Door, T146–T147 *Literacy Activity Book* Comprehension Skill, p. 18 Phonics and Spelling, pp. 19–22 High-Frequency Words, p. 23 Vocabulary Skill, p. 24 Language and Writing, p. 25 **Audio Tape** for The World Outside My Door: *Citybook* The Learning Company's new elementary writing center software

✓ *Indicates Tested Skills. See page T47 for assessment options.*

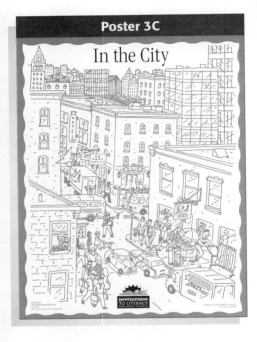

In the City

1 Introduce *the* Literature

Preparing to Read and Write

INTERACTIVE LEARNING

Warm-up

Looking at a Picture

- Invite children to look carefully at the picture on Poster 3C and describe what they see.

- Ask them to tell how the picture makes them feel. If they stepped inside this picture, would it be noisy or quiet? Why do they think so?

Prior Knowledge/Building Background

Key Concept What cities are like

Ask children to draw pictures that show what they think a city is like. Then invite them to share their pictures and talk about where they got their ideas about cities. Encourage children to tell what they know about a city near you, or a city they have visited. Point out that a city is where many people live and work; it usually has many tall buildings, many places for people to shop and eat, and museums and places that offer plays and musical performances.

There are many buildings in a city.

Take a picture walk through *Citybook.* Invite children to return to their drawings of cities and add new details they may have just learned.

Social Studies

Teacher FactFile

Cities

You may want to share the following information about cities with children. Help them find these places on a map or globe.

- The oldest subway system in the United States is in the city of Boston, Massachusetts. Building began in March 1895.
- The city of Boston is often called Beantown, because of the famous baked beans that are made there.
- The tallest building in the world is the Sears Tower, in the city of Chicago.
- Chicago is called the Windy City because of the strong winds that blow from Lake Michigan.
- New York City, the city featured in *Citybook,* is often called the Big Apple.

Selection Vocabulary

Key Words: *city, sights*

High-Frequency Words: *go, long, many, of, on, people, walk*

Help children practice words from *Citybook*. Display Transparency 3–1 and read the sentences aloud. Then ask children to identify any words they already know. Discuss letter sounds and context clues children can use to figure out the words.

Vocabulary Practice Have children complete *Literacy Activity Book* page 15.

Word Web

Help children become familiar with words they can use to describe cities. Brainstorm with children a list of words associated with a city and organize the words in a word web like the one shown below. Record your web on chart paper and encourage children to add to it as they explore *Citybook*.

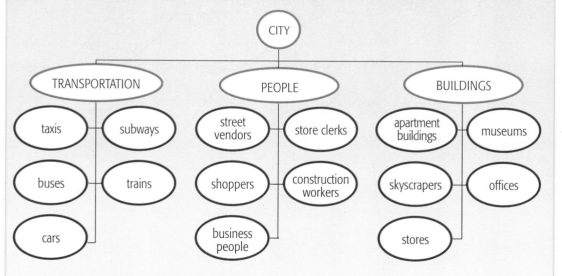

Students Acquiring English Invite children to choose words from the web to illustrate. Encourage them to look through *Citybook* for pictures of each word.

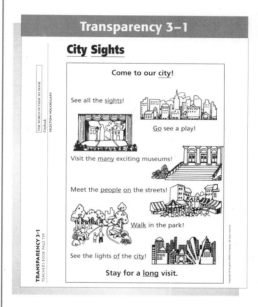

Transparency 3–1

City Sights

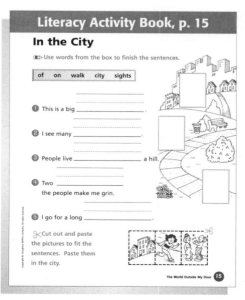

Literacy Activity Book, p. 15

In the City

2

Interact *with* **Literature**

More About the Authors

Shelley Rotner

Shelley Rotner became interested in writing books for children after her daughter, Emily, was born. Having been a professional photographer, a photography instructor, and an assistant to a museum curator, she then created her first children's book, *Changes.* The book was an immediate success and was named an Outstanding Science Trade Book for Children by the National Science Teachers Association. Other books by Shelley Rotner include *City Streets, Faces,* and *Nature Spy,* which was also an Outstanding Science Trade Book winner. She has won many awards for her photography, including a grand prize in a competition sponsored by *Natural History* magazine.

Shelley Rotner, her husband, and her daughter live in Massachusetts.

Ken Kreisler

Ken Kreisler has had a successful partnership with Shelley Rotner. Besides *Citybook,* he has been her co-author for *Nature Spy* and *Ocean Day.* In the past, Ken Kreisler has been a college professor, a commercial fisherman, and the captain of a yacht. Besides writing books for children, he has written the script for a film about whales, and he is also working on screenplays and novels for young adults.

Ken Kreisler and his wife and daughter live in New York City.

Shelley Rotner often visits New York City with her daughter, Emily. They like to shop, see the museums, and of course, take photographs! Shelley Rotner lives with her family in Massachusetts.

Meet Shelley Rotner and Ken Kreisler

Ken Kreisler has written four other books with Shelley Rotner. Their latest book is called *Faces.* Mr. Kreisler also likes to work with his daughter, Samantha. They live in New York City.

45

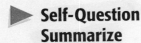

Interact
with
Literature

Reading Strategies

▶ **Self-Question**
Summarize

Discussion Remind children that they can do many things to help themselves become good readers. They can ask questions about a selection and read to find the answers. They can also find the most important parts to remember.

Have children tell how they can get ideas for questions about *Citybook*. As necessary, point out that they can look at the title and the pictures and think about what they know about cities from real life.

Predicting/Purpose Setting

Have children look through the selection and suggest questions they have about it. Record their questions on chart paper for later use. Have children look for answers to their questions as they read.

Kevin loved to go to the city.

46

Choices for Reading

Teacher Read Aloud

Have children ask questions about the selection, based on the title and the pictures. As you read the selection aloud, children should listen for answers. Stop periodically for discussion and for children to ask new questions.

Shared Reading

Read the selection aloud, as children echo-read it after you. Be sure to allow time for them to look at and discuss the pictures on each page. Then use one or more of the other choices for rereading.

Guided Reading

Have children preview pages 46–53, pose questions, and read to find the answers. Follow up with Guided Reading on page T108.

Cooperative Reading

Have partners discuss questions they have about the selection. Then have them take turns reading pages aloud. Encourage them to stop periodically to discuss what they have read and to pose new questions.

Independent Reading

Help children read page 46 and establish some purpose-setting questions about Kevin's trip to the city. Then have them read silently to the end of the selection to find the answers.

There was so much to see —

47

QuickREFERENCE

High-Frequency Words

go

Have children find the word on page 46 that means the opposite of *stop*. *(go)*

Phonics/Decoding Review

Consonant Sounds Call attention to the name *Kevin* on page 46. Remind children that the letter *k* stands for the sound at the beginning of *Kevin*.

Interact
with
Literature

lots of people on the go —

48

QuickREFERENCE

High-Frequency Words
of, people, on

Have children find the words *of, people,* and *on,* and use them in oral sentences.

riding buses,

49

Visual Literacy

Invite children to see how many times they can spot Kevin in the photos throughout the selection.

Journal

Invite children to begin a list in their journals of all the things Kevin sees in the city.

Interact
with
Literature

taking taxis,

50

 MEETING INDIVIDUAL NEEDS

Extra Support

Vocabulary Some children may not know what a *taxi* is. A *taxi* is a car that carries passengers for money. *Taxi* comes from the word *taximeter,* the machine inside a taxi that automatically shows how much the ride costs.

QuickREFERENCE

Phonics/Decoding Review

Consonant Sounds Call attention to the sound for *t* at the beginning of the words *taking* and *taxis.*

catching trains,

51

Anthology p. 51

Phonics/Decoding

Clusters with *r*

REVIEW & MAINTAIN

Teach/Model

Ask children to find a word on page 51 that begins with the same two sounds as *travel.* *(train)* Remind children that when a consonant and an *r* come together at the beginning of a word we say them almost as if they were one sound. Have children say *travel* and *train* again and listen for the beginning sounds.

Have children turn to page 66 and find another word that begins with a consonant and an *r.* *(bridges)*

Practice/Apply

Write the consonant clusters *tr, br, gr,* and *dr* in a chart as shown and provide children with examples of words that begin with each one. Help children to think of other words that begin the same way as the examples. Then ask them to use the words in oral sentences.

tr	br
train	bridge
(try)	(bright)
(trail)	(brown)

gr	dr
grand	dry
(great)	(drain)
(gray)	(drink)

SKILL FINDER

Phonics and Spelling, pp. T76, T77, T190, T191

Minilessons, pp. T65, T181

Interact *with* Literature

Reading Strategies

► **Summarize**

Ask children what they think is important to remember about the pages they just read. Have them name the boy in the selection and tell in their own words what he saw.

Guided Reading

Comprehension/Critical Thinking

Discuss whether any of children's questions about the selection have been answered so far. Then ask:

1. Why did Kevin like going to the city? (There was a lot to see there.)

2. How do people in the city get around? (They ride buses, taxis, and trains; they walk, run, and roller blade.) Do you think it is easy to get around in the city? Why or why not?

Predicting/Purpose Setting

Have children preview pages 54–59, add new questions to the list begun earlier, and look for answers to their questions. See page T114 for discussion.

Informal Assessment

Oral Reading Use pages 46–53 to assess children's oral reading fluency. See the Oral Reading Checklist in the *Teacher's Assessment Handbook* for criteria.

walking, running, roller blading.

52

Students Acquiring English

Have children act out *riding buses, taking taxis, catching trains, walking, running,* and *roller blading.*

QuickREFERENCE

High-Frequency Words

walk

Ask volunteers to find the word *walking,* identify its base word *walk,* then use the word *walk* in an oral sentence.

53

Comprehension

Text Organization and Summarizing

REVIEW & MAINTAIN

Teach/Model

Have children reread pages 48–52. Ask them what all these pages tell about. (how people move around the city) Use children's responses to begin a chart. Explain that how people move around the city is the topic of these pages, or what they tell about.

Citybook, pages 48–52	
Topic	How people move around the city
Main Idea	
Different Ways	

Help children to compose a sentence that tells the most important idea of those pages. (Example: People move around the city in many ways.) Explain that their sentence tells the main idea of those pages, and then enter it on the chart.

Practice/Apply

Invite children to name the ways of traveling mentioned in the selection. List these ways on the chart and have volunteers add a picture to go with each one.

SKILL FINDER

Full lesson/Reteaching, pp. T74–T75; Themes 7, 10

Minilessons, pp. T61, T69

Background: FYI

Rollerblade is a brand name for in-line skates, which are like roller skates with the wheels arranged in a single line.

Safety Link

Discuss with children the importance of wearing protective elbow and knee pads and helmets when roller blading or roller skating.

Window shopping,

54

Extra Support

Idioms Discuss with children what *window shopping* means. If necessary, explain that window shopping is looking at things for sale in store windows without buying them.

Quick REFERENCE

Science Link

Have children guess what kind of skeleton is in the store window. (a horse) Ask children to find places on their bodies where they can feel the bones. Explain that skeletons give bodies a shape for support and motion.

Interact *with* Literature

Reading Strategies

 Self-Question

Discuss with children the questions they are asking themselves as they read and how this helps them better understand the selection. Do the pictures answer any of their questions? As they look longer at the pictures, do they have new questions?

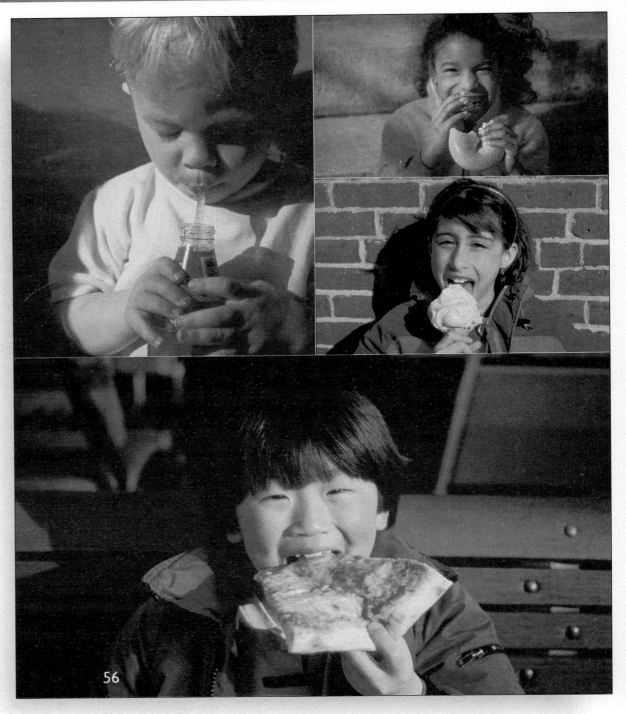

56

Self-Assessment

Have children ask themselves these questions:

- Am I looking for answers to my questions?
- Am I looking for the most important parts to remember?

 QuickREFERENCE

★★★ Multicultural Link

Tell children that many of the foods we eat in the United States come to us from cultures around the world: the bagel is Jewish; pizza, Italian; hot dogs and pretzels, German. Invite children to name other foods and the cultures from which they come.

sometimes stopping.

57

Anthology p. 57

Concepts of Print

Poetry Point out that the words on pages 54 and 57 do not form a sentence. Explain that because this selection is written like a poem, lines begin with capital letters and end with periods even though they are not sentences. You may wish to write the selection text on chart paper to show how the text forms a poem.

Interact *with* Literature

Mimes, music, museums.

58

Reading Strategies

▶ Summarize

Have children look at pages 53–59 and summarize what Kevin saw: many things for sale, performers, a museum exhibit. Ask them what they think is important to remember about this part of the selection.

Guided Reading

Comprehension/Critical Thinking

Discuss which of children's questions were answered in this part of the selection. Then discuss the following questions:

1. What are some things people can buy in the city? (coats, sunglasses, ice cream, pizza, bagels)

2. What are some things people do to have fun in the city?

Predicting/Purpose Setting

Have children preview through page 65. What questions do they have as they look at the pictures? Record children's responses and have them read to see if their questions are answered.

Informal Assessment

If children's responses indicate that they are understanding the selection, have them finish reading it cooperatively or independently.

Quick**REFERENCE**

Vocabulary

Explain that a *mime* is someone who does pantomime, the acting out of a story or activity without using words. Invite a volunteer to demonstrate what a mime does.

Music Link

Many children may not know what a saxophone sounds like. They may enjoy hearing recordings by great jazz sax players such as Coleman Hawkins, Lester Young, or Charlie Parker.

59

Science Link	**Phonics/Decoding Review**
Ask the dinosaur experts in your class to identify the dinosaur in the photo (tyrannosaurus) and tell something about it. Have any children seen a real dinosaur skeleton in a museum?	**Consonant Sounds** Have children identify the letter that stands for the beginning sound in the words *mime, music,* and *museum. (m)*

Anthology p. 59

Citybook **T115**

Interact
with
Literature

60

Quick REFERENCE

Visual Literacy

Discuss what information the paintings on the walls give about the store in the photo on pages 60–61.

 Home Connection

Have children ask their parents, guardians, or grandparents to help them draw a picture and write a story about a pet the family has or knows. Invite volunteers to share their pet project with the class.

Painted walls

61

 Technology Link

Children may want to find out more about New York and other cities by using a CD-ROM encyclopedia, other software, and on-line services.

Phonics/Decoding Review

Consonant Sounds Have children identify the letter that stands for the beginning sound in the word *walls*. *(w)* Have them find words on pages 52 and 54 that begin with the same sound. *(walking, window)*

2

Interact
with
Literature

and neon signs.

62

QuickREFERENCE

Vocabulary

You may wish to explain to children that *neon* is used to make certain kinds of lights. Contained in a tube, neon glows reddish-orange when electricity runs through it.

Phonics/Decoding Review

Consonant Sounds Point out that children hear the sound for *n* at the beginning and at the end of the word *neon*. Help them identify the word on page 73 that begins with the sound for *n*. (*nights*)

★★★ **Multicultural Link**

The photo in the lower right corner shows characters in the Chinese language. Invite children who can write in languages other than English to write words on the board and translate them for the class.

2

Interact
with
Literature

Reading Strategies

▶ **Summarize**

Point out that the pages children just read show the writing, drawing, and other things Kevin saw. Ask children what information they want to remember about this part of the selection.

Guided Reading

Comprehension/Critical Thinking

Discuss with children any answers they found to their questions. Were their questions answered by the words, the pictures, or both? Then discuss the following questions:

1. Where do you see writing on these pages? (on walls, in signs)

2. What information do the painted walls and the signs give people?

3. How are the two lines in the pictures on page 64–65 different?

Predicting/Purpose Setting

Have children page through to the end of the selection and suggest any questions they want answered about this last part. Have them read to find answers to these and their earlier questions.

Long

64

QuickREFERENCE

High-Frequency Words
long

Ask children to find the word on this spread that describes the lines. Then ask a volunteer to use *long* in a sentence.

Science Link

Children may be able to identify the birds as pigeons. Ask children to speculate about what pigeons eat in the city. Where might they make their nests?

lines.

65

Interact
with
Literature

Fountains,   bridges,

66

statues,

flags.

67

Phonics/Decoding

Clusters with *l* and *s*

TESTED SKILL

Teach/Model

Ask children to find a word on page 67 that begins with the same sounds as *state*. *(statues)* Write *statues* on the board and ask a volunteer to underline the two letters that stand for the beginning sounds.

Point out that when two consonants are side by side at the beginning of a word, such as *st* in *statues,* the sounds for *s* and *t* are so close together they almost seem to be one sound. Have children reread page 61. Print *wall* on the board, then replace the *w* with *sm* and have children read the word.

Next, ask children to find a word on page 67 that begins with the same sounds as *fly*. *(flags)* Ask them to suggest some other words that begin with *fl*. *(flute, flood, flame, Florida)*

Practice/Apply

Write the following story words on the board: *blading, stopping.* Ask a volunteer to read each word and to underline the letters that stand for the beginning sounds. Then have children name other words that begin with *bl* and *st.*

SKILL FINDER

Phonics and Spelling, pp. T136, T137, T190, T191

Minilessons, pp. T67, T181

QuickREFERENCE

Background: FYI

The statue shows Alice in Wonderland sitting on a toadstool. You may wish to show children illustrations from *Alice in Wonderland* and invite them to compare the drawings to the statue.

Social Studies Link

Invite children to use an encyclopedia or almanac to identify the nations represented by the flags in this photograph.

QuickREFERENCE

Media Literacy

Encourage children to notice in newspapers, television shows, and movies events that take place in cities. What can children find out about cities from these sources?

Background: FYI

The ducks in the picture on page 69 are being cured, or preserved, with soy sauce, which helps turn them brown. Later they will be served as Peking Duck.

So many sights.

69

Comprehension
Noting Details

Teach/Model

TESTED SKILL

Explain to children that paying attention to the pictures and the things that happen in a selection can make it more interesting and help them to understand it better.

Read aloud the text on page 69. Then model how to note details.

Think Aloud

The words on that page tell me there are many sights. I wonder what they are. At the top of page 68, I see Kevin looking at someone riding a bike and someone walking on the sidewalk. I see a dollar bill painted in a rainbow of colors. There are a lot of interesting sights to see.

Ask children to name some more sights on that page.

Practice/Apply

Have children note details in the pictures on pages 54–55 that help them to understand what Kevin means when he says *window shopping.*

SKILL FINDER

Full lesson/Reteaching, pp. T134–T135; Themes 1, 7, 10

Minilesson, p. T175

Phonics/Decoding Review

Consonant Sounds Have children identify the letter that stands for the beginning sound in *so* and *sights.* (s)

High-Frequency Words
many

Have children find the word *many.* Invite volunteers to repeat the following sentence, supplying the name of something Kevin saw: *Kevin saw many _____ in the city.*

Interact *with* Literature

Reading Strategies

▶ **Think About Words**

Point to the word *lights* on page 70 and ask children how they could figure out this word. Discuss the following:

- **What makes sense** This word describes something the city has many of. *Windows, people, cars,* and a number of other words might make sense.

- **Sounds for letters** How does the word begin? (with *l*) How does the word end? (with *s*) Does the ending make the word mean more than one? (yes) If we take the *s* off, what does the word end with? (*t*) What word begins with *l*, ends with *t* and *s*, and names something the city has many of? (*lights*)

- **Picture clues** The pictures on pages 70–71 show many lights shining in the city.

Have a volunteer read page 70 again, using the word *lights*. Discuss the meaning of the text and its connection with the picture.

So many lights.

70

Quick**REFERENCE**

Science Link

Discuss, and demonstrate if possible, how glass can act as a mirror to reflect objects around it, as the windows in the building on page 70 do.

71

Phonics/Decoding

Base Words and Endings: *-s*, *-es*, *-ing*

Teach/Model

Remind children that a word in its simplest form—with no endings added—is called a *base word*. Ask children to point to the word *lights* on page 70 and identify its base word. *(light)* Continue with *buses* on page 49 and *walking* on page 52. Write these words and their base words on the board as shown:

Base Word	With an Ending
light	lights
bus	buses
walk	walking

- Explain that with many naming words like *light,* we just add *-s* to mean more than one. When a word already ends with *-s,* like *bus,* we add *-es* to mean more than one.

- Explain that with many action words like *walk,* we can add *-ing* to make a new word.

Practice/Apply

Help children find other words in the story to which the endings *-s* and *-ing* have been added. *(lines, signs, blading, running)* Write them on the board and help children find the base word in each.

SKILL FINDER Full lesson/Reteaching, Themes 9, 10

72

Technology Link

Children may enjoy using electronic mail to write to other children and tell them about life where they live.

City nights.

73

Interact *with* Literature

 **Guided Reading**

Comprehension/Critical Thinking

Discuss with children any answers they found to their questions and where in the selection they found these answers. Then discuss the following questions:

1. What were some of the things Kevin saw in the last part of the selection?

2. Why do you think Kevin fell asleep at the end of the selection?

Reading Strategies

▶ **Self-Question Summarize**

Discuss which of children's questions have not been answered in the selection. Can children use what they know to figure out what the answers might be?

Have children retell the most important parts of the selection in their own words. If they have difficulty remembering information, have them look back through the selection.

74

 Self-Assessment

Encourage children to ask themselves these questions:

● What questions did I ask myself? Were they answered?

● Can I retell the most important parts of this selection?

QuickREFERENCE

 Journal

Have children use the pictures in the selection to check and complete their lists of the things Kevin saw. Children can use their lists to help them retell the selection.

 Extra Support

Rereading To develop fluency and confidence, invite children to do a choral reading of the story with you.

Multi-Age Classrooms Pair children of different ages and reading abilities. More proficient readers can assist their partners with unfamiliar words and concepts.

Build a City!

Work in a group. Use boxes or blocks to make buildings. Label each part of your city.

RESPONDING

Post Office

Bank

Police

Store

75

Responding Activities

 Personal Response

- Invite children to draw and label pictures that show their favorite part of the story or how they feel about the story.
- Allow children to respond to the selection in any way they wish.

Anthology Activity

Set up a table or clear some floor space for children to complete the activity on page 75. Provide them with milk cartons, scissors, construction paper, and paste to create buildings and roads for their city. If you don't have the space or the materials, have children draw pictures of things they would include in their city.

 Home Connection

Have children share their Personal Response pictures with family members. Encourage children to ask family members if they have ever visited or lived in a big city and what it was like.

 MEETING INDIVIDUAL NEEDS

Students Acquiring English

Encourage children to look through *Citybook* for signs with words and pictures on them. Discuss the meaning of each sign.

 Informal Assessment

Use the Comprehension Check or any of the Responding Activities on pages T132–T133 to assess children's understanding of the story.

Additional Support:

Reread any confusing sections aloud to help children understand the story.

Interact
with
Literature

Responding

N.Y. Convention and
Visitors Bureau
2 Columbus Circle
New York, NY 10019

To whom it may concern:

Please send our class information
about New York City. Please tell us
what museums you have that children
would like to visit. Please also tell us
what other sights we could see.
Thank you.

Yours truly,

Mr Tom Rayburn

The children in
Mr. Rayburn's class
Memorial School
Woodbridge, NY 10026

More Responding Activities

All About Cities

Invite children to generate a list of questions they have about cities after reading *Citybook.* Help them write a class letter requesting more information about cities. Questions about the city nearest you may be directed to the visitors bureau in that city. (Most have toll-free phone numbers.) Questions about New York City can be directed to:

> New York Convention and Visitors Bureau
> 2 Columbus Circle
> New York, NY 10019
> 1–800–692–8474

Different Cities, Big and Small

Have children look at other books about cities, such as *City Sounds* by Craig Brown and *The Inside-Outside Book of New York City* by Roxie Murno. Children can compare the information and pictures in these books to *Citybook.*

Literature Discussion
Cooperative Learning

Divide the class into groups of three or four children. Ask the following questions to prompt discussion in the groups:

- What did you think of the pictures in *Citybook*? Did they make you want to go to the city? Why or why not?

- Would you like to go to the city with Kevin for a day? Where would you ask him to take you? Why would you like to go there?

- Have you ever been to a big city? What was it like? Or, if you've never been, what do you think it would be like? Do you think you would enjoy it? Why or why not?

Informal Assessment

The Comprehension Check or the Literature Discussion can be used to informally assess children's understanding of the selection. See pages T132 and T133.

Additional Support:

Use the Guided Reading notes and questions to review the selection, rereading as necessary.

More Responding Activities

Your Town vs. New York City

Challenge Have interested children create a class chart that compares their city or town to New York City or another large city. Encourage them to use information not only from *Citybook* but also from sources such as an almanac, so they may include information such as size and population that can't be found in *Citybook*.

Hometown Book

Invite children to use *Citybook* as a model for writing and illustrating their own books about their hometown or another city or town they like to visit. Encourage volunteers to share their Hometown Books with the class.

Like or Dislike?

Kevin seemed to like everything he saw in the city. How do children feel? Invite children to create charts telling what sights in *Citybook* they did or didn't like. Encourage children to share their charts.

Comprehension Check

To determine children's understanding of the selection, use these questions and/or *Literacy Activity Book* page 17.

1. What did Kevin do in the city?
(He saw all the sights of the city.)

2. Why did Kevin like the city?
(There was so much to see.)

What I Liked	What I Didn't Like
trains museum bridges	lines too many people

City Collage

Invite children to create a city collage.

Materials
- large sheet of butcher paper
- old magazines and newspapers
- construction paper, scissors, paste

1 Draw pictures of city things on construction paper. Then cut them out.

2 Cut city pictures from old magazines. Paste the pictures onto butcher paper.

3 Display the collage on a bulletin board.

Literacy Activity Book, p. 17
What a Sight!

Portfolio Opportunity

As a writing sample, save children's work from the Hometown Book activity.

Instruct *and* Integrate

Comprehension

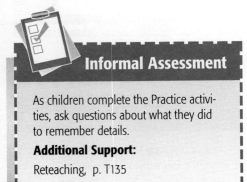

INTERACTIVE LEARNING

TESTED SKILL ✓ Noting Details
LAB, p. 18

Teach/Model

- Look through the story with children, pointing out the many things there are to name in the pictures.

- Then have children work in pairs to find one interesting detail they think others may have missed. When children come together, have each pair ask the question shown.

> "Who knows where the _____ is?"

- Reread with children what the author says at the beginning of the selection, on pages 46–47. (*Kevin loved to go to the city. There was so much to see ...*) Ask children to explain how the details they found helped them to understand Kevin's feelings about the city.

- Ask volunteers to choose their favorite photograph in the selection. Have them tell what details in the picture made the page more interesting and helped them read the words.

Practice/Apply

- Have pairs of children look for book covers with many details in the art. Ask them to find as many interesting details in the pictures as they can and then share what they found with others. Explain that looking at details on book covers can give us clues about the story inside the book.

- Have children complete *Literacy Activity Book* page 18.

Informal Assessment

As children complete the Practice activities, ask questions about what they did to remember details.

Additional Support:

Reteaching, p. T135

SKILL FINDER Minilessons, pp. T125, T175

More Practice Activities

Now You See It, Now You Don't

Arrange on a tabletop some common classroom objects. Tell children they may look at the objects for a while and then you are going to take one away. After thirty seconds or so, ask children to cover their eyes as you remove an object. Then ask if they can name what's missing. Continue the game, removing other items or sometimes adding new ones and asking children to note what's different.

Brilliant!

Ask children to name every kind of light they can find in the pictures of *Citybook*. (headlights, streetlights, traffic lights, sunlight, train lights, sign lights, fountain lights, office lights, others)

Have them make a poster entitled *Lights in the City,* drawing pictures of different kinds of lights and labeling them.

Details, Details

Ask each child to think of an object in the classroom and describe it for others to name.

Reteaching ## Noting Details

Reread the story *My River* with children. Then, as you page through the story again, ask children to dictate a list of details in the text and the pictures that help them learn more about river life and remember whose river it is.

Portfolio Opportunity

Save *Literacy Activity Book* page 18 as a record of children's ability to note details.

Instruct
and
Integrate

Phonics and Spelling

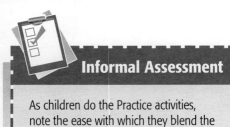

Informal Assessment

As children do the Practice activities,
note the ease with which they blend the
consonant sounds in the clusters and
identify the words.
Portfolio Opportunity Save *LAB* pp.
19–22 as a record.

INTERACTIVE LEARNING

Consonant Clusters with *l*

LAB, pp. 19, 20

- Read the words on page 52 with children.

- Write *blading* on the chalkboard and underline the beginning consonants.
  Have children say *blading* and listen to the sounds for the letters *b* and *l*
  together at the beginning.

- Remind children that *l* often appears together with some other consonant
  in words and that we say the sounds for those letters so close together that
  they almost seem to be one sound.

- Write the following words on the chalkboard: *floor, class, glad.* Read them
  aloud, asking children to listen for the beginning sounds in each one. Ask
  volunteers to underline the beginning letters as you say the words again.

- Write the consonant clusters *bl, fl, cl, gl,* and *pl* on the chalkboard. Have
  partners write one word that begins with each cluster. Invite children to
  share their words by using them in oral sentences.

- Have children complete *Literacy Activity Book* pages 19, 20.

SKILL FINDER | Minilessons, pp. T67, T123, T181

More Practice Activities

Wheeee!

Write the words *blading, flying,* and *gliding* on the chalkboard and underline the beginning clusters. Read the words for children, asking them to
listen for the beginning sounds. Then have children imagine that they are
doing one of those things. Ask them to write a sentence that tells what
they are doing and draw a picture to go with it.

INTERACTIVE LEARNING

Consonant Clusters with *s*

LAB, pp. 21, 22

Turn to page 57 in *Citybook*. Read the words with children. Then write *stopping* on the chalkboard and underline the beginning cluster. Remind children that the letter *s* often appears in front of other consonants in words, and that we say the sounds for those letters so close together they almost seem to be one sound.

Write the following on the chalkboard.

Point to *st* and ask what word begins with *st* and names a place to buy something. *(store)* Complete the word *store* and ask children to read it with you. Then point to *sk* and ask what word begins with *sk* and names the place where the clouds are. *(sky)*

Write the following words on the chalkboard and read them with children.

sky   skin   skirt   stop   store   stand   spend   speak

Assign words to pairs of children. Ask them to look for pictures to go with their words and share where they found them. Children can write the words, add illustrations, and post them on the Word Wall.

Have children complete *Literacy Activity Book* pages 21, 22.

SKILL FINDER — Minilessons, pp. T67, T123, T181

More Practice Activities

Rhyme Time

MEETING INDIVIDUAL NEEDS

Challenge Make copies of the puzzles shown for children or put them on the board.

Help children to spell words that rhyme with *spin, skate,* and *still*. Then challenge them to make up a sentence or a couplet using two rhyming words.

sp	sk	st
spin	skate	still
--in	--ate	--ill

A Walk in the City

WATCH **ME** READ

A Walk in the City
by Tanner Ottley Gay

This story includes words with *l* and *s* clusters for decoding practice.

Literacy Activity Book, p. 21

What's in the Park?   sk   sp   st

☞ Think of the beginning or ending sounds.
Write **sk**, **sp**, or **st**.

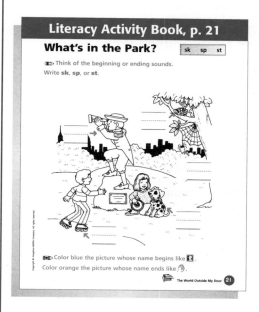

☞ Color blue the picture whose name begins like 🎺.
Color orange the picture whose name ends like 🐦.

The World Outside My Door 21

Literacy Activity Book, p. 22

Busy Day in the City   sk   sp   st

☞ Draw a line from the picture to the word it goes with.

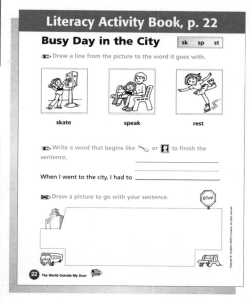

skate   speak   rest

☞ Write a word that begins like ✂ or 🎺 to finish the sentence.

When I went to the city, I had to ____

☞ Draw a picture to go with your sentence.

22   *The World Outside My Door*

Instruct *and* Integrate

Vocabulary

A Walk in the City
by Tanner Ottley Gay

A Walk in the City

This story provides practice and application for the following skills:

- **High-Frequency Words:** *go, long many, of, on, people, walk*
- **Phonics/Decoding Skills:** Clusters with *s* and *l*
- **Cumulative Review:** Previously taught decoding skills and High-Frequency Words

Literacy Activity Book, p. 23

City Sentences

Read each sentence. Draw a picture to go with it.

| Two people walk. | Many people run fast. |
| Here is a long line of people. | People go on this. |

Write about the city. Use some words from the box.

| go | long | many | of | on | people | walk |

The World Outside My Door 23

Informal Assessment

As children read *A Walk in the City* or complete the other activities on this page, note the ease with which they recognize the High-Frequency Words.

High-Frequency Words

 High-Frequency Words: *go, long, many, of, on, people, walk*

Vocabulary Password

Give each pair a sand timer and a set of High-Frequency Word cards.

- Place the cards in a pile face down.

- One player takes a word card without showing it to the other player, then starts the sand timer. The player gives a clue to help the other player guess the word.

- If the player doesn't guess the word, the first player provides another clue, and the player guesses again. Play continues until the word is guessed or the sand runs out. Then the players switch roles.

- For every word a player guesses correctly, the player gets two points and the clue-giver gets one point. The highest score wins.

Materials
- word cards for the High-Frequency Words
- sand timers

Vocabulary Musical Chairs

 Extra Support Set up chairs so that there is one less chair than there are children and place a word card on each chair. (Include any High-Frequency Words introduced to date.)

Play music as children walk around the room. When the music stops, each child tries to sit in a chair. The child who remains standing is out of the game.

The children sitting in the chairs must each use their High-Frequency Word in a sentence. If a child cannot, he or she is also out of the game, and a chair is removed. Play continues until only one child is left in a chair.

City Sentences

LAB, p. 23

Together, read the directions on *Literacy Activity Book* page 23. Have children complete the page and share their work with a partner.

MINILESSON

Vocabulary Skill
Word Family: *shop*

LAB, p. 24

Teach/Model

Read aloud page 54. Then write the word *shopping* on the chalkboard. Circle the base word *shop* and ask children how many words they can think of that have the word *shop* in them. Write their responses in a word web.

shopped · shop (a store) · shop (to buy) · SHOPPING · shopping · shopper

Practice/Apply

- Write the word *paint* on the chalkboard as the center of a word web. Have children supply words from the word family for a web. *(paint—as a noun and a verb—painted, painter, painting)*

- Invite volunteers to use words from the word web in oral sentences.

- Explain that many words have several other words that are related to them. Suggest that children might think of a group of words like this as a "word family."

- Have children complete *Literacy Activity Book* page 24.

Literacy Activity Book, p. 24

People in the City

Read the sentences about people in the city.
Write the best word to finish each sentence.

1. Joan is _____
   shop   shopped   shopping

2. Lee is a _____.
   painted   painter   painting

3. The police officer _____ the car.
   stop   stopped   stopping

4. Will is _____ many dogs.
   walked   walker   walking

24 The World Outside My Door

MINILESSON

Vocabulary Expansion
City Words

Teach/Model

Point out that *Citybook* names some things that you might find anywhere, like trains and buses, but others that you would probably only find in a city, like taxis and museums. Ask children to name some other things often found in cities.

skyscrapers	train stations
theaters	apartment buildings
stadiums	subways

Practice/Apply

Have children find pictures of city scenes, mount them on construction paper, and label them, using this sentence frame: *Cities have _____.*

Cities have restaurants.

Portfolio Opportunity

- Children's work on *Literacy Activity Book* page 23 will show how well they read the High-Frequency Words.

- Save *Literacy Activity Book* page 24 as a record of children's familiarity with word families.

Instruct and Integrate

Language and Writing

MINILESSON

Writing More Names for Places

LAB, p. 25

- Show children page 55 in *Citybook*. Ask children what kinds of stores are pictured. (Samples: electronics store, clothing store, toy store, eyeglasses store) Ask children to think of possible names for these stores. Write their responses on the board. Remind children that special names of places are written with capital letters.

- Tell children that you have to run errands after school today. On the chalkboard write a list of things you need to do. Have children tell you the special names of the places you need to visit. Write the names next to the items on your list.

- Have children complete *Literacy Activity Book* page 25 for practice in writing names of community places.

buy milk	Ed's Grocery
return book	Cary Library
deposit check	First Bank
buy medicine	Annie's Drug Store
buy flowers	Sonia's Flowers

Practice Activities

A Class Community

Set up your classroom to resemble a small community. Design areas to be the post office, the bank, the grocery store, the restaurant, and the library. Help children plan and create signs for the services and shops. The following are ideas for things children can make as they work in the different areas.

Post Office	Restaurant	Store	Library	Bank
• letters	• menus	• sale signs	• list of books	• checks
• post cards	• orders	• grocery lists		• savings books
• stamps		• coupons		

Autograph Books

To give children practice in writing their addresses, help them create their own small autograph book out of construction paper or tag board. Guide them to draw a bookplate that says, *If this book is lost, return to _____* for the first page, and have them write their name and address there. Tell children that they can ask friends and family members to write notes in their autograph books.

Extra Support Have children dictate their addresses to you. Children can then copy their addresses as you have written them.

Informal Assessment

Check children's ability to write the names of places and their understanding of using capital letters for the names of special places.

More Practice Activities

Saying Your Address

Oral Language Development Have children turn to partners and say their address. If children have difficulty doing this, suggest they practice memorizing their address at home. Repeat the activity in a few days.

Language Experience Stories

Plan field trips to see the sights in your community. Take a walk around the school block or a special tour of a business, museum, or library. When you return to school, have children dictate their thoughts about the experience.

Children can use The Learning Company's new elementary writing center to write, illustrate, and publish their work to share with others.

Business Cards

Grammar Connection Collect business cards from your friends and from local businesses. Post the cards on a bulletin board. Explain their uses to children. (You may want to play a search game using the cards. Children can search for the names of businesses such as a drugstore, a car sales shop, and so on.)

- Ask children what jobs they know about or would like to do when they grow up. Suggest they create their own business cards with their name, the name of their job or business, and a drawing or logo. Remind children to capitalize special names.

- Post their cards on the board with the others, or put them in the appropriate places in your class community, if you created one.

The Children's Choice

Invite children to brainstorm a list of fast-food restaurants, museums, toy stores, or fun places to play. Have each child pick his or her favorite in the category and write why he or she picked it. Let children help you tally their choices. On chart paper, write the name of the most popular place, and list children's reasons beneath it. You may want to publish your own "Children's Choice" newsletter about local places.

Portfolio Opportunity

- Save *Literacy Activity Book* page 25 as a sample of children's ability to write the names of places.

- Save children's written responses to activities on these pages as samples of their writing development.

Instruct *and* Integrate

Communication Activities

Audio Tape for The World Outside My Door: *Citybook*

Tell children to pay special attention to the things people do in the city as they follow the words the narrator reads.

Listening and Speaking

I Love the City!

Remind children how much Kevin liked the city. Then ask volunteers to put themselves in Kevin's shoes, come to the front of the room, and give a brief talk about why the city is such a great place to visit. Review the Tips for Giving a Talk.

Students Acquiring English Have children practice their talks with a partner.

Tips for Giving a Talk
- Know what you are going to say.
- Speak clearly.
- Look at the audience.

Sounds of the City

Review with children some of the sounds they might hear on a visit to a city. Invite volunteers to come to the front of the room and imitate different city sounds and have the other children guess what the sounds are. Encourage children to pick a city sound they like and draw a picture of what makes that sound.

Beep Beep!

Viewing

Signs All Around Us

Review with children all the different examples of print that Kevin saw in the city. Invite children to look for examples of signs in *Citybook*. Have them record their findings in chart form and explain the kind of information each sign gives. Then encourage children to find other examples of signs in their school or community and add them to the chart.

Example	Kind of Information
taxi fare $1.50 initial charge	prices
Erasmo's Laundry	kind of store

Informal Assessment

Check children's speaking skills, using the Tips for Giving a Talk as criteria for evaluation.

Independent Reading & Writing

Student-Selected Reading

Reading Range

The children in your class may be reading a wide range of books. Those reading easier books may be self-conscious about their choices. You can encourage them by

- letting children know that it is fine for different people to be reading different books
- introducing some books that are easier and some that are more difficult
- inviting confident readers to revisit old favorites from time to time
- suggesting children read with a partner

Student-Selected Writing

Emergent Writers

To help children make the transition from drawing to adding text to a page, encourage them to talk about their pictures. Then focus on the main idea and ask where it might go on a page, for example: "A dog is chasing a rabbit. If you were going to write that down, where would you put it?" Locating a place on a page can prompt children to write about their pictures.

A dog is chasing a rabbit.

Talking Allowed

Permit children to talk during writing time. Quiet conversation between students is often a form of rehearsal for prewriting. Children writing side by side might spontaneously seek each other's help in sounding out words, brainstorming ideas, and responding to each other's work.

Books for Independent Reading

Encourage children to choose their own books. They might choose one of the following titles.

Hats Hats Hats!
by Ann Morris
illustrated by Ken Heyman

A Walk in the City
by Tanner Ottley Gay

Citybook
by Shelley Rotner and Ken Kreisler

Have children reread this selection silently or aloud to a partner.

See the Bibliography on pages T42–T43 for more theme-related books for independent reading.

Ideas for Independent Writing

Encourage children to write on self-selected topics. For those who need help getting started, suggest one of the following activities:

- an **advertisement** for a billboard or the side of a bus
- an **adventure** set in a city
- a **map with labels** from their home to a favorite place in town

Portfolio Opportunity

Save examples of the writing children do independently on self-selected topics.

Cross-Curricular Activities

Punch holes through the paper and tie with string or yarn.

Choices for Social Studies

Getting from Here to There
Cooperative Learning

- Have children examine the photographs in *Citybook* to find ways people travel from place to place. List the modes of transportation on the chalkboard. Encourage children to add to the list.

- Invite small groups to choose a method of transportation and to make a shape book about it.

- Have each group draw the shape of the vehicle on oak tag and cut it out.

- Then have groups trace around their oak-tag shape on pieces of construction paper and cut out the shapes.

- Ask children to write a sentence on each of the shapes describing the method of transportation.

- Punch holes through the paper and tie with string or yarn.

Materials
- construction paper
- oak tag
- crayons
- scissors
- stapler
- string or yarn

Cities and Towns in Pictures

Invite children to create a photographic or picture essay about their city or town.

- Have children brainstorm a list of places in their town or city. Their list might include parks, schools, churches, the library, the post office, monuments, or shopping malls.

- Ask children to find photographs, take their own photographs, or draw pictures of these places.

- Have them mount each picture or photograph on construction paper and write sentences describing it.

- Display the essay on a bulletin board.

Materials
- construction paper
- felt-tip markers
- camera and film (optional)

Science

What Is Around Me?

Ask children to pretend they are standing on a busy street corner in the city pictured in *Citybook.* Encourage them to describe what they can see, hear, touch, taste, and smell. List their responses on the chalkboard.

- Take children on a sensory walk in the school neighborhood. After the walk, have children describe what they saw, heard, touched, tasted, and smelled. Record their responses on the chalkboard.

- Together, compare the two lists.

- You might have children start a sensory notebook to record what they see, hear, touch, taste, and smell when they visit new places.

Book List

Science

City Sounds
by Craig Brown

Wake Up, City
by Alvin Tressalt

Taxi: A Book of City Words

Music

Traveling Songs

- Have children recall the various ways people travel in the city.

- Explain that children will be singing a song about traveling.

- Write the first verse of "The Bus Song" on chart paper. Have children stand in a circle and sing the song.

- Encourage children to create their own lyrics, for example: "The wheels on the trains go clickety-clack . . . all down the track."

- Children might want to make up their own motions to go with the music.

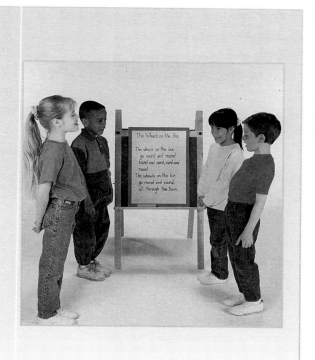

The Bus Song

The wheels on the bus go round and round, round and round, round and round. The wheels on the bus go round and round, all through the town.

SCHOOL BUS

Reading-Writing Workshop

The World Outside Your Door

Connecting to *Citybook*

Review *Citybook* with children, and have them talk about what they learned about a city neighborhood. Discuss how the book presents information with pictures and words.

Discussing the Student Models

Tell children that Shaleesha and Sheronda drew pictures of their neighborhoods and wrote about what they drew. Invite children to look at the pictures as you read aloud the captions. Discuss what Shaleesha and Sheronda tell about the world outside their door.

Prewriting

Choose a Topic Ask children to think about what they see outside their door at home, at school, or in a special place. Have them brainstorm things they might want to draw and write about. Write their ideas on the board. Then have children choose an idea to write about.

Plan the Writing Have children work with a partner as they plan what they want to tell about their neighborhoods. Encourage partners to ask questions and to share ideas.

My Neighborhood

What is your neighborhood like? Shaleesha and Sheronda wanted to write about theirs.

Shaleesha Rice

William Blackstone Elementary School

Boston, Massachusetts

Shaleesha likes to ride her bike on her neighborhood playground. She's very good at drawing, reading, and doing math. Shaleesha likes to help her friends with their schoolwork, too. Her great-grandmother says that Shaleesha is always happy.

76

My. neighborhood has beautiful trees.
I have lots of friends to play with.

SKILL FINDER

RESOURCES FOR INSTRUCTION	
Theme Resources	**Theme Resources**
Writing	*Grammar*
● Writing Names for Places, pp. T82–T83	● Special Names for Places, p. T83
● Writing More Names for Places, pp. T140–T141	● More Special Names, p. T141
● Writing to Describe Places, pp. T194–T195	

lots of people

a house

a cat

BE A WRITER

Sharonda Fulton

Roy Clark Elementary School

Tulsa, Oklahoma

Sharonda likes to play in her neighborhood. She often rides her bike and visits her friend across the street.

Sharonda also walks her dog Buster, but she doesn't go very far because he's too big!

77

Drafting

Have children sketch a picture of what they see outside their door. As children draw, you may want to walk around the room, offering help and encouragement as needed. Ask children to tell you about what they have drawn, and help them think of other things they might show. Some children may also be ready to write about what they have drawn, using standard spelling or temporary/ invented spelling.

Revising

Encourage children to meet with a writing partner to share their work. Have them ask their partners questions such as these: Can you picture my neighborhood by looking at what I have shown? Is there anything I should add to my drawing? Tell them to add details to their work, based on their writing conferences.

Publishing and Sharing

Have children finish their drawings. Help those who want to dictate sentences about what they have drawn. Bind the final drafts, and make a class book called *The World Outside Our Door.*

Children can use The Learning Company's new elementary writing center to write, illustrate, and publish their work to share with others.

Building Background

Have children look around the classroom and identify as many signs as they can. Ask them why they think signs are useful. Explain that a sign is a quick way to say something. Have children name examples of signs they see often, such as stop signs, restroom signs, and telephone signs. You might draw distinctive shapes on the chalkboard, such as an octagonal stop sign, and challenge children to identify the sign that has that shape.

Find the Signs

A sign is missing from each picture.
Can you find it?

Lemonade
10¢

78

Discussion

Read pages 78–79 with children, and have them discuss what is happening in the pictures. Then have them match the correct sign with each picture and answer the question at the bottom of page 79.

STOP

Wet
Paint

You didn't use all the signs.
Where would you see the others?

79

Social Studies

Making Signs Have children make signs for the classroom using pictures, words, or a combination of both.

Materials
- oak tag, cut into various shapes and sizes
- markers, crayons, or pencils
- letter stamps and a stamp pad

Encourage children to make signs to put in special areas of the classroom. Have them brainstorm different locations for their signs, such as the bulletin board, the Learning Center, or the coat closet. Help them label their posters. They can also make signs to take home.

Social Studies

International Signs Show children pictures of international road signs. (Travel guides are a good source.) Explain that these signs can be found in countries all around the world. Ask if they can guess why these signs have pictures with no words. Explain that the signs are useful because they can be understood by all people, no matter what language they speak. Encourage children to interpret some of the signs.

Building Background

Have children tell what time of day sunrise happens. Ask why they think it is called *sunrise.* Explain that the sun is coming up, or rising. Then ask if they ever yawn or rub their eyes when they wake up in the morning. Explain that another word for *getting up* in the morning is *rising.*

Finally, ask children if they have ever seen anyone bake bread. Explain that before the bread is baked, the dough must *rise,* or get higher. Tell children that they will read a poem about sunrise in the city.

Reading the Poem

Read the poem with children. Then challenge them to figure out the poet's comparisons by asking the following questions:

- What does the city in the poem do that a person waking up also does? (yawns)

- What does the city in the poem do that bread dough also does? (rises)

Then have children look at the picture to find things that show it is morning.

Sunrise

The city YAWNS
And rubs its eyes,
Like baking bread
Begins to rise.

by Frank Asch

80

Social Studies

Comparing Environments Have children compare the city in the picture to their community. Ask them what things they see and hear each morning on their way to school. Depending on where they live, they may find many similarities or many differences between the two. Help children create a comparison chart with their responses.

Sing Along with Ella Jenkins

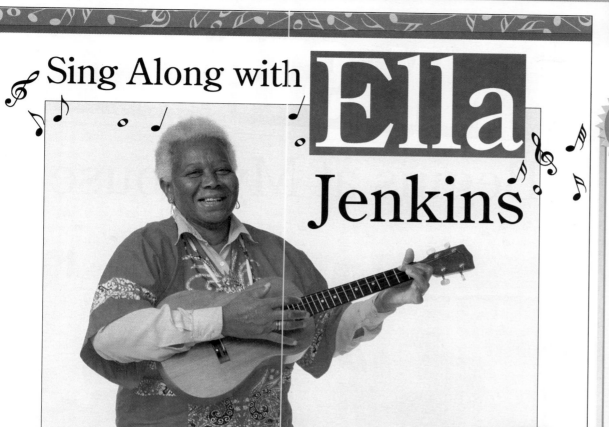

Here is a picture of Ms. Jenkins with her baritone ukulele.

Ella Jenkins has performed in concerts all over the world. She also teaches music classes called rhythm workshops. There, children share songs, dances, games, and chants from different countries.

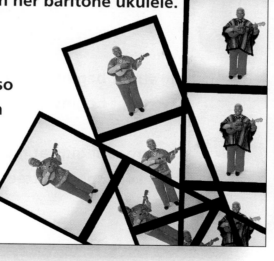

Introduce *the* Literature

Prior Knowledge

Invite children to picture in their minds the street or road on which they live. You might ask them to share descriptions by asking questions such as these:

- What is the name of your street?

- What is the tallest building on your street?

- Are there trees on your street? If so, are they big or little?

- Are the houses close together or far apart?

- What vehicles besides cars do you often see on your street?

Tell children that they are going to read one boy's description of the street where he lives. Explain that the boy's description is part of a song by Ella Jenkins. Then have them look at the picture and read about Ella Jenkins on page 81.

Discussion

Read pages 82–87 with children. Then have them look at the pictures and point out the boy whose street it is.

Invite children to discuss the following questions:

- What are some things you see in the pictures that *go up and down?* (the stairs, the swing)

- What things do you see that might *go round and round?* (the two boys going around the sign pole, tires on the wagon)

- Why do you think the boy says that some things on the street *go upside down?*

- Why do you think the street is a *very special street?*

MY STREET Begins at My House

My street begins at my house,
My street begins at my house.

My street begins at my house,
It's a very special street.

82

On my street things go up and down,
On my street things go round and round.

83

Rhythm Workshop

Ask children to find some repeated verses or patterns in the song. Tell them that these repetitions and patterns help give the song rhythm. Encourage them to clap their hands to the rhythm of the words. Invite children to tap on their desks or stomp their feet as they say the words.

**On my street things go upside down,
It's a very special street.**

84

My street begins at my house,
My street begins at my house.

85

Visual Literacy

Snapshots Invite children to look at the snapshots that are included in this photo essay. Ask them who the other boys in the photos are. Do they look like they are having fun? Have children predict why the boy might be taking their pictures.

Discussion

Have children discuss these questions:

- What is the boy doing to show others what his street looks like? Do you think that taking pictures is a good idea? Why?

- The boy is sending his description to a very special person. Who is it? (his grandmother)

- Why might the boy be sending this description to his grandmother right now? (One possible answer is that the boy has just moved to a new street and wants to show his grandmother what it is like.)

- Do you think the boy likes the street where he lives? Why?

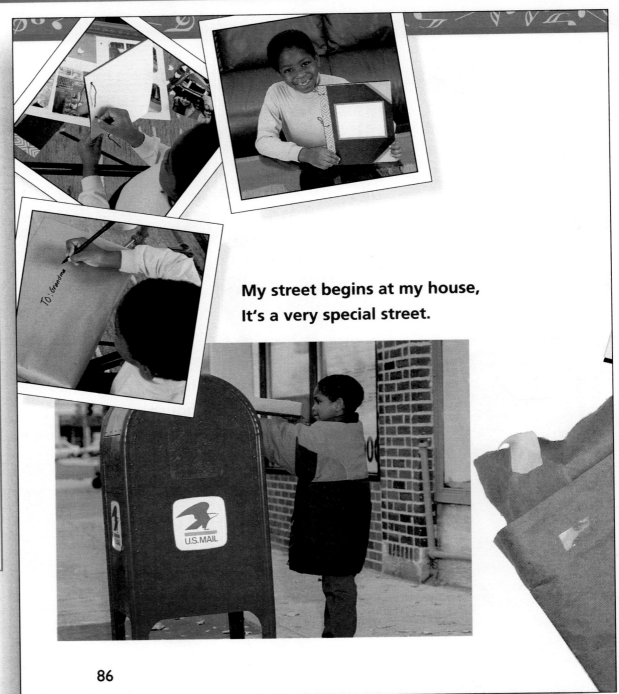

My street begins at my house,
It's a very special street.

86

87

✏️ **Writing**

Challenge Encourage children to write to a relative or friend about their home. They might include descriptions of their street, their friends, or things that happen on their street. Help children prepare the envelopes for mailing by reviewing with them the important things to include:

- The name and complete address, including the ZIP code, of the person receiving the mailing

- A stamp for the right amount of postage

- The child's name and return address in the upper left corner

Social Studies

My Neighborhood Encourage children to create their own picture essay about their street, road, or neighborhood. Some may wish to draw a map showing their street with its houses, stores and other buildings, as well as green areas. Others may prefer to draw photolike scenes and caption them.

ANTHOLOGY

SELECTION:

Listen to the Desert/Oye al desierto

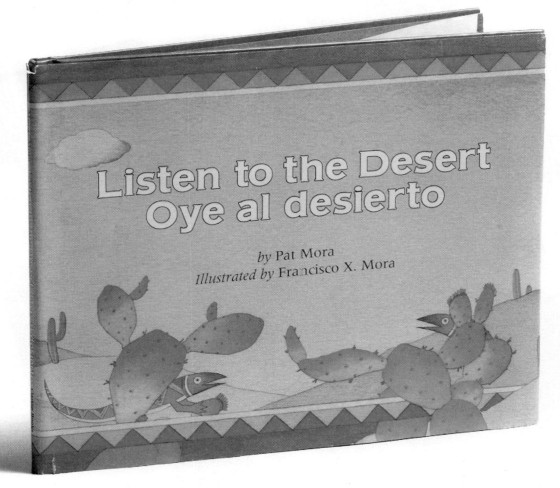

by Pat Mora

Other Books by the Author

A Birthday Basket for Tia

Pablo's Tree

Agua, Agua, Agua

The Desert Is My Mother

Selection Summary

In this poetic work, the author invites the reader to stop and listen — in both English and Spanish — to the fascinating sounds of the desert. One can hear the hoot of an owl, the hiss of a snake, the call of a coyote, and the spin of the wind. There's much more to hear when you explore the desert. Come listen!

Lesson Planning Guide

	Skill/Strategy Instruction	Meeting Individual Needs	Lesson Resources
1 **Introduce** *the* **Literature** *Pacing: 1 day*	**Preparing to Read and Write** Warm-up, T160 Prior Knowledge/Background, T160 **Key Words**, T161 • desert **High–Frequency Words**, T161 • call • eat • fish • say • to	**Other Choices for Building Background**, T161 **Students Acquiring English**, T161 **Extra Support**, T161	**Poster** Warm-up, 3D **Transparency** Selection Vocabulary, 3–2 *Literacy Activity Book* Selection Vocabulary, p. 27
2 **Interact** *with* **Literature** *Pacing: 1–3 days*	**Reading Strategies** Predict/Infer, T164, T170 Evaluate, T164, T178, T184 Think About Words, T168 Monitor, T172 **Minilessons** Noting Details, T175 ✔ Making Generalizations, T177 Clusters with *r, l, s,* T181 **Responding**, T186	**Choices for Reading**, T164 **Guided Reading**, T164, T172, T178, T184 **Students Acquiring English**, T178 **Extra Support**, T168, T174, T180, T185 **Challenge**, T171, T175, T177, T181 **Responding Choices**, T187	**Reading Writing Workshop** The World Outside Your Door, T146–T147 *Literacy Activity Book* Comprehension Check, p. 29 **Study Skills** Following Directions, T203, H4 The Learning Company's new elementary writing center software
3 **Instruct** *and* **Integrate** *Pacing: 1–3 days*	✔ **Comprehension** Making Generalizations, T188–T189 ✔ **Phonics and Spelling** Consonant Clusters Review, T190, T191 ✔ **Vocabulary** High-Frequency Words, T192 Sense Words, T193 Onomatopoeia, T193 **Language and Writing** Writing to Describe Places, T194–T195 **Communication Activities**, T196 **Independent Reading & Writing**, T197 **Cross-Curricular Activities**, T198–T200	**Activity Choices/Reteaching** Making Generalizations, T189 **Activity Choices** Consonant Clusters Review, T190–T191 **Activity Choices** High-Frequency Words, T192 **Activity Choices** Language and Writing, T194–T195	**Reading Writing Workshop** The World Outside Your Door, T146–T147 *Literacy Activity Book* Comprehension Skill, p. 30 Phonics and Spelling, pp. 31–34 High-Frequency Words, p. 35 Vocabulary Skill, p. 36 Language and Writing, p. 37 **Audio Tape** for The World Outside My Door: *Listen to the Desert/Oye al desierto* The Learning Company's new elementary writing center software

✔ *Indicates **Tested Skills.** See page T47 for assessment options.*

1

Introduce
the
Literature

Preparing to Read and Write

Poster 3D

Listen!

INTERACTIVE LEARNING

Warm-up

Animal Talk

• Use Poster 3D to engage children in some "animal talk." Begin by having children name the animals they see and identify the sounds each animal makes.

• Identify the function of the speech balloons. Help children record the animal sounds in the speech balloons.

• Invite children to imagine what it would sound like if all the animals were "talking" at once.

Prior Knowledge/Building Background

**Key Concept
Desert life**

• Collect photographs or realistic pictures of desert landscapes and desert animals. (See Anthology page 113 and the Bibliography on pages T42–T43.)

• Display the pictures you have collected.

• Encourage children to identify by name things in each picture, such as sandy soil, rocks, plants, and animals.

• Have children share what they know about deserts. Help them understand that the desert is a unique natural environment with its own animals and plants.

Geography

Teacher FactFile

Deserts

Help children understand more about what deserts are like by sharing this information. You may want to help children find the places mentioned on a map.

• The largest desert in the world is the Sahara Desert in Africa.

• There are no deserts in Europe.

• Most people think of deserts as being hot, dry places. Yet many cold, dry places are deserts, too. These places are often called cold deserts, or tundra. Antarctica is an example of a cold desert.

• Camels survive in the desert by making water from the fat they store in their humps.

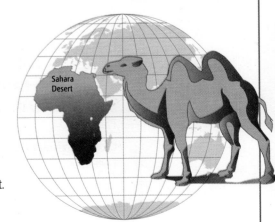

Sahara Desert

Other Choices for Building Background

Selection Vocabulary

Key Words: *desert*

High-Frequency Words: *call, eat, fish, say, to*

Use Transparency 3–2 to introduce the selection vocabulary. Read the sentences aloud. Then talk briefly about the words using these prompts:

Reread the sentences and invite children to chime in with the sound-effect words *croak, splish splash,* and *munch.*

Which two words mean to use one's voice? *(call, say)*

What animal name rhymes with *wish*? *(fish)*

How would you describe a desert? *(very hot)*

What do you do when you're hungry? *(eat)*

Which short word sounds just like a number word? *(to)*

Vocabulary Practice Have children work independently or in pairs to complete *Literacy Activity Book* page 27.

Picture Play

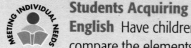

Students Acquiring English Have children compare the elements in the pictures you prepared for display with those in the selection. Are there any matches? Help children make a list. Ask students acquiring English if they know any words in their first language for items on the list. Have these children help their classmates say the words.

Quick-Write

Have children quick-draw a desert scene. Ask them to label the things in their pictures. Encourage them to write a sentence that tells how they would feel about spending time in a desert.

A Listening List

Extra Support The selection is in essence a list of desert sounds described onomatopoetically. To ready children for the form of the selection, use the animal names and animal sounds from Poster 3D to create a Listening List. Record children's ideas on chart paper.

Transparency 3–2

What Is Here?

The desert is a hot, hot place.
The sand slips over your toes.
The sky is wide and blue.
At first it looks like no one is here.
Stop and listen. What do you hear?
You can hear birds call.
You can hear toads say, "Croak, croak!"
You can hear fish splish splash in hidden pools.
You can even hear mice eat, "Munch, munch!"
It's fun to visit the desert.

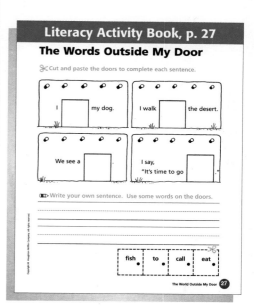

Literacy Activity Book, p. 27

The Words Outside My Door

Cut and paste the doors to complete each sentence.

I ____ my dog.   I walk ____ the desert.

We see a ____   I say, "It's time to go ____"

Write your own sentence. Use some words on the doors.

fish • to • call • eat

Listening List

Listen to the owl speak, *Whoo, whoo, whoo*

Listen to the cat sing, *Meow, meow, meow*

Listen to the cow cry, *Moo, moo, moo*

Interact *with* **Literature**

More About the Author

Pat Mora

Born and brought up in El Paso, Texas, Pat Mora speaks and writes in both Spanish and English. She has written books of poetry for adults, and her poetic style is reflected in *Listen to the Desert/Oye al desierto.* She is also the author of other books for young readers, such as *Pablo's Tree* and *Tomás and the Library Lady.*

Meet Pat Mora

Pat Mora grew up in the southwestern United States, where she learned English and Spanish. She says that she can hear the sounds of the desert in both languages. Now Ms. Mora writes books and poetry in both languages, too.

Meet Francisco X. Mora

Francisco X. Mora grew up in Mexico. He likes to paint flowers, lizards, armadillos, and other things he saw there as a child.

"My paintings are to be enjoyed," he says. "They talk about friendship, joy, and the beauty of nature and life."

88

More About the Illustrator

Francisco X. Mora

Born in Mexico and now living in Wisconsin, Francisco X. Mora's work has been shown in exhibitions throughout the United States and Mexico. In his books for children, he often paints animals, flowers, and other things as he remembers them from his childhood in Mexico. He especially loves to show his animals living together in peace.

Francisco X. Mora has illustrated many other books for children and is also the author of three of them: *Juan Tuza and the Magic Pouch, The Legend of the Two Moons,* and *La Gran Fiesta de Navidad.*

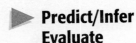
Interact *with* Literature

Reading Strategies

▶ **Predict/Infer Evaluate**

Student Application Ask children to describe some of the things they do to help themselves understand what they read. Then have them preview *Listen to the Desert*. Invite them to tell what they find out about the story.

Get children started in using their reading strategies by asking what is different about this selection. Talk about how it is written in English and Spanish and how it looks more like a poem than a story. Ask if children think they will enjoy reading this particular selection and why or why not.

Predicting/Purpose Setting

Ask children what sounds they think they will "hear" in *Listen to the Desert*. Record their predictions and have children read to see which of the predictions match the selection.

Listen to the desert, pon, pon, pon.
Listen to the desert, pon, pon, pon.
Oye al desierto, pon, pon, pon.
Oye al desierto, pon, pon, pon.

90

Choices for Reading

Teacher Read Aloud

Help children set a purpose for reading. Then read aloud the entire selection as children follow along. Switch to Guided Reading for a second pass. Use the Guided Reading questions on pages T172, T178, and T184 to check children's comprehension.

Shared Reading

Following purpose setting, read the entire story aloud as children follow along. Encourage them to chime in on each repeated line. Then use one or more of the other choices for rereading.

Guided Reading

Have children read pages 90–99 to see how each animal makes a sound. Follow up with the questions under Guided Reading on page T172.

Cooperative Reading

If possible, pair children whose first language is Spanish with others whose primary language is English. The first-language speaker can read aloud the first line in either English or Spanish. The other reads the repeated line.

Independent Reading

Have children record predictions about the sounds in *Listen to the Desert*. Then have them read silently to the end of the selection and compare their predictions with what the author wrote.

91

Interact *with* **Literature**

Listen to the owl hoot, whoo, whoo, whoo.
Listen to the owl hoot, whoo, whoo, whoo.
   ¡Oye! La lechuza, uuu, uuu, uuu.
   ¡Oye! La lechuza, uuu, uuu, uuu.

92

Informal Assessment

Oral Reading Use pages 90–93 to informally assess children's oral reading fluency. See the Oral Reading Checklist in the *Teacher's Assessment Handbook* for criteria.

QuickREFERENCE

High-Frequency Words
to

Have children find and read the word *to*. Point out that this word is part of the repeating group of words *Listen to the.* . . .

Multicultural Link

Spanish Vocabulary Some children may know other words for *lechuza* (owl), such as *búho* or *tecolote*.

Background: FYI

The Spanish in this poem is not a literal translation of the English. The poet exhibits at times certain liberties with the Spanish to maintain the poem's rhythm and meter, as well as to reflect her own dialect.

93

Visual Literacy

Ask what time of day the picture shows it to be. Have children identify specific clues in the illustration.

Science Link

Owls Explain that an owl's eyes are so sensitive it can see in even the dimmest light. Owls cannot move their eyes from side to side, so they have to move their heads: they can turn their heads almost all the way around!

Interact *with* Literature

Reading Strategies

▶ **Think About Words**

Talk about how children could figure out the word *toad* on page 94 if they did not know it.

- **What makes sense** I know that the sentence tells about an animal. It is an animal that can hop.

- **Sounds for the letters** What word begins with *t*, ends with *d*, and names an animal that can hop?

- **Picture clues** The picture shows a little animal that looks like a frog, but *frog* does not begin with *t*. A toad is like a frog. I'm pretty sure the word is *toad*.

Have children read the first sentence aloud with you and discuss whether *toad* makes sense here.

Listen to the toad hop, plop, plop, plop.
Listen to the toad hop, plop, plop, plop.
Oye al sapito, plap, plap, plap.
Oye al sapito, plap, plap, plap.

94

Self-Assessment

Encourage children to think about how they usually figure out words.

- Do I have a favorite way of figuring out words? Why does that way seem to work for me?

- Do I sometimes use more than just one way to figure out a word? What ways do I use?

QuickREFERENCE

 ★★★ **Multicultural Link**

Spanish-speaking children may recognize the diminutive-forming suffix *-ito* on *sapito*, which means "little toad."

Extra Support

Help children understand that it is the toad's hopping that makes the sound.

95

Science Link

Toads and Frogs Most people have trouble telling toads and frogs apart. A toad's skin is warty-looking, dry, and thick, while a frog's skin is smooth and moist. It is the desert toad's warty skin that helps protect it from the intense heat.

Reading Strategies

▶ **Predict/Infer**

Discuss the patterns that can help children predict what will come next in the selection. These patterns can also help them understand what they read.

- Call attention to the pattern created by the repeated words *Listen to the....*

- Point out that each time children turn the page they see these words and read about a new sound in the desert.

- The pictures can help children understand what the sound words mean.

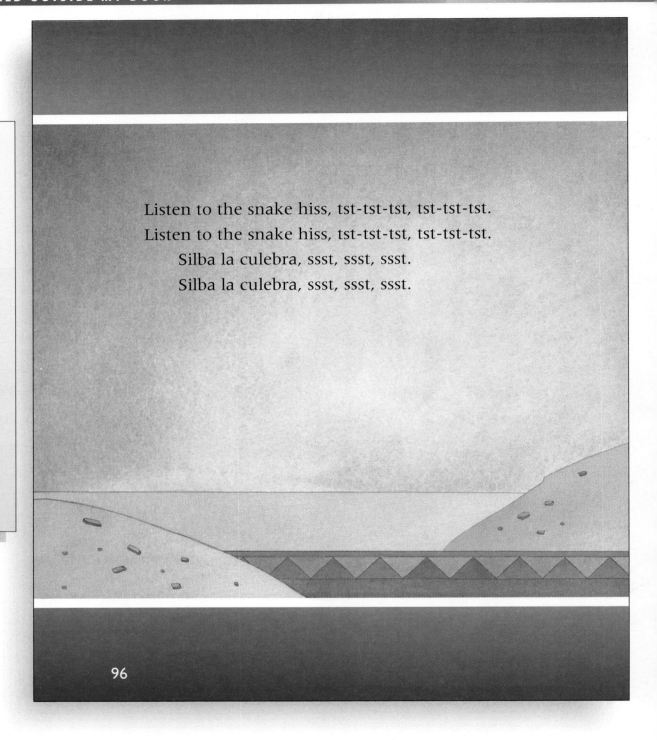

Listen to the snake hiss, tst-tst-tst, tst-tst-tst.
Listen to the snake hiss, tst-tst-tst, tst-tst-tst.
      Silba la culebra, ssst, ssst, ssst.
      Silba la culebra, ssst, ssst, ssst.

96

Quick**REFERENCE**

Phonics/Decoding Review

Consonant Sounds Have children find and read aloud the words that tell what the animals do on pages 92, 94, and 96. *(hoot, hop, hiss)* Point out that all of these words begin with the sound for *h*.

 Multicultural Link

Spanish Vocabulary Some Spanish-speaking children may be familiar with the word *serpiente* for snake instead of *culebra*.

97

Challenge

MEETING INDIVIDUAL NEEDS

Have volunteers demonstrate how a snake moves through the sand.

Anthology p. 97

Interact
with
Literature

Reading Strategies

▶ **Monitor**

Some children may be confused by the author's use of *say* in reference to the sound the dove makes. Have them use the selection's content pattern and the picture to clarify that the author is still reporting the sounds animals make.

 **Guided Reading**

Comprehension/Critical Thinking

Have children compare their predictions about sounds with what the author wrote. Then ask:

1. How are the owl and dove alike? (Both are birds. Both make "oo" sounds.)

2. Are the sounds you've read about so far loud or soft? Explain.

Predicting/Purpose Setting

Invite children to add to or change their predictions about sounds they will "hear" in the selection. Then have them read pages 100–105. Use the questions on page T178 to check comprehension.

Informal Assessment

If children's responses indicate that they are understanding the selection, have them finish reading it independently or cooperatively.

Listen to the dove say coo, coo, coo.
Listen to the dove say coo, coo, coo.
    La paloma arrulla, currucú, currucú, currucú.
    La paloma arrulla, currucú, currucú, currucú.

98

QuickREFERENCE

High-Frequency Words
say

Relate the word *say* to *says* and *said*. Have children create oral sentences using each of the forms.

Background: FYI

In Spanish, *ll* is a distinct letter of the alphabet and is generally pronounced as the consonant *y* is pronounced in English.

99

Anthology p. 99

Science Link

Ask children if the dove in the picture reminds them of any other bird they are familiar with. Explain that doves are smaller than, but related to, pigeons.

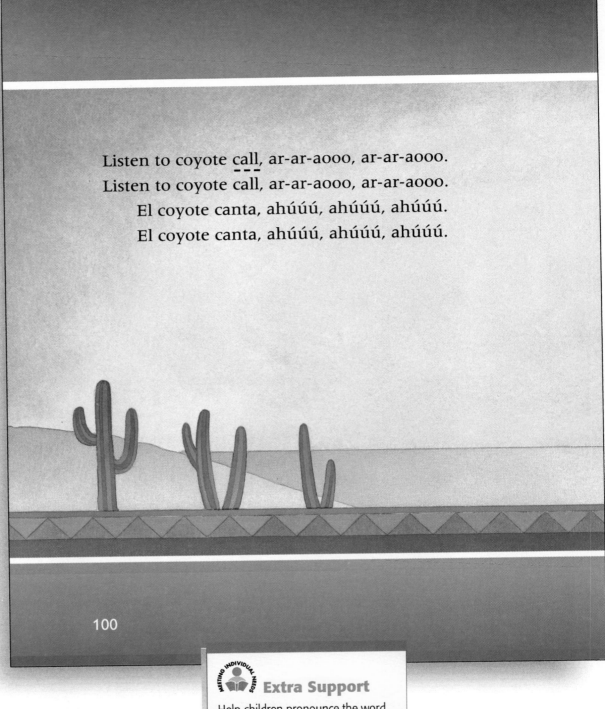

Listen to coyote call, ar-ar-aooo, ar-ar-aooo.
Listen to coyote call, ar-ar-aooo, ar-ar-aooo.
El coyote canta, ahúúú, ahúúú, ahúúú.
El coyote canta, ahúúú, ahúúú, ahúúú.

100

QuickREFERENCE

MEETING INDIVIDUAL NEEDS **Extra Support**

Help children pronounce the word *coyote*. If necessary, explain that a coyote is a wolflike animal that lives in the deserts of the American Southwest, among other places. Coyotes are sometimes called *prairie wolves*.

High-Frequency Words
call

Have children identify the word *call*. Help them understand that in this poem *call* is used as an action word. Explain that *call* can be used as a naming word, too, as in "I made phone call to my doctor."

101

Science Link

Tell children that the coyote is famous for its evening serenade of howls and yelps. In fact, its scientific name, *Canis latrans*, means "barking dog."

Challenge

Have children make the coyote's nighttime sound. Challenge them to take the coyote's howling stance as they try out their calls.

Comprehension

Noting Details

REVIEW & MAINTAIN

Teach/Model

Recall with children that paying attention to all the words and pictures in a story helps to make it interesting to read. Ask how the sound effects help us to enjoy this story.

Review some of the children's favorite sounds. Then help them conclude that the sound-effect words and the special action words the author chooses, as well as the details in the pictures, all make us feel like we are really in a desert.

Work with children to identify some of the action words the author uses. *(hoot, hop, hiss, call)*

Practice/Apply

Have children identify details in the pictures that help them understand more about the desert and make the selection interesting.

SKILL FINDER

Full lesson/Reteaching, pp. T134–T135; Themes 1, 7, 10

Minilessons, p. T125

Interact
with
Literature

Listen to the <u>fish</u> <u>eat</u>, puh, puh, puh.
Listen to the fish eat, puh, puh, puh.
¡Oye! Los pescaditos, plaf, plaf, plaf.
¡Oye! Los pescaditos, plaf, plaf, plaf.

102

Quick**REFERENCE**

High-Frequency Words
fish, eat

Have children read the first sentence on page 102 aloud with you and identify the words *fish* and *eat*. Explain that the plural form of *fish* can be either *fish* or *fishes*.

Phonics/Decoding Review

Consonant Sounds Ask children to identify other words that begin with the same sound as *fish*. Then ask them to think of words that end with the same sound as *eat*.

103

Comprehension
Making Generalizations

Teach/Model

TESTED SKILL

Ask children if they can tell by reading the selection that the author has spent some time in the desert. Have them tell how they came to that conclusion. (She identifies different kinds of desert animals and can describe how they sound.)

Then ask children what they think the author would want them to do if they had a chance to spend some time in the desert. Guide them in making the generalization that the author probably would tell them to listen and watch carefully to get the most out of the experience. Point out that, even though the author doesn't say this, they can tell from the things she does say about sounds in the desert what her advice might be.

Practice/Apply

Tell children that during the hottest part of the day, the desert looks empty and lifeless. Ask them why that might be. (Animals sleep or hide in cool places.) Ask children to think about the clues in the selection and tell where they think the animals might be during the day. (underground, in the shade of a plant, behind or under rocks)

SKILL FINDER
Full lesson/Reteaching, pp. T188–T189; Theme 8

Minilessons, p. T71

Challenge
MEETING INDIVIDUAL NEEDS

Have volunteers demonstrate the sound and action of the fish eating.

Background: FYI

The word *pescaditos* ("little fish," from the Spanish word *pescado*) is most often used to denote prepared-to-eat fish, while *pez* identifies a live fish. However, in some dialects, *pescado* refers to "river fish."

Interact *with* Literature

Guided Reading

Comprehension/Critical Thinking

Have children compare their predictions with the sounds described on the pages they just read. Then ask these questions:

1. What animals did you read about in this part of the selection? (coyote, fish, mice)

2. Do you think *scrrt, scrrt* is a good description of how mice sound? Why or why not? What sound words would you use to describe mice noises?

Predicting/Purpose Setting

Have children predict what else they might "hear" in this selection. Then have them read to the end to discover what other sounds can be heard if they listen to the desert.

Reading Strategies
 Evaluate

Ask children if they were surprised by any of the sounds the author included. Which sounds do they think would be easiest for them to hear if they were actually in a desert? How else might the author have described the sound for each animal?

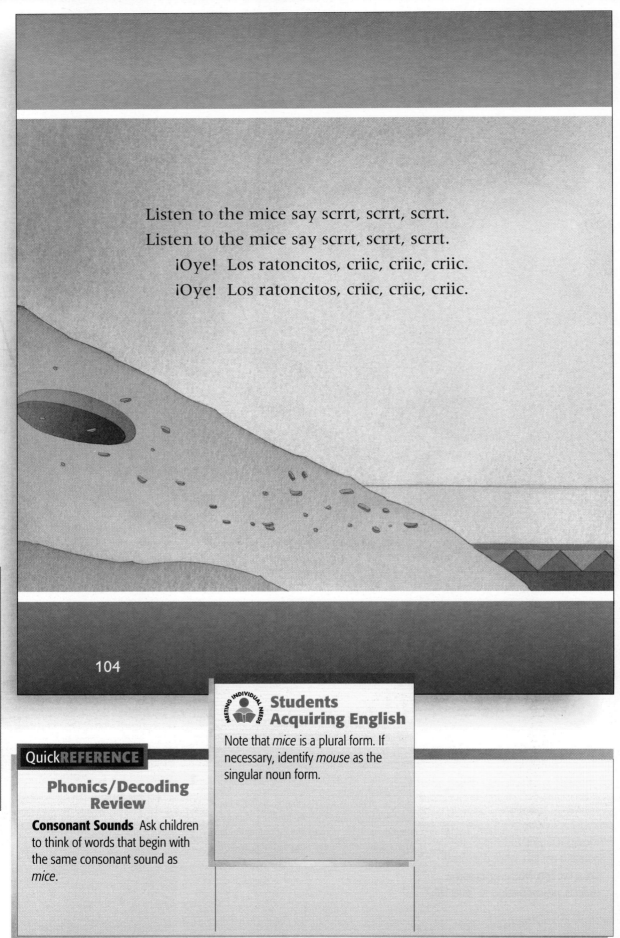

Listen to the mice say scrrt, scrrt, scrrt.
Listen to the mice say scrrt, scrrt, scrrt.
¡Oye! Los ratoncitos, criic, criic, criic.
¡Oye! Los ratoncitos, criic, criic, criic.

104

Quick**REFERENCE**

Phonics/Decoding Review

Consonant Sounds Ask children to think of words that begin with the same consonant sound as *mice*.

Students Acquiring English

Note that *mice* is a plural form. If necessary, identify *mouse* as the singular noun form.

105

Anthology p. 105

Visual Literacy

Ask children to use the illustration to tell where mice live in the desert. Explain that many small animals burrow deep into the sand to keep cool during the hot daytime hours. They come out and move around at night when it is cool.

 Journal

Ask children to write the name of the animal they would most like to see up close in the desert. Some children may want to add an illustration. Some may want to write about why they would like to see a particular animal.

Interact *with* Literature

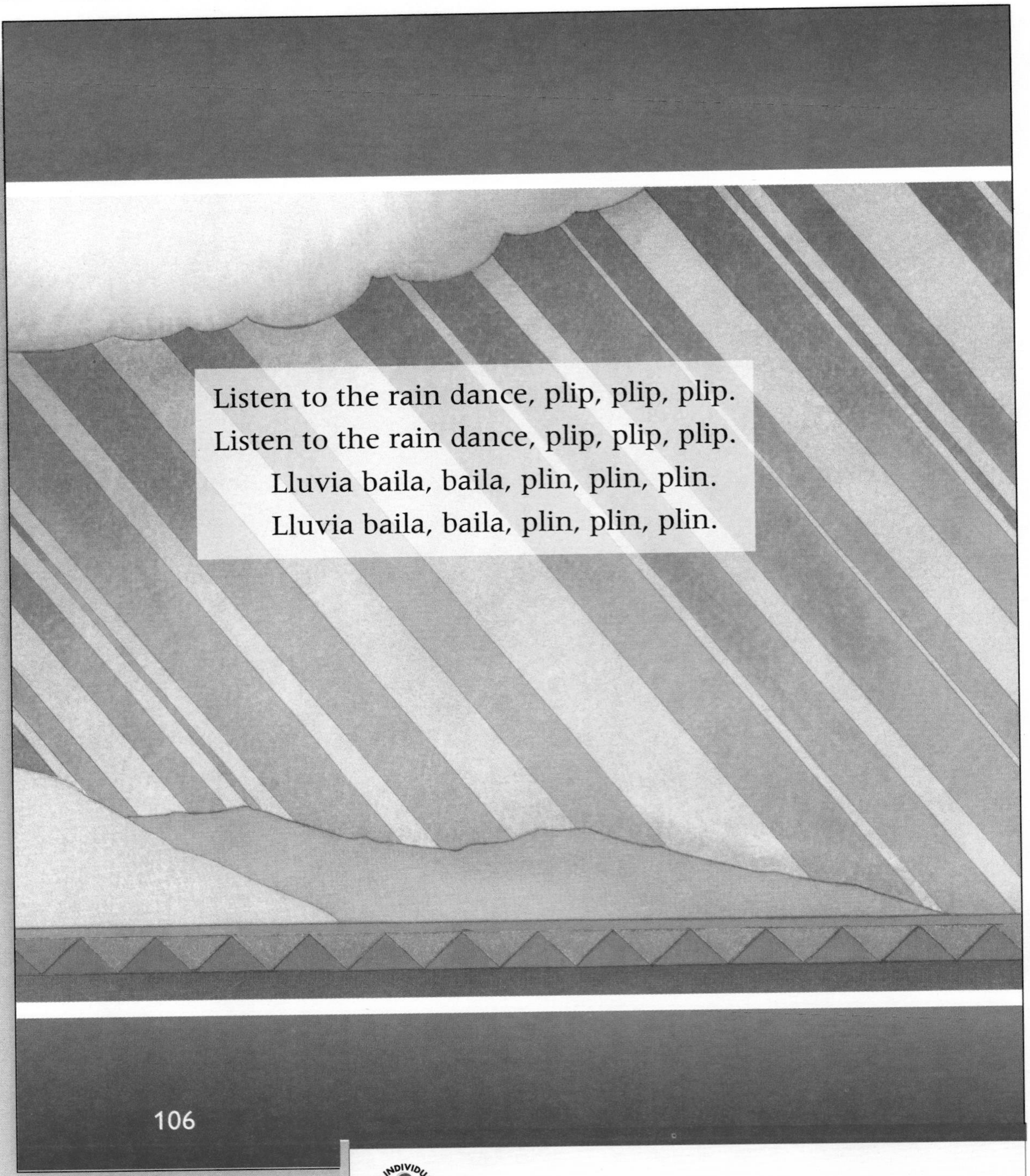
Listen to the rain dance, plip, plip, plip.
Listen to the rain dance, plip, plip, plip.
Lluvia baila, baila, plin, plin, plin.
Lluvia baila, baila, plin, plin, plin.

106

Meeting Individual Needs: Extra Support

Some children may need help with the idea of personifying the rain, as the author does here by saying that it dances. Explain that this is the author's way of creating a picture in the reader's mind of how the rain is falling. Ask children how they think the rain is falling. Is there a heavy downpour or a light, gentle rain?

QuickREFERENCE

Phonics/Decoding Review

Consonant Sounds Ask children to think of words that begin or end with the same sound as *rain*.

107

Phonics/Decoding

Clusters with *r, l, s*

TESTED SKILL

Teach/Model

Have children say the sound the rain makes as it dances. Write *plip, plip, plip* on the board. Remind children that when *p* and *l* come together in a word their sounds almost seem to be one sound.

Create the following web:

Have volunteers complete each section of the web, making words that rhyme with *plip*.

Practice/Apply

Write *stack* on the board. Have a volunteer underline the two letters that stand for the beginning sounds. Then display these clusters: *tr, bl, sn*.

Have children write *stack* on paper and below it write rhyming words using the clusters on the board. Invite them to illustrate the words and read them to a partner.

SKILL FINDER

Phonics and Spelling, pp. T76, T136, T190

Minilessons, pp. T65, T67, T107, T123

MEETING INDIVIDUAL NEEDS

Challenge

Ask children to think of other sound effect words to describe a "dancing" rain.

2

Interact
with
Literature

Listen to the wind spin, zoom, zoom, zoom.
Listen to the wind spin, zoom, zoom, zoom.
Oye, zumba el viento, zuum, zuum, zuum.
Oye, zumba el viento, zuum, zuum, zuum.

108

QuickREFERENCE

Vocabulary

Synonyms See if children can substitute a synonym for *spin*. They might suggest *whirl, twirl,* or other words.

Visual Literacy

Ask children to describe how the artist shows that it is windy. (streaks across the picture; bending cactuses)

109

Phonics/Decoding Review

Consonant Sounds Remind children that the letter *z* stands for the sound they hear at the beginning of *zoom*. Have them think of words that begin with this sound.

At this time, you may also wish to review the sound of final *x* by asking children to identify the letter that stands for the last sound in *box, fix,* and *wax.*

Interact with Literature

 Guided Reading

Comprehension/Critical Thinking

Discuss which of children's predictions match what the author wrote in the last part of the selection. Then ask:

1. How are the sounds in this part of the selection different from those you read about earlier? (They are made by rain and wind rather than animals.)

2. What sound do you think the words *pon, pon, pon* describe? (The words probably describe all the sounds of the desert together.)

Reading Strategies

▶ **Evaluate**

Encourage children to talk about what they liked or didn't like about the selection. Did they enjoy the sound words? Did they find it interesting to see the poem in two languages? Then ask what they think the author wants readers to know about the desert.

Listen to the desert, pon, pon, pon.
Listen to the desert, pon, pon, pon.
Oye al desierto, pon, pon, pon.
Oye al desierto, pon, pon, pon.

110

Self-Assessment

Have children ask themselves:

● How did the story pattern help me predict what would come next?

● What did I think of the way this selection was written?

QuickREFERENCE

Visual Literacy

Ask children what is unusual about the pictures on these pages. Help them see that all the desert animals are depicted together. Note that this would most likely not occur in real life. The artist is making the point that all of these creatures, plus the rain and the wind, make up the sounds of the desert.

111

Extra Support

Rereading Have children reread the selection in small groups, with a different child reading each spread.
Multi-Age Classrooms Pair younger children with older ones and have the partners reread the selection chorally.

Phonics/Decoding Review

Consonant Sounds Point out that all the animals children see on pages 110–111 live in the desert. Write *live* on the chalkboard and remind children that the letter *v* stands for the sound they hear at the end of *live*. Invite them to suggest words that begin with *v*, then words that end with *v*.

Interact with Literature

Responding Activities

Personal Response

Ask children to draw and write about what they learned about the desert. Have them tell whether the desert is a place they would like to visit and why.

Anthology Activity

Before children begin to draw and write, encourage them to talk about the different animals they met in the selection. Invite children who know about other desert animals to share what they know. When children are finished drawing and writing, use a hole punch and yarn to bind their pages into a book.

Informal Assessment

Use the Comprehension Check or the Literature Discussion on page T187 to assess children's general understanding of the story.

Additional Support:

- Take a picture walk through the story. Call on volunteers to summarize what is happening on each page.
- Discuss with children the author's purpose or purposes for writing the selection.

RESPONDING

Our Guide to Desert Animals

Draw and write about a desert animal. Work in a group. Put your pages together to make a book.

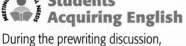

This is a mouse.

112

QuickREFERENCE

Students Acquiring English

During the prewriting discussion, suggest that children jot down ideas, words, and phrases that they think they may like to use in their own writing.

Home Connection

Suggest that children draw pictures with captions to help them share what they have learned about the desert with family members.

More Responding Activities

Literature Discussion
Cooperative Learning

Have children discuss what they liked and didn't like about the stories in this theme. Ask these questions to prompt discussion:

- Which story did you like the most? Why?
- What would you tell a friend about the stories in this theme?

Desert March

Provide children with assorted cutouts of the desert animals mentioned in the selection. Have each child select his or her favorite to use to make a stick puppet. Ask children to color their animals and paste them on craft sticks. Group children according to their animal selections and ask them to march around the "desert" (classroom). Each animal group should recite in turn its sound as identified in the selection: *Listen to the mice say scrrt, scrrt, scrrt.*

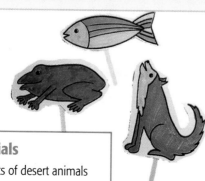

Materials
- cutouts of desert animals
- craft sticks
- paste
- crayons or markers

Listen Once Again

Invite children to add another verse to the poem. Have them use the *Listen to the...* pattern and come up with a sound word for one of these desert natives: tumbleweeds, sand, spiders. Provide children with verbs appropriate to each item, for example:

- Listen to the tumbleweeds roll, ...
- Listen to the sand swirl, ...
- Listen to the spiders scurry, ...

Have children illustrate the new verse.

Shared Writing: *A Class Poem*

Invite children to work together to create their own "Listen to the ..." poem for a familiar setting, such as the playground or the classroom. Work with them to list things someone might hear in that setting. Call on individual children to supply the appropriate sounds to complete each verse, for example:

- Listen to the children laugh, ha-ha, ho-ho.
- Listen to the ball bounce, boing, boing, boing.

Record the poem on chart paper and display it on the bulletin board.

Comprehension Check

To determine children's overall understanding of the selection, use these questions and/or *Literacy Activity Book* page 29.

1. Who lives in the desert?
2. What sounds do some of the desert animals make?
3. Is the desert a loud place or a quiet place? Explain your thinking.

Literacy Activity Book, p. 29

I Hear the Desert

☞ What can you hear in the desert? Write and draw about it. These pictures may help to remind you.

The World Outside My Door **29**

Portfolio Opportunity

- As a record of selection comprehension, save *Literacy Activity Book* page 29.
- As a writing sample, save children's Personal Response.

3 Instruct *and* Integrate

Comprehension

INTERACTIVE LEARNING

TESTED SKILL ✓ Making Generalizations
LAB, p. 30

Teach/Model

Take children for a listening walk near the school (or just have them imagine they are doing that). Have them name things that make noise and use sound words to tell what sounds they heard. List their responses on the chalkboard. Then have children close their eyes as you read them their list in the style of the story. (Example: "Listen to the truck roar, vroom, vroom, vroom. Listen to the pigeon call, coo, coo, coo.") Ask children what their list tells them about the neighborhood around the school. (There are many sounds.)

Ask children to name some of the animals and sound words in *Listen to the Desert/Oye al desierto*. List them on the chalkboard. Then ask children what the lists tell us about the desert. (that many animals live there; that there are sounds even in a quiet desert)

Story Animals	Sounds	The Desert
snake	tst	Many different
dove	coo	kinds of animals
toad	plop	live in the desert
coyote	ar-ar-aooo	
fish	puh	

Ask children if they think the author of the selection named every animal that lives in that desert. Then pose this question: If you went to the desert and listened and watched carefully, what might you discover?

Practice/Apply

• Read the following partial sentences with children. Then have them copy one onto a piece of paper and complete it.

> I would like to go to that desert because_____.

> I would not like to go to that desert because_____.

• Have children complete *Literacy Activity Book* page 30.

SKILL FINDER Minilessons, pp. T71, T177

Informal Assessment

Children's ability to make a generalization and apply it to a new situation relies on their skill in drawing logical conclusions. Ask questions occasionally to determine how children arrived at a conclusion.

Additional Support:
Reteaching, p. T189

More Practice Activities

Let's Go Back to the City

Look through the pages of *Citybook* with children, asking them to name some sounds they would hear in the places shown, for example, horns beeping and cash registers ringing. List the sound words on the chalkboard. Then ask children if they would expect to hear sounds like that in the selection they just read.

Invite children to use what they've learned about the city and the desert to write a class poem. You may want to use the frame shown here.

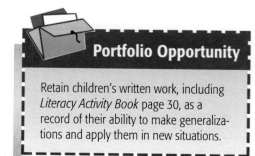

____s in the city go ____,
____, ____.
____s in the desert go ____,
____, ____.
____s in the city go ____,
____, ____.
____s in the desert go____,
____, ____.
The city sounds so _____,
and the desert sounds so
_____.
I think I like the _____ best of all.

Weather or Not

Ask children to think of some weather words. (*sunny, cloudy, thunder, lightning, hail, rain, sleet, snow, windy*) Write their words on the chalkboard. Then have them think of sound words to go with each one. Ask children to think of sentences that compare what they hear during storms and calmer weather.

Listen to the Marker, Squeak, Squeak

Help children to write a story about the classroom in the style of *Listen to the Desert/Oye al desierto*. Write the story on chart paper, and help children make generalizations about classroom sounds.

Students Acquiring English Children may enjoy sharing words in other languages that describe the sounds named.

Reteaching

Making Generalizations

Have children look closely at the plants that are pictured in the selection. Ask them what they can learn about desert plants from looking at those pictures. (Examples: Plants are generally low to the ground; they don't have leaves like other plants; stems are thick; some are brownish green; there aren't many plants.) Ask children to draw a desert plant.

Extra Support Instead of asking children to draw any desert plant, you may wish to be more specific. Provide photos of some thick cactus plants and conventional leafy trees, and have them decide which would be more appropriate for the desert.

Portfolio Opportunity

Retain children's written work, including *Literacy Activity Book* page 30, as a record of their ability to make generalizations and apply them in new situations.

Instruct *and* **Integrate**

Phonics and Spelling

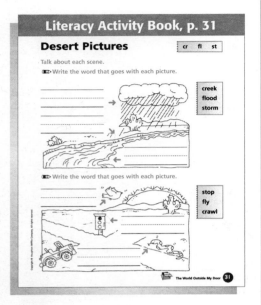

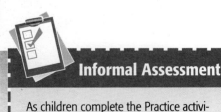

Informal Assessment

As children complete the Practice activities, note the ease with which they are able to read words with initial clusters. **Portfolio Opportunity** Save *Literacy Activity Book* pp. 31–34 as record.

INTERACTIVE LEARNING

TESTED SKILL

Consonant Clusters Review

LAB, pp. 31, 32

- Ask children to recall the sound words for the toad (*plop, plop, plop*) and the movements of the wind (*spin*) in *Listen to the Desert/Oye al desierto.* Print the words on the chalkboard. Ask a volunteer to underline the first two letters in each word and tell what they know about the sounds for those letters. (They often come together in a word; we say the sounds so close together they almost seem to be one sound.)

- Next, write these sentences on the chalkboard, underlining as shown.

- Read the sentences with children. Have volunteers tell what two letters stand for the beginning sounds in each underlined word and name another word that begins the same way. Then have children read the sentences with you.

- Have children complete *Literacy Activity Book* pages 31, 32.

"Caw, caw," cried the crow.
"Fly by," said the fly.
Skip, skip, went the little skunk.

SKILL FINDER | Minilessons, pp. T65, T67, T107, T123, T181

More Practice Activities

Sing Along

Print the phrases shown below on the chalkboard and help children read them. Then use these words to sing "*If You're Happy and You Know It. . .*"

- clap your hands
- blink your eyes
- stamp your feet
- smile a smile
- give a grin
- snap your fingers

Students Acquiring English The repetition of the words and actions will help reinforce the connection between the words and their meanings.

Riddles

Print these clusters on the chalkboard: *cr, gr, tr, fl, bl, st, sm, sk.* Then ask riddles such as these and have children think of answers that begin with the clusters.

- This is the color of grass. (green)
- A magician does these. (tricks)
- You might throw this for a dog to fetch. (stick)
- You use your nose to do this. (smell)
- Birds can do this with their wings. (fly)

INTERACTIVE LEARNING

Consonant Clusters Review

LAB, pp. 33, 34

Write the following words on the chalkboard, omitting the first two letters in each one as shown: *(fl)ower, (cl)oud, (sp)ace.* Have children listen as you pronounce each word, and ask a volunteer to write the letters that stand for the beginning sounds. Read the words with children.

Have children look through *Listen to the Desert/Oye al desierto* and point out flowers, clouds, and space. Then write the following titles on the chalkboard and read them with children: *A Desert, A City, A School.* As you read each of the following words, have children tell you which title or titles you should list them under: *bridge, flag, skates, sweater, snow, steps, store, grass, snake, bricks, truck, grapes, swing, clown, spoons.*

Ask children to draw a desert, city, or school picture that contains one or more of the things named on the lists. Have them label the pictures and write a sentence as a caption.

Have children complete *Literacy Activity Book* pages 33, 34.

SKILL FINDER
Minilessons, pp. T65, T67, T107, T123, T181

A Fish Trip

A Fish Trip
by Margo Lemieux

This story includes words with some of the initial clusters taught in these lessons.

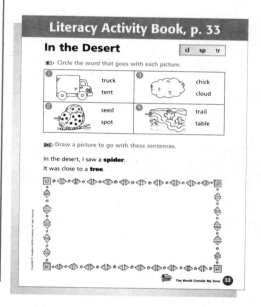

Literacy Activity Book, p. 33

More Practice Activities

Wisdom from Mother Goose

- Write the rhyme shown on chart paper. Read it with children and discuss its meaning. Have children use what they know about consonant clusters to identify the underlined words.

- Gather a spoonful of earth from outside the school and place it on a piece of drawing paper. Have children examine it with a magnifying glass and note whether any "little drops of water" are soaking into the drawing paper.

- Have them record what they see in their science journals.

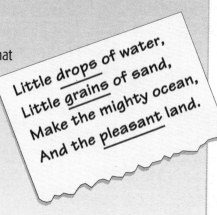

Little drops of water,
Little grains of sand,
Make the mighty ocean,
And the pleasant land.

Literacy Activity Book, p. 34

Instruct *and* Integrate

Vocabulary

A Fish Trip

A Fish Trip
by Margo Lemieux

This story provides practice and application for the following skills:

- **High-Frequency Words:** *call, eat, fish, say, to*

- **Phonics/Decoding Skills:** Clusters with *r, l,* and *s*

- **Cumulative Review:** Previously taught decoding skills and High-Frequency Words

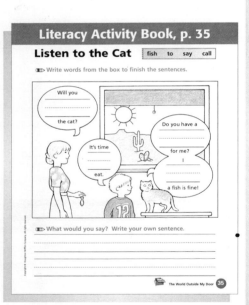

Literacy Activity Book, p. 35

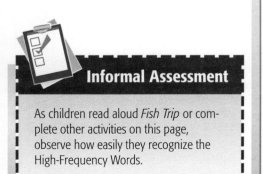

Informal Assessment

As children read aloud *Fish Trip* or complete other activities on this page, observe how easily they recognize the High-Frequency Words.

High-Frequency Words

 High-Frequency Words: *call, eat, fish, say, to*

Listen to the Cat

LAB, p. 35

Review the High-Frequency Words with children. Together, read the directions on *Literacy Activity Book* page 35. Have children complete the page and share their work with a partner.

See It and Say It

Suggest that children draw pictures relating to the sounds different animals make. Have them use the High-Frequency Words to help them label or caption their pictures.

Sentence Stretch

Cooperative Learning

Challenge children working in small groups to use as many of the High-Frequency Words as they can in one super-stretched-out sentence. Have the groups dictate their sentences. Compare the sentences and decide which group's sentence is the longest.

Listen Up!

List the High-Frequency Words on the chalkboard. Have children copy them on paper. Explain that they will take turns making up oral stories. They should try to include in their stories as many of the words as possible, as many times as possible. Listeners should write the name of each speaker as a column heading over columns next to the word list. They should make a mark next to each word as they hear it spoken. The storyteller who earns the most marks is the winner.

	Kara	Will
call	✓	✓✓
eat		✓
fish		
say	✓✓	
to	✓✓	

MINILESSON

Vocabulary Skill
Sense Words
LAB, p. 36

Teach/Model

Remind children that *Listen to the Desert/Oye al desierto* is about the many sounds in a desert. Explain that writers often use words that tell how something sounds, looks, tastes, feels, or smells. Ask children if they can find the words on pages 90–91 that tell how the desert sounds. (*pon, pon, pon*)

Practice/Apply

- Ask children to imagine that they are in a favorite place, perhaps a park or beach.

- Have children work together to name at least one thing there that appeals to each of the five senses: hearing, sight, taste, touch, and smell. Put their ideas into a word web.

- Then have children draw pictures of the place, showing things that appeal to three or more of the senses. Ask volunteers to share their pictures with the class, identifying the things and the senses they appeal to.

- Have children complete *Literacy Activity Book* page 36.

Literacy Activity Book, p. 36

Sensing the Desert

see	hear
smell	taste
touch	

☞ Finish each sentence.

I have sharp points.

Don't _____ me.

I am water.

I _____ good when you are thirsty.

You can _____ me howl.

Don't forget me. I help you _____ in the sun.

Put your nose near me. Do I _____ sweet?

☞ Write a sentence about the desert. Use words from the box.

_____

36 The World Outside My Door

MINILESSON

Vocabulary Expansion
Onomatopoeia

Teach/Model

Read aloud pages 94–95. Point out that *plop* is a word that sounds like the thing it describes. Explain that English has many words like this and that writers use them to recreate sensations like the crash of a wave or the roar of a lion.

Practice/Apply

Write the following on the chalkboard: *bang, buzz, splash, toot, zoom.* Ask volunteers to name something that makes the sound each word describes. Ask other volunteers to use the word in a sentence.

Portfolio Opportunity

- *Literacy Activity Book* page 35 will show children's understanding of the High-Frequency Words.

- Save *Literacy Activity Book* page 36 as a record of children's ability to recognize and use sense words.

Instruct and Integrate

Language and Writing

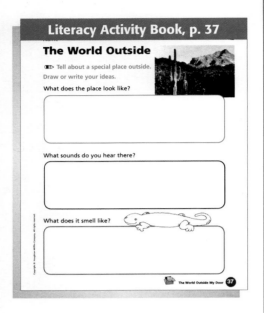

MINILESSON

Writing to Describe Places

LAB, p. 37

- Point out that Pat Mora, the author of *Listen to the Desert/Oye al desierto*, describes the sounds of the desert. But she could also have described the desert by telling what it looks or smells like.

- Choose a familiar outdoor place, such as a local park. Have children tell you what the place sounds, smells, and looks like. Record their ideas.

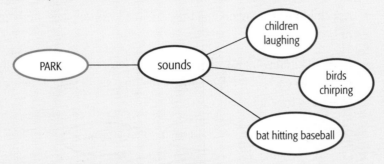

- Have children complete *Literacy Activity Book* page 37 for practice in describing places.

Practice Activities

Writing Post Cards

- Invite children to write a post card to the class telling about a place they have visited. Remind them to write about how the place looked, smelled, and sounded.

- Encourage children to draw a picture of the place on the back of the card.

- Put the cards on a bulletin board.

Travel Logs

- Have children brainstorm a list of things they might see and do if they visited the desert for a week. Then have them make travel logs.

- Show them how to date the pages, or have them begin each page with the day of the week. For example, *On Monday I . . . .*

- Encourage children to illustrate their logs and share them with the class.

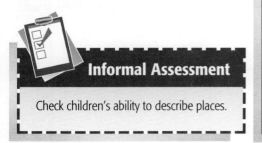

Informal Assessment

Check children's ability to describe places.

More Practice Activities

Where Am I?

Invite children to write riddles that describe a place. You may want to give them some examples. Have them write four or five riddles and then challenge different classmates to write answers to the riddles.

I can see rows and rows of corn, and I hear the sound of mooing. Where am I?

It is dark and I smell popcorn as I search for a seat. Where am I?

Children can use The Learning Company's new elementary writing center to write, illustrate, and publish their work to share with others.

Making Nature Sounds

Oral Language Development Have children recall the sounds that some of the animals made in *Listen to the Desert.* You may want to read them another book that includes sounds of nature, such as *Why Mosquitoes Buzz in People's Ears* or *Borreguita and the Coyote,* by Verna Aardema.

- Have children make sounds that occur in nature. Ask them, "How does the wind sound? How does sand sound under your feet?"

- Suggest that children record sounds in a tape recorder for other children to guess.

- Encourage children to use sounds in their own stories when appropriate.

The Owl Says "Whoo"

Grammar Connection Write the sentences on the board as shown.

> The owl says "Whoo."
> The doves say "Coo."

Underline *says* and *say.* Point out that the first sentence uses *says* because there is one owl; the second sentence uses *say* because there is more than one dove. Have children work with a partner to practice using *say* and *says.* Ask partners to make up sentences about what different animals say. One partner stands alone and says a sentence using *says,* such as "The snake says 'Hiss'." The other partner then joins in, and they both say the sentence, this time using *say*: "The snakes say 'Hiss'."

Portfolio Opportunity

- Save *Literacy Activity Book* page 37 as a sample of children's ability to describe places.

- Save children's written responses to activities on these pages as samples of their writing development.

Instruct and Integrate

Communication Activities

Audio Tape
for The World Outside My Door: *Listen to the Desert/Oye al desierto*

Encourage children to pay special attention to the sounds of the animals and the desert as they follow the words the narrator reads.

Listening and Speaking

Echo-Reading

Divide the class into two groups. Have the first group read the first line on each page. The second group can read the second, or repetition, line to create an echo effect. After children have had some practice, you may wish to tape-record their reading.

Sounds Like ...
Cooperative Learning

Have children pick a favorite animal and demonstrate the sound it makes for the class. Invite children to tape-record their animal noises. Make sure that they understand how to operate the tape recorder.

When the tape is complete, have children play it for another class and ask that class to guess what sounds they hear.

How-to Tips for Tape-Recording
- Have children practice their sounds before recording them.
- Remind children to speak loudly and clearly.
- After children record their sounds, have them listen to the tape. If they wish to re-record their sounds, allow them to do so.

Viewing

Desert Colors

Invite children to review *Listen to the Desert/Oye al desierto* and make a list of the different colors they see in the illustrations. Ask them: What colors make the desert seem hot? (tan, brown, yellow) Explain that artists use different colors to give their illustrations different feelings. Have children write words next to the colors on their list to tell how each color makes them feel.

Color	Feeling
Blue	cool
tan	warm
yellow	hot

Portfolio Opportunity

You may want to keep children's color charts in their portfolios.

Independent Reading & Writing

Student-Selected Reading

Model Self-Correction

When you read aloud to children, point out the times you self-correct by repeating a word or going back to a sentence and beginning again. You may even say from time to time, "I didn't understand that paragraph. I'm going to read it one more time." Let children know that everyone stumbles now and then and that rereading or self-correcting is necessary to understand what we read.

Turn to a Partner

At the end of independent reading time, have children turn to a partner and share what they were reading. Encourage children to ask each other questions about the books. Invite children to tell you if they have discovered any new books that they would like to read.

Books for Independent Reading

Encourage children to choose their own books. They might choose one of the following titles.

Hats Hats Hats!
by Ann Morris
illustrated by Ken Heyman

PAPERBACK **PLUS**

A Fish Trip
by Margo Lemieux

WATCH **ME** READ

Listen to the Desert/Oye al desierto
by Pat Mora
illustrated by Francisco X. Mora

Have children reread this selection silently or aloud to a partner.

See the Bibliography on pages T42–T43 for more theme-related books for independent reading.

Self-Selected Writing

Responding to Writing

When responding to children's work, give as much specific feedback as possible. For example, you might say, "You used a lot of details in telling me about your house. I feel as if I've been there." That way, the child can apply this knowledge to future writing projects.

The Same Drawing

You may find that some children draw the same thing over and over again during independent writing time. Talk with children about what they have drawn. The discussion may prompt them to add words to the drawing.

Ideas for Independent Writing

Encourage children to write on self-selected topics. For those who need help getting started, suggest one of the following activities:

- a **drawing with captions** of a desert scene
- a **post card** from the desert
- a **sound** book

Portfolio Opportunity

Save examples of the writing children do independently on self-selected topics.

Instruct *and* Integrate

Cross-Curricular Activities

Cactus Plants from Seeds

Challenge Have children examine the illustrations in *Listen to the Desert/Oye al desierto* to find desert plants (cacti). Explain that they will be growing their own cactus plants from seed.

Materials

- cactus seeds
- gravel
- plastic bag
- rubber band
- seed labels
- seed tray
- soil mixture (one part sand, one part perlite, and one part potting soil)

1 Poke several small drainage holes in the bottom of the seed tray and cover with 1/2" of gravel. Fill with the soil mixture to about 1/2" from the top.

2 Place the cactus seeds on the top of the soil, about 1/4" apart. Sprinkle a thin layer of soil mixture over the seeds. Put the tray in a sink filled with about 1 1/2" of water. Let it soak until the soil is moist (about one minute).

3 Cover the soil with a thin layer of very fine aquarium gravel.

Now do the following:

- Push two small seed labels into the soil, on opposite sides of the tray. Place the tray in a plastic bag and seal with a rubber band. The labels will prevent the bag from touching the soil.

- Put the tray in a place that is always at least 70° Fahrenheit and has an indirect light. When the seeds have sprouted (in one or two weeks), open the bag to let air circulate. When the seedlings have spines, remove the tray from the plastic bag.

- Every two or three days, have children observe and record the changes in the plants' heights.

When you are finished observing the plants, transplant each cactus into a small pot. Let each child take one home and care for it.

Math

Weighing Sand

Have children examine the illustrations in *Listen to the Desert/Oye al desierto*. Ask them what covers the ground. (sand) Explain that they will be comparing the weight of sand with the weight of other things.

- Have children fill another cup with the same amount of chalk and place it in the other pan of the balance scale.

- Have children compare the weights. Encourage them to use the comparison words *heavier* and *lighter*.

Materials
- balance scale
- chalk
- clay
- flour
- pencil shavings
- salt
- sand
- sugar
- two yogurt cups

Have children fill a cup about halfway with sand and place it in one pan of the balance scale.

Invite them to continue comparing the weight of the sand with the same amount of other things.

Art

Colored Sand Bottles

Cover desktops or tabletops with newspaper. Provide each child with a plastic bottle, a funnel, and two to four different kinds of colored sand in cups. Have children follow the steps shown.

1 Place a funnel in the top of the bottle. Pour one kind of colored sand through the funnel until it forms a thin layer on the bottom of the bottle.

2 Choose a different colored sand and pour it through the funnel on top of the first layer. Tilt the bottle to make thick, thin, or wavy layers.

3 Repeat the process, alternating colors until the sand reaches the top of the bottle. Put on the cap and display the bottles in the classroom.

Materials
- small, clear, plastic soda bottles
- colored sand
- funnels (cone-shaped water cups with bottom cut off)
- plastic or paper cups

Instruct
and
Integrate

Cross-Curricular Activities (continued)

Social Studies

Creating a Desert Relief Map

Have children look at the illustrations in the selection. Ask them to describe the landscape. (few plants, sand dunes, hills and mountains) Ask them why few plants grow in the desert. (There is little rainfall.) Display a topographical map of the United States. Lead children to see that the colors represent different geographical regions: forests, deserts, mountains, and coastal plains. Have them locate desert areas on the map. Help children create their own desert area relief map.

Materials
- cardboard
- flour
- paintbrushes
- topographical map of the United States
- salt
- water
- watercolors

Combine three parts salt and one part flour with enough water to bring the mixture to the consistency of dough.

Have children model the dough on heavy cardboard. Have them create sand dunes, hills and mountains. Use watercolors to paint the map.

Encourage children to describe the map features to their classmates.

Drama

Acting Out *Listen to the Desert/Oye al desierto*

MEETING INDIVIDUAL NEEDS

Extra Support Have children recall the sounds and movements of the animals, wind, and rain in *Listen to the Desert/Oye al desierto*. Explain to them that they will be recreating the story.

- Choose volunteers to play the roles of the desert, owl, toad, snake, dove, coyote, fish, mice, rain, and wind. Encourage them to practice the sounds and the movements of the animals.

- You might have children create scenery by painting a desert landscape on mural paper.

- As a volunteer reads the selection, children can act out the movements and sounds of the animals.

- You may wish to invite another class to the performance.

Materials
- brushes
- mural paper
- tempera paint

Desert Critter Fun Facts

 This dune cricket uses its feet to keep from sinking into the sand.

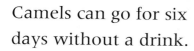

Camels can go for six days without a drink.

Roadrunners can run five blocks in just one minute!

113

Introduce the Literature

Building Background

Ask children to tell what they have learned so far about the desert. Remind them that a desert is a very dry area that is not near any waterways (such as rivers or lakes) and that does not get much rain. If possible, show them photographs from magazines or books of large deserts, such as the North African Sahara or California's Mojave. Tell children that although the desert may look lifeless, there are many interesting animals that live there.

Interact with Literature

Reading the Article

Learning About Desert Animals
Read page 113 with children. Point out the name *dune cricket* and ask if they know what a dune is. If necessary, explain that a dune is a hill of sand. Ask children why they think the dune cricket doesn't sink in the sand. Then invite children to share things they know and things they have learned about camels and roadrunners.

Instruct and Integrate

Art

Desert Display Invite children to make a Desert Display using sand, construction paper, scissors, craft sticks, paste, and a cardboard box. Have children draw desert animals and plants on construction paper, cut them out, and paste a craft stick on the back of each one. Cut the sides of a cardboard box low and fill the box with sand. Then have them place their desert animals and plants in the sand to create a desert scene.

Introduce the Literature

Building Background

Bring in sand of various colors (often available in craft supply shops or toy stores), and have children feel the tiny grains. Explain that sand is formed by the gradual crumbling and wearing away of rocks over many years.

Explain that some Native Americans, especially the Navajo, make paintings out of sand. Tell children that they are going to learn about Navajo sand art and also how to make their own sand paintings.

Interact with Literature

Discussion

Read pages 114–115 with children and have them look at the photographs. Then discuss the following:

- How is the painting that the Navajo are making different from other paintings you have seen? How is it like other paintings?

- Above the photograph there are some designs often used in sand painting. Which one of those designs looks the most like the one the Navajo are using?

Sand Painting

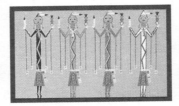

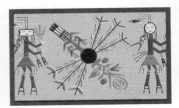

These Navajo men are making a painting from sand.

114

You can draw using sand!

1

Draw a picture.

Spread glue on one part.

2

Choose one color. Sprinkle the sand on the glue. Let it dry.

3

Shake off the extra sand.

Repeat with another color.

115

Instruct and Integrate

MINILESSON

Study Skill

Following Directions

TESTED SKILL

Teach/Model

Tell children that it is very important to read and follow directions carefully. Have a volunteer read the directions for making sand paintings on page 115. Help children create a list of things they will need to complete the project.

Materials
- oak tag or other heavy paper
- pencils, crayons, or markers
- sand of various colors
- glue
- newspapers

Practice/Apply

Have children follow the steps.

Invite volunteers to share their completed sand paintings with the class.

SKILL FINDER   Full lesson, p. H2

Interact with Literature

Background: FYI

Here are some facts about the tradition of Navajo sand painting.

- Five traditional colors are used in Navajo sand painting. They are white, yellow, red, black, and gray-blue.
- A traditional Navajo sand painting is made by trickling colored sands on the floor of a hogan (a dwelling). After the painting is used in a ceremony, it is destroyed.

Introduce the Literature

Building Background

Have children discuss how they feel about the dark. Then ask them if they have ever camped outdoors overnight. Invite volunteers to share their experiences and to tell what they saw and heard. If no children have slept outside, encourage them to imagine what sounds they might hear, what the ground would feel like, if the air would be cold or not, and so on. Then tell children that they are going to read two poems: one about sleeping outdoors, and another poem written by a boy their own age.

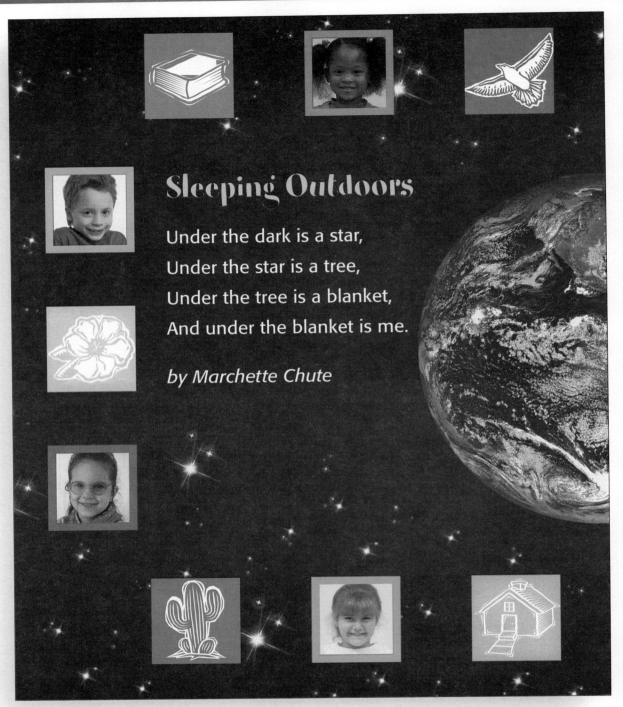

Sleeping Outdoors

Under the dark is a star,
Under the star is a tree,
Under the tree is a blanket,
And under the blanket is me.

by Marchette Chute

Interact with Literature

Reading the Poems

Choral Reading Read both poems with children. Then divide them into four groups and have them read "Sleeping Outdoors" chorally, with each group reading one line aloud. For the second poem, have all the children read it aloud together.

I Love the World

I love you, Big World.
I wish I could call you
And tell you a secret:
That I love you, World.

by Paul Wollner
Age 7

117

Anthology p. 117

Instruct and Integrate

✏ Writing

Write a New Poem Some children might enjoy the challenge of making up their own original poems, just as Paul Wollner did. Others may prefer to use the pattern from "Sleeping Outdoors" to create new poems about camping out or another subject that interests them. Write this frame on the chalkboard to help them:

Under the _____ is _____.
Under the _____ is _____.
Under the _____ is _____.
And under the _____ is _____.

Instruct and Integrate

✏ Writing

Write a Letter to the World Ask children what the boy who wrote "I Love the World" said he wished he could do. (call the world and tell it a secret) Ask children: If you could write a letter to the world, what would you say? Encourage children, either individually or in small groups, to dictate and/or write a letter to the world telling something important to them.

Theme Assessment Wrap-Up

Time: About 1 hour

Evaluates

1 **Theme Concept:** People and animals live in many different environments.

2 **Skills:** Noting Details, Making Generalizations

This is a brief, informal performance assessment activity. For a more extended reading-writing performance assessment, see the Integrated Theme Test.

Literacy Activity Book, p. 38

Many Homes

▸ Plan what you will draw on other paper.
Sketch or write your ideas.

Homes for People

Homes for Animals

Check your work.

☐ I showed different places where people and animals live.
☐ I showed what the places are like.
☐ I can tell about the places.

38 The World Outside My Door

Portfolio Opportunity

- *Literacy Activity Book* page 38
- Save the children's drawings.

PERFORMANCE ASSESSMENT

Many Homes

LAB, p. 38

Materials
- construction paper
- markers or crayons

Introducing

Ask children to draw pictures of four different kinds of places where people and animals live. You might want to help them recall environments they have read about or know about. Help children use *Literacy Activity Book* page 38 to plan their work.

1 On one sheet of paper, draw a line through the middle, and draw two places where people live. Think about what people do there. Show someone in each picture.

2 On another sheet, draw two places where animals live. In each picture show an animal that lives there and many other details.

3 Try to think of ways the homes are like each other.

Evaluating

Read aloud the checklist on *Literacy Activity Book* page 38. Have children show their pictures. Let classmates ask questions about the pictures. Ask the child who drew the pictures to tell of one way the four homes, or environments, are alike. Evaluate, using the scoring rubric.

Scoring Rubric

Criterion	1	2	3	4
Child's pictures show four environments.	Child cannot draw or name the places.	Child identifies one or two environments.	Child draws three or four places adequately.	Child draws interesting pictures of four environments.
Child recalls and supplies details.	Child supplies almost no details.	Child supplies some details, not all correct.	Child supplies several correct details.	Child supplies many accurate details.
Child makes a generalization about homes.	Child cannot make a generalization.	Generalization does not fit all four homes.	Child only repeats what has been said in class.	Generalization is accurate and thoughtful.

Choices for Assessment

Informal Assessment

Review the Informal Assessment Checklist and observation notes to determine:

- Which selections did children enjoy most?
- How well did children apply comprehension skills to the theme?
- In what areas do children need more practice or support?

Formal Assessment

Select formal tests that meet your classroom needs:

- Integrated Theme Test for The World Outside My Door and Get the Giggles may be given after Get the Giggles
- Theme Skills Test for The World Outside My Door

See the *Teacher's Assessment Handbook* for guidelines for administering tests and using answer keys, scoring rubrics, and children's sample papers.

Portfolio Assessment

Conferencing with Children

Plan to meet regularly with children, individually or in small groups, to review their work and to select materials for their portfolios. Encourage children to select work that represents important learning.

Early in the year set children's expectations by discussing ways they can prepare for a special conference with you. Also discuss your expectations of others during conference time.

Let children know of conferences one day in advance. Set up a conference board where you can place children's names.

Sending Work Home

Here are two ways to encourage children to take work home to share:

- Have children keep their work in collection folders. About every two weeks, review the folders with them to select items for the portfolio. Then have children prepare a packet of the remaining work to take home.

- Send a positive note to parents with the child's work, or encourage children to write their own note, telling what they've done well.

Managing Assessment
Testing Options

Question: How can I assess children's overall progress at the end of a theme?

Answer: *Invitations to Literacy* includes a range of assessment options. Select the options that best meet your needs:

Performance Assessment

The Performance Assessment at the end of each theme is a hands-on activity that evaluates children's understanding of the theme concept and major comprehension skills. A rubric is provided for evaluation.

Integrated Theme Test

The Integrated Theme Test provides a new theme-related reading selection. It uses written and multiple-choice formats to evaluate children's abilities in reading strategies, comprehension, critical thinking, phonics/decoding, word skills, and writing.

Theme Skills Test

The Theme Skills Test evaluates discrete literacy skills of the theme, including comprehension, phonics/decoding, high-frequency words, writing, spelling, grammar, and study skills, when applicable.

Benchmark Progress Tests

The Benchmark Progress Tests can be given two times a year to evaluate overall progress in reading and writing. They are not theme-related. Many teachers choose to use these tests at midyear and at the end of the year.

For more information on this and other topics, see the *Teacher's Assessment Handbook*.

Celebrating the Theme

Choices for Celebrating

Travel Folders

Cooperative Learning

Have children create travel folders about places they would like to visit.

- Bring in travel posters or brochures for children to study. Point out that the art and the words are intended to make people want to travel to that place.

- Divide children into small groups. Assign each group a place, such as a specific city or geographical region.

- Have groups draw pictures or cut pictures out of magazines that show their places.

- Invite children to paste their pictures on blank paper and write words or sentences that tell about their places.

- Have groups decorate the outside of a file folder and put their pages inside.

Materials

- travel brochures
- construction paper
- crayons
- old magazines
- scissors
- paste
- file folders

See the **Teacher's Resource Disk** for theme-related Teacher Support material.

Self-Assessment

Have children meet in small groups to discuss what they learned in the theme. Use the following prompts to foster their discussion:

- What did you learn about the different environments in this theme that you didn't know before?

- If you could travel to the city, the desert, or the river, which one would you choose? What might you see there?

- Which book in this theme was your favorite? Why did you choose that book?

A Field Trip

Take a day to visit an outdoor place near the school. Before you go, help children plan the trip by following these steps:

- Brainstorm what things to bring and clothes to wear.

- Make a list of things you might see on a walk. (You might want to duplicate the list and add boxes for check marks. Children can use the checklists on the trip.)

- Meet with someone who can expand children's knowledge of the history or ecosystem of the place you chose.

Display Dioramas

If children created the dioramas suggested for the Ongoing Project on page T48, provide time for them to share the settings they created.

- Children show dioramas and tell three things they included that are important to that environment.

- Provide a time for other students or special guests to ask questions about the dioramas.

Get the Giggles
HaHaHa

Table of Contents
THEME: Get the Giggles

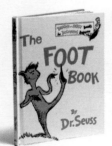

Each title is also available in black and white.
This version includes a home activity.

WATCH ME READ Books *PRACTICE FOR HIGH-FREQUENCY WORDS AND PHONICS SKILLS*

Where IS My Baby?
by Deborah Eaton

Fox and Chick
by Cass Hollander

Hank and Lin
by Stu Goodwin

PAPERBACK **PLUS** *LITERATURE FOR SMALL GROUP INSTRUCTION*

AVERAGE/CHALLENGING

Hooray for Snail!

After Snail hits a baseball out of this world, he must try to make it around the bases.

In the same book . . .

Find out more about how to play baseball, learn fun baseball facts, and discover where team names come from.

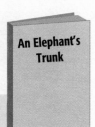

Reading Rainbow Review Book

by John Stadler

EARLY SUCCESS

AN INTERVENTION PROGRAM

On the Farm
illustrated by Luisa Laino

After a Bath
by Aileen Fisher

An Elephant's Trunk
by Valerie Tripp

Bibliography
Books for Independent Reading

 Multicultural

 Science/Health

 Math

 Social Studies

 Music

 Art

VERY EASY

Oink
by Arthur Geisert
Houghton 1991 (32p)
Eight adventurous piglets sneak away from their sleeping mother in an almost wordless story.

Shake My Sillies Out
 by Raffi
Crown 1988 (32p) paper
Sleepless forest animals and campers jump, jiggle, and wiggle their sillies away.

Ten Cats Have Hats
 by Jean Marzollo
Scholastic 1994 (24p)
From one bear to ten cats, a young girl presents animals and their silly possessions.

Who Sank the Boat?
by Pamela Allen
Sandcastle 1990 (32p) paper
Five animal friends decide to go rowing in a very small boat, but disaster's not far behind.

More Spaghetti, I Say!
by Rita Golden Gelman
Scholastic 1993 (32p) paper
Minnie the monkey is so busy eating spaghetti that she can't play with Freddy.

Frogs in Clogs
by Sheila Samton
Crown 1995 (32p)
Frogs in clogs and pigs wearing wigs are some of the silly animal antics in this book.

EASY

Shoes
by Elizabeth Winthrop
Harper 1986 (32p) also paper
Exuberant rhyming verse celebrates all kinds of different shoes.

Silly Sally
by Audrey Wood
Harcourt 1992 (32p)
Silly Sally and her animal friends parade into town walking backwards and upside down.

The Surprise Party
by Pat Hutchins
Macmillan 1969 (32p) also paper
Rabbit's having a party, but as each animal tells the next, the message becomes completely garbled.

Peanut Butter and Jelly
 by Nadine Bernard Westcott
Dutton 1987 (32p)
Puffin paper
A rollicking rhyme pays homage to the peanut butter and jelly sandwich.

Green Eggs and Ham
by Dr. Seuss
Random 1960 (64p) also paper
Sam I Am convinces another creature to eat green eggs and ham.
Available in Spanish as *Huevos verdes con jamón.*

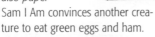

The Grumpalump
by Sarah Hayes
Clarion 1990 (24p)
A strange grumpalump turns out to be a hot-air balloon in this cumulative story.

Five Little Monkeys Sitting in a Tree
by Eileen Christelow
Clarion 1991 (32p) also paper
Five mischievous monkeys discover the risks in teasing a crocodile.

The Missing Tarts
by B. G. Hennessy
Viking 1988 (32p) also paper
The Queen of Hearts involves Jack and Jill and other Mother Goose characters in a lively search for her missing tarts.

AVERAGE

My Mom and Dad Make Me Laugh
by Nick Sharrat
Candlewick 1994 (32p)
Mom adores spots and Dad only wears stripes, but in this funny family, a boy dresses in gray because he loves elephants.

The Cow Buzzed
by Andrea Zimmerman and David Clemesha
Harper 1993 (32p) also paper
When a bee sneezes, all the farm animals get the sniffles and the wrong voices in a funny cumulative tale.

Ten Tiny Turtles
 by Paul Cherrill
Ticknor 1995 (32p)
From worms wearing sunglasses to fish playing hockey, silly counting rhymes capture animals' activities.

El libro tonto (The Silly Book)
by Babette Cole
A young boy points out the many silly things that people do. **Text in Spanish.**

Sheep Take a Hike
by Nancy Shaw
Houghton 1994 (32p)
When six sheep set out for a hike, they have a series of comic misadventures.

April Showers
by George Shannon
Greenwillow 1995 (32p)
A group of frogs dancing and jumping and leaping in the rain don't notice a snake.

The Right Number of Elephants
by Jeff Sheppard
Harper 1990 (32p) also paper
Helpful pachyderms solve some problems for a young girl in this counting book.

CHALLENGING

Zoodles
by Bernard Most
Harcourt 1992 (32p)
The answers to this book of playful riddles are hybrid animals like the camelephant.

Caps for Sale
by Esphyr Slobodkina
Harper 1947 (48p) also paper
A poor peddler loses his caps to a group of mischievous monkeys.
Available in Spanish as *Se venden gorras.*

CHALLENGING (continued)

Laughing All the Way
by George Shannon
Houghton 1992
(32p)
Duck's bad day
gets even worse
after he's grabbed by Bear.

Old Turtle's Riddle and Joke Book
by Leonard Kessler
Greenwillow 1986 (48p)
Dell 1990 paper
Old Turtle and his friends tell easy jokes and riddles.

Duncan the Dancing Duck
by Syd Hoff
Clarion 1994 (32p)
A dancing duck finds fame in the big city.

No Peas for Nellie
by Chris Demarest
Macmillan 1988 (32p) also paper
Nellie goes through an outlandish list of all the things she'd rather eat than peas.

Amelia Bedelia
by Peggy Parish
Harper 1963 (64p) also paper
The literal-minded housekeeper follows one funny mix-up with another.

Books for Teacher Read Aloud

A Poem for a Pickle: Funnybone Verses
by Eve Merriam
Greenwillow 1989 (40p)
These bouncy, funny poems will delight children.

The 500 Hats of Bartholomew Cubbins
by Dr. Seuss
Random 1989 (48p)
Every time Bartholomew doffs his hat before the king, another hat appears.

King Bidgood's in the Bathtub
by Audrey Wood
Harcourt 1985 (32p) also paper
A king refuses to get out of the bathtub to rule his kingdom.

Moira's Birthday
by Robert Munsch
Firefly 1993 (32p) paper
Moira's birthday party turns out to be even bigger than she expected.
Available in Spanish as El cumpleaños de Mariela.

Books for Shared Reading

Rachel Fister's Blister
by Amy MacDonald
Houghton 1990 (32p)
A blister on a girl's toe prompts all of the adults to try a series of silly cures.

It's Raining, It's Pouring
by Kin Eagle
Whispering Coyote 1994 (32p)
Six new verses add humor to a traditional rhyme.

The Cake That Mack Ate
by Rose Robart
Little 1987 (32p) also paper
Mack the dog eats a birthday cake in a humorous cumulative story.

Pardon? Said the Giraffe
by Colin West
Harper 1986 (24p) paper
Giraffe is so tall, he can't hear a word that Frog says to him.

Technology Resources

Software

C.D.'s Story Time Macintosh CD-ROM software. Houghton Mifflin Company.

"Wild Animals, Come Out!" CD: Digraphs *ch* and *sh*
"Scared Silly" CD: Cause and Effect
"Working Together" CD: Sequence

Writing Software The Learning Company's new elementary writing center. Macintosh or Windows software. The Learning Company®.

Internet See the Houghton Mifflin Internet resources for additional bibliographic entries and theme-related activities.

Teacher's Resource Disk Macintosh or Windows software. Houghton Mifflin Company.

Video Cassettes

Hop on Pop by Dr. Seuss. Filmic Archives

Green Eggs and Ham by Dr. Seuss. Filmic Archives

I Know an Old Lady by Nadine Bernard Westcott. Listening Library

Moira's Birthday by Robert Munsch. Listening Library

Funny Farm Animals Media Basics

Audio Cassettes

Shoes by Elizabeth Winthrop. Live Oak

King Bidgood's in the Bathtub by Audrey Wood. Listening Library

Something Big Has Been Here by Jack Prelutsky. Listening Library

Audio Tapes for Get the Giggles Houghton Mifflin Company

Filmstrips

The Foot Book by Dr. Seuss. Am. Sch. Pub.

Caps for Sale by Esphyr Slobodkina. Weston Woods

Chicken Soup with Rice by Maurice Sendak. Weston Woods

AV addresses are on pages H13–H14.

Theme at a Glance

Selections	Reading			Writing and Language Arts	
	Comprehension Skills and Strategies	Vocabulary	Phonics	Writing	
On Top of Spaghetti	✓ Cause and effect, T235, T242–T243 Sequence, T237; Inferences: drawing conclusions, T239; Reading strategies, T228, T230, T234, T238; **Responding, T240–T241**	✓ High-frequency words, T248 Rhyming words, T249 Foods that go together, T249	✓ Digraphs *sh, th,* T233, T244, T245 Digraph *wh,* T229 ✓ Think about words, T246–T247	Class song, T224 Telling where, T250–T251	
On Top of Spaghetti				Song lyrics, T256	
Aaaah . . . Choo!					
Make Pasta Art!, What's Silly?					
The Foot Book	✓ Fantasy and realism, T283, T298–T299; Categorize/classify, T285; Reading strategies, T268, T270, T272, T274, T280, T292; **Responding, T296–T297**	✓ High-frequency words, T265, T302 Antonyms, T303 Alliteration, T303	✓ Digraph *ch,* T289, T300, T301 Digraphs *sh, th,* T287	Describe a person, animal, or thing, T304–T305	
Knock, Knock! Who's There?				Knock-knock jokes, T312	
Funny Faces in Funny Places					
Reading-Writing Workshop **Be a Writer: Giggle Time**				Writing about something silly, T316–T317	
Poems and Drawings by Shel Silverstein		Rhyming game, T319		Poems, T318	
The Lady with the Alligator Purse	✓ Sequence, T333, T350–T351; Fantasy/realism, T329; Cause and effect, T335; Reading strategies, T324, T326, T330, T332, T334, T340 **Responding, T348–T349**	✓ High-frequency words, T323, T354 Contractions with *not,* T355 Career words, T355	✓ Digraphs *sh, th, ch,* T327 ✓ Initial digraphs review, T352 ✓ Final digraphs review, T353 Clusters with *r, s,* T331	Names for people, T356–T357	
Bath Time for Calvin				Comic strip, T363	
She Fell into the Bathtub					
Shake My Sillies Out		Action words, T366			

✓ *Indicates Tested Skills.* See page T217 for assessment options.

Theme Concept
Some stories make us laugh!

Pacing
This theme is designed to take 2 1/2 to 4 weeks, depending on your students' needs and interests.

Multi-Age Classroom
This theme can be used in conjunction with themes found in other grade levels.
Kindergarten: Just for Fun
Grade 2: That's Incredible!

Cross-Curricular

Spelling	Grammar, Usage, and Mechanics	Listening and Speaking	Viewing	Content Areas and Study Skills
✓ Digraphs *sh, th,* T244, T245	Position words, T251	Singing and playing instruments, T252	Viewing from different angles, T252 Art in motion, T252	**Study Skills:** parts of a book, T227, H3 **Math:** pasta patterns, T254 **Art:** pasta frames, T254 **Science:** foods that grow on trees, T255; investigating spaghetti, T255
		Sing-along, T256		
				Health: taking care of a cold, T257
			Observing details, T259	**Art:** making pasta art, T258; making silly pictures, T259 **Creative Movement:** playing silly games, T261
✓ Digraph *ch,* T300, T301	Using *foot/feet, tooth/teeth,* T305	Tying shoes, T306 Be kind to your feet, T306	Investigating animal tracks, T306	**Math:** graphing shoes, T308; measuring with a foot, T308 **Science:** neat animal feet, T309 **Social Studies:** special shoes for special jobs, T309 **Art:** making silly feet and shoes, T310 **Music:** new verses for a silly song, T310
		Homophone riddles, T312 Sound words, T312		**Art:** drawing funny things, T313 **Social Studies:** role-playing, T313
				Science: going on a funny-faces hunt, T314 **Art:** making funny faces, T315
✓ Initial digraphs review, T352 ✓ Final digraphs review, T353	Names for people, T357	Telephone time, T358 How to eat pizza, T358	Following an animal through the story, T358	**Math:** equal parts, T360 **Social Studies:** interviews with workers, T360 **Science:** floating and sinking, T361 **Health:** staying healthy, T361 **Art:** making animal purses, T362 **Creative Movement:** jumping rope, T362
				Art: making footprint pictures, T364
		Singing, T365		**Art:** drawing sillies, T366; **Social Studies:** identifying emotions, T367; conquering scary things, T367

Theme at a Glance **T215**

Meeting Individual Needs

Key to Meeting Individual Needs

Students Acquiring English

Activities and notes throughout the lesson plans offer strategies to help children understand the selections and lessons.

Challenge

Challenge activities and notes throughout the lesson plans suggest additional activities to stimulate critical and creative thinking.

Extra Support

Activities and notes throughout the lesson plans offer additional strategies to help children experience success.

Managing Instruction

Independent Work: Free Reading

The best independent work is self-selected reading. If many of your children are unaccustomed to self-selected reading, begin by building the routine. Place many easy and engaging books in your classroom. Start with five minutes of reading aloud to your children, followed by five minutes of free reading. Be consistent and persistent and gradually increase the amount of time for reading. When children can read independently for fifteen minutes, begin small, flexible groups.

For further information on this and other Managing Instruction topics, see the *Professional Development Handbook*.

PERFORMANCE STANDARDS

During this theme, children will

- *recognize that some stories make us laugh*
- *apply comprehension skills: Cause and Effect; Fantasy and Realism; Sequence*
- *decode and spell words with the digraphs* th, sh, *and* ch
- *retell or summarize each selection*
- *write lyrics together for a class song*
- *identify opposites*
- *make inferences and predictions about future outcomes*

Students Acquiring English	Challenge	Extra Support
Develop Key Concepts Children focus on Key Concepts through a song, opposites flash cards, and taking a picture walk.	**Engage in Creative Thinking** Opportunities for creative expression include creating new names for plants and animals and writing a poem and a make-believe story.	**Receive Increased Instructional Time** Background-building suggestions give children time to explore concepts related to the literature. Minilessons provide individualized instruction.
Expand Vocabulary Opportunities for expanding vocabulary throughout the theme include using context clues, identifying opposites and pairs of rhyming words, and sorting ideas and words into categories.	**Apply Critical Thinking** This theme offers opportunities to apply critical thinking. These include problem-solving activities, comparing and contrasting illustrations, and making inferences about story events.	**Increase Independent Reading** Easy and engaging books in the classroom motivate children to self-select independent reading. (See Bibliography, T212–T213.)
Show Understanding Children are provided with opportunities to show their understanding of concepts through physical responses and graphic or physical representations.	**Explore Topics of Interest** Each piece of literature serves as a springboard for independent research on trees, different animal feet, and different types of occupations.	**Enhance Self-Confidence** This theme provides extra support opportunities for reading and responding. Because of this, children will see themselves as active, competent members of the reading community.

Additional Resources

Invitaciones
Develop bi-literacy with this integrated reading/language arts program in Spanish. Provides authentic literature and real-world resources from Spanish-speaking cultures.

Language Support
Translations of Big Books in Chinese, Hmong, Khmer, and Vietnamese. *Teacher's Booklet* provides instructional support in English.

Students Acquiring English Handbook
Guidelines, strategies, and additional instruction for students acquiring English.

Extra Support Handbook
Additional theme, skill, and language support.

Early Success: An Intervention Program
Additional instructional support for at-risk students in a small-group setting. Includes little books and daily lesson plans, plus a consumable book of take-home story summaries.

Writing Software
The Learning Company's new elementary writing center software.

Planning for Assessment

Informal Assessment

Informal Assessment Checklist

- Reading and Responding
- Cause and Effect; Fantasy and Realism; Sequence
- Writing Skills
- Phonics and Spelling
- Phonics/Decoding
- Listening and Speaking
- Attitudes and Habits

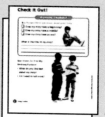

Literacy Activity Book

- Comprehension Check, pp. 49, 60
- Comprehension Skills, pp. 39, 50, 61
- Language and Writing, pp. 47, 57, 69
- Phonics and Spelling, pp. 40–43, 51–54, 63–66

Performance Assessment

- Making a Funny Story, p. T368
- Scoring Rubric, p. T368

Retellings—Oral/Written

- *Teacher's Assessment Handbook*

Formal Assessment

Integrated Theme Test

This test applies the following theme skills from Get the Giggles as well as The World Outside My Door to a new reading selection.

- Reading Strategies
- Comprehension Skills
- Digraphs *sh, th, ch*
- Writing Fluency
- Self-Assessment

Integrated Theme Test

Theme Skills Test

- Cause and Effect; Fantasy and Realism; Sequence
- Digraphs *sh, th, ch*
- High-Frequency Words

Theme Skills Test

Managing Assessment

Running Records

Question: How can I keep running records of children's reading?

Answer: Running records can be kept any time a child reads aloud. Use these tips to keep it simple:

- Have children read a short section of text during a conference with you. Simply listen and, on a blank piece of paper, note with a check every time the child reads a word correctly. When the child misreads a word, jot down the word missed and the child's miscue. Immediately afterward, jot down your impressions.

- Use the procedure above as you work with a small group of children. Don't try to take a running record for every child in the group. Focus on different children over time.

- Appropriate texts and more detailed suggestions for recording can be found in the *Teacher's Assessment Handbook*.

For more information on this and other topics, see the *Teacher's Assessment Handbook*.

Portfolio Assessment

The portfolio icon signals portfolio opportunities throughout the theme.

Additional Portfolio Tips:

- Evaluating *Literacy Activity Book* Pages, p. T369

Launching the Theme

INTERACTIVE LEARNING

Launching Activity

Giggle Game   Here's a game that's sure to give your class the giggles!

- Divide the class in two teams. Ask the teams to line up facing each other about five feet apart. Name one team *Heads,* the other *Tails.*

- Flip a coin. If it's heads, the Heads try to make the Tails laugh while the Tails try to keep a straight face. Any Tails that laugh must join the other team. Each round lasts a minute.

- Introduce the theme title, "Get the Giggles," and have the children guess what types of books they will be reading next.

Interactive Bulletin Board

What Makes You Laugh? Celebrate the funnier things in life with this bulletin board. Have children search for and create items that make them laugh and post them on the bulletin board. These might include

- comic strips
- funny pictures from magazines
- a joke written or copied by a child
- zany words
- silly rhymes
- pictures of funny incidents drawn by the children

Ongoing Project

Our Class Funnies   What makes something funny? Children will explore this concept while creating their own comic strips.

- Invite children to look at the comics in a newspaper. Assist them in recognizing the sequence in each strip and the funny endings.

- Ask children to sketch their own comic strip characters and, during the theme, to think of a funny situation for their characters. Then, provide them with paper and have them draw their own comic strips.

Portfolio Opportunity

The Portfolio Opportunity icon highlights other portfolio opportunities throughout the theme.

Choices for Centers

Creating Centers

Use these activities and materials to create learning centers in the classroom.

Phonics and Word Study

Materials: large plastic jar or bowl, construction paper, markers

- **Let's Fish,** T244
- **Chain Champs,** T300
- **Three Cheers,** T352

Science

Materials: chart paper, magazines and reference materials about trees and bushes that bear fruit, uncooked and cooked spaghetti, magnifying glasses, tub of water, small objects

- **Some Food Really Grows on Trees,** T255
- **Why Spaghetti Gets Soft When It's Cooked,** T255
- **Floating and Sinking,** T361

Writing and Computer

Materials: writing paper, pencils, pens, scissors, old magazines, newspapers, push-pins, bulletin board

- **What a Mess!,** T241
- **How Many, Many Feet You Meet,** T297
- **Crazy-Creature Posters,** T304

Art

Materials: different types of pasta, cardboard, glue, half-gallon cartons, liquid detergent, tempera paint, tag board, scissors, construction paper, elastic, markers, stapler

- **Pasta Frames,** T254
- **Making Silly Feet and Shoes,** T310
- **Animal Purses,** T362

BIG BOOK

SELECTION:

On Top of Spaghetti

Little Big Book Plus

Big Book Plus

illustrated by
Katherine Tillotson

Selection Summary

This illustrated version of the popular children's song will have everybody laughing. A little girl loses her meatball when her brother sneezes. The meatball rolls off her plate of spaghetti, off the table, and out the door, and it keeps on rolling until it ends up under a bush in the garden. Then the family dog buries it. Has your class ever heard of a spaghetti-and-meatball tree?

Lesson Planning Guide

	Skill/Strategy Instruction	Meeting Individual Needs	Lesson Resources
1 **Introduce** *the* **Literature** *Pacing: 1 day*	**Preparing to Read and Write** Warm-up, T222 Prior Knowledge/Background, T222 **High-Frequency Words**, T248 • as • be • big • could • tree • under • when • your	**Other Choices for Building Background**, T223 **Students Acquiring English**, T223 **Extra Support**, T223	**Poster** Warm-up, 4A
2 **Interact** *with* **Literature** *Pacing: 1–3 days*	**Shared Reading and Writing**, T224 **Reading Strategies** Monitor, T228, T230 Evaluate, T228, T234, T238 Think About Words, T234 **Minilessons** Digraph *wh*, T229 ✓ Digraphs *sh, th*, T233 ✓ Cause and Effect, T235 Sequence, T237 Inferences: Drawing Conclusions, T239	**Choices for Rereadings**, T225 **Choices for Reading**, T228 **Guided Reading**, T228, T232, T236, T238 **Students Acquiring English**, T230, T233, T235 **Extra Support**, T229, T238 **Challenge**, T234, T236 **Responding Choices**, T240–T241	**Reading-Writing Workshop** Writing About Something Silly, T316–T317 **Sentence Strips**, 1–21 **Study Skills** Parts of a Book, T227, H3 **Audio Tape** for Get the Giggles: *On Top of Spaghetti* The Learning Company's new elementary writing center software
3 **Instruct** *and* **Integrate** *Pacing: 1–3 days*	✓ **Comprehension** Cause and Effect, T242–T243 **Phonics and Spelling** ✓ Digraph *sh*, T244 ✓ Digraph *th*, T245 ✓ Think About Words, T246 Using Context, T247 **Vocabulary** ✓ High-Frequency Words, T248 Rhyming Words, T249 Foods That Go Together, T249 **Language and Writing** Writing to Tell Where, T250–T251 **Communication Activities**, T252 **Independent Reading & Writing**, T253 **Cross-Curricular Activities**, T254–T255	**Activity Choices/Reteaching** Cause and Effect, T243 **Activity Choices** Digraph *sh*, T244 Digraph *th*, T245 **Activity Choices** High-Frequency Words, T248 **Activity Choices** Language and Writing, T250–T251	**Reading-Writing Workshop** Writing About Something Silly, T316–T317 **Transparency** Comprehension, 4–1 *Literacy Activity Book* Comprehension Skill, p. 39 Phonics and Spelling, pp. 40–43 High-Frequency Words, p. 44 Vocabulary Skill, p. 45 Language and Writing, p. 47 **Sentence Strips**, 1–21 **Audio Tape** for Get the Giggles: *On Top of Spaghetti* The Learning Company's new elementary writing center software

✓ *Indicates Tested Skills. See page T217 for assessment options.*

Introduce *the* Literature

Preparing to Read and Write

Poster 4A

Spaghetti! Spaghetti!

Spaghetti! spaghetti!
I love you a lot,
you're slishy, you're sloshy,
delicious and hot.
I gobble you down
oh, I can't get enough,
spaghetti! spaghetti!
you're wonderful stuff.

by Jack Prelutsky

INVITATIONS
TO LITERACY

INTERACTIVE LEARNING

Warm-up

Sharing Poetry

- Read aloud the poem "Spaghetti! Spaghetti!" on Poster 4A.

- Read the poem again, encouraging children to join in.

- Ask if children love spaghetti as much as the poet does. Have them draw pictures of foods they love.

Prior Knowledge/Building Background

**Key Concept
What are meatballs?**

Call children's attention to the meatballs pictured on Poster 4A. Then ask the following questions:

- Does anyone know what these are called?

- Why do you think they are called meatballs?

- How do you think meatballs are made?

If possible, follow this simple recipe with children to make meatballs. If an oven is not readily available, you might ask a parent volunteer to bring in some meatballs for children to try, or they could help prepare a batch of meatballs to be baked later.

Meatballs

Materials
medium bowl
shallow baking pan

Ingredients
1 envelope of onion soup mix
1 pound ground beef
1/2 cup plain bread crumbs

1/4 cup water
2 eggs slightly beaten
tomato sauce (optional*)

1. Preheat oven to 375 degrees.
2. Combine all of the ingredients in a bowl.
3. Shape the mixture into one-inch balls.
4. Place meatballs in a baking pan and bake 18 minutes or until done.
5. Serve with tomato sauce.

Makes about 4 dozen meatballs

Other Choices for Building Background

Sing It!

Students Acquiring English This selection is even more fun if you sing it. Teach children the first verse of the song and sing it with them before they read the selection. Refer to page 26 of the Big Book Plus for the words and the music.

Teacher Read Aloud

Part of the humor of this selection is the fantasy of meatballs growing on trees. To introduce children to other stories based on food fantasies, choose a book from the Teacher Read Aloud category in the Bibliography on pages T212–T213. You might consider the following: *The Bread That Grew*, by Robert L. Duyff; *The Night Kitchen*, by Maurice Sendak (also available in Spanish); or *Strega Nona*, by Tomie dePaola.

Does It Roll?

Extra Support In this story, a meatball rolls off a plate of spaghetti when someone sneezes. To help children better understand what types of things roll, invite them to help you sort shapes according to how they move. Provide small groups with objects of different shapes. Encourage them to explore whether the objects roll, slide, or both when pushed along the ground. Have them sort the objects on a floor graph.

Materials
- floor graphs
- real objects of varying shapes

Multicultural Link
Teacher FactFile
Everybody Eats Pasta!

Most people think of pasta as an Italian dish, but pasta was invented by the Chinese, who have eaten noodles as a traditional food for thousands of years. The Italian trader Marco Polo encountered pasta during his travels in Asia, and he brought the knowledge of how it is made back to Venice. From that time, pasta has been a mainstay of Mediterranean cuisine. In modern times, it has become a popular American food as well.

2

Interact *with* Literature

Shared Reading and Writing

INTERACTIVE LEARNING

Shared Reading

Preview and Predict

- Display the Big Book Plus *On Top of Spaghetti.* Explain to children that this book is based on silly lyrics that children like themselves created to go with the music of an old folk song.

- Invite volunteers who know the song to sing it or describe what it's about. Ask children what they think will happen in the story version.

Read Together

- Invite children to read the story with you to check their predictions. Run your hand under the words as you read, and encourage children to chime in. As you read, discuss the illustrations and events with children.

- Pause after reading page 23 of the story. Ask what advice the storyteller might give someone who is about to eat a spaghetti dinner.

Personal Response

Have children look back at the story. Ask them what they think makes the story funny. Then have them name foods they wish grew on trees.

Shared Writing: *A Class Song*

Prewriting

Brainstorm a list of other places the meatball in the story might have rolled. Have children choose two or three favorite places from the list and make a word web for each one to generate ideas for new verses.

Drafting

Have volunteers contribute lines for the song and record their suggestions on chart paper. (You might want to first teach the Exploring Language Patterns activity on the next page.)

Think Aloud

I know that the last word in the second and fourth lines need to rhyme, like the rhyming words *floor* and *door* and *bush* and *mush.* I also know the first two lines tell where it rolled and the last two lines tell what happened. I could say, "It rolled into the street, and under a *car,* and then my flat meatball, could not roll too *far.*"

Publishing

Invite volunteers to illustrate each verse and display the class song on a bulletin board. Sing it to the music printed on Big Book Plus page 26.

Where the Meatball Rolled

★**1.** Into the street

2. Into the water

3. Onto a roof

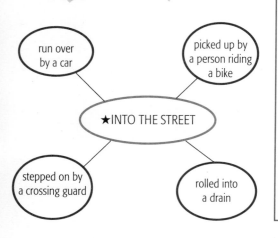

run over by a car

picked up by a person riding a bike

★INTO THE STREET

stepped on by a crossing guard

rolled into a drain

Cloze Reading

On every other page, use a self-stick note to cover an end-of-line rhyming word. Reread the story aloud, omitting each covered word. Ask children to supply it. Children can check their responses by removing the notes to reveal the words.

Sing It Chorally!

Have children read the story aloud as a group. Then designate half the class as "ones" and the other half as "twos." Using the music on page 26 of the Big Book Plus, have the "ones" sing one line from the story and the "twos" sing the next.

 More Choices for Shared Writing

- Write a silly recipe for meatballs.
- Write a letter to a friend telling him or her about a meatball tree that has appeared in the schoolyard.
- Write a story about a tree that produces ice cream cones or some other favorite food.

Listen and Read

Audio Tape for Get the Giggles: *On Top of Spaghetti*

Extra Support Invite small groups of children to listen to the Audio Tape. Encourage them to follow along in their books and to chime in with familiar words.

Exploring Language Patterns

- Have children identify the patterns in the text: the repeating phrases *(It rolled…* and *all covered with…)* and the rhyming words.

- Reread the story and ask children to count the number of times they hear each repeating phrase.

- Read the story again and have children clap when they hear the words that rhyme. Invite volunteers to explain how patterns in a story (rhyming or repeated words) can help them read more of the words.

Sentence Strips

- Distribute Sentence Strips 2–5 to children. Have them recreate the first four pages of the story by arranging the four strips in the pocket chart. Then reread the first four pages aloud. Have children follow the sentences in the pocket chart to confirm they are in the correct order.

- Continue the activity with the rest of the story.

  On top of spaghetti

  All covered with cheese,

  I lost my poor meatball

  When somebody sneezed.

Interact *with* Literature

More About the Illustrator

Katherine Tillotson

Sketching and painting from as early as she can remember, Katherine Tillotson left her hometown of Minneapolis, Minnesota, to attend the University of Colorado, where she earned a degree in fine arts. After graduating, Katherine continued her illustration; her designs have won awards from Bookbuilders West and Communications Arts.

Katherine Tillotson lives in San Francisco with her husband, Bob, and her fine furry friend, Alex.

Meet
Katherine Tillotson

Katherine Tillotson started to draw and to paint as a child.

Ms. Tillotson drew the pictures for this well-known story and song because she loves to eat pasta!

Katherine Tillotson with her furry friend, Alex

On Top of Spaghetti

LITTLE BIG BOOK
PLUS

In the same book...
Learn why we sneeze,
and how to make pasta
art. Then figure out
what's silly.

A Traditional Story and Song
illustrated by
Katherine Tillotson

Study Skill
Parts of a Book

Teach/Model

Display the table of contents in the Big Book Plus for children. Ask them to tell what they think a table of contents page is used for. Help children conclude that books with more than one story or with many parts have a table of contents page so the reader knows what is in the book and on what page each new selection begins.

Read aloud all of the selection titles. Invite volunteers to pick a selection title, read it, tell what page it begins on, and then turn to that page to check.

Practice/Apply

Invite pairs to take turns choosing a selection from the table of contents page in their Little Big Book Plus, reading the page number it begins on and then turning to that page in their Little Big Books Plus to check.

SKILL FINDER   Full lesson, p. H3

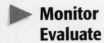

Interact
with
Literature

Reading Strategies

▶ **Monitor**
Evaluate

Teacher Modeling Tell children that good readers stop now and then to ask whether they have understood what has happened in a story. They also ask themselves how they feel about it. Model this strategy for children.

Think Aloud

As I read *On Top of Spaghetti,* I'll stop now and then to ask myself whether I understand what I've read so far. Now I know this is a silly story—so I might expect some things *not* to make much sense. When I come to a part that doesn't seem to make sense, I'll look at the pictures to see if they help and then I'll read on. I'll ask myself: What makes this story so funny? Why does it make people laugh?

Predicting/Purpose Setting

Suggest that as children reread the story, they decide what things are silly about it and note them in their journals.

LITTLE BIG BOOK
PLUS

On top of spaghetti

2

I lost my poor meatball

4

Choices for Reading

Guided Reading

Have children read pages 2–13, noting in their journals things they think are silly in the first part of the story. Follow up with the questions on page T232.

Cooperative Reading

Have small groups of children sing as they read the verses. Remind them to stop now and then to see if they understand what is happening and to decide what is silly.

Independent Reading

Have children read silently to the end of the selection, making note of things they think are silly. When children have finished, ask each reader to choose the one event that he or she thinks is silliest.

All covered with cheese,

3

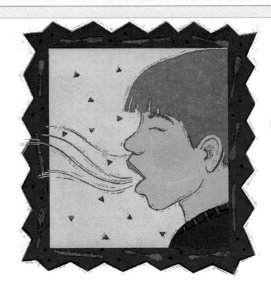

When somebody sneezed.

5

Phonics/Decoding

Digraph *wh*

Teach/Model

Read aloud page 5. Then write *when* on the board. Have children read the word and listen for the beginning sound. Remind them that sometimes two letters together stand for one sound, as at the beginning of *when*.

Underline the letters *wh* in *when*. Ask children these questions:

- What two letters stand for the beginning sound in *when*? *(wh)*

- Have you seen other words that begin like *when*? *(where, white, whale, whistle, why, which)*

List the words on the board and ask volunteers to underline the letters *wh* at the beginning of each word.

Practice/Apply

Write this silly sentence on the board and help children read it:

The white whale whistles when it sees a wheel.

Have pairs work together to write a silly sentence using as many words from the list as possible.

High-Frequency Words
when

Have children identify the word *when* on page 5. Point out that, as it is used here, *when* suggests that the girl lost her meatball *because* someone sneezed.

Extra Support

To help children understand how the girl's meatball gets lost, trace a route from page 5—where the boy's big sneeze must have shaken the table and caused a breeze—across to the top of the spaghetti on page 4 where the meatball used to sit, and then down to where the meatball is rolling. Point out the motion lines.

Interact
with
Literature

Reading Strategies

▶ Monitor

Model for children how to use the Monitor strategy during reading.

Think Aloud

This is a good place to ask myself if I understand what happens to the meatball after it falls on the floor. The story says that it rolled out the door, but I don't think a meatball would roll so far. Yet, the picture on page 9 shows the meatball going out the door. Now I know this story is silly, so I'll read on to see what happens next.

LITTLE BIG BOOK
PLUS

It rolled off the table

6

And then my poor meatball,

8

QuickREFERENCE

Students Acquiring English

MEETING INDIVIDUAL NEEDS

To help children acquiring English better understand the story, reread pages 6–9 and ask them to trace with a finger the lines showing where and how the meatball moved.

And onto the floor,

7

It rolled out the door.

9

Phonics/Decoding Review

Reread page 7. Ask children what two letters stand for the beginning sounds in *floor*. *(fl)* Remind children that *f* and *l* often come together in a word and that their sounds are so close together they seem to blend. Invite children to find other words in the story that have the following initial clusters: *sp, sn, gr, tr.* *(spaghetti, sneeze, grew, tree)*

Interact *with* Literature

Guided Reading

Comprehension/Critical Thinking

Ask children to share what things they thought were silly in the first part of this story. Then discuss the following questions:

1. Where did the meatball roll? *(off the table, onto the floor, out the door, into the garden, under a bush)*

2. What caused the meatball to start rolling? *(Somebody sneezed.)*

3. Do you think a meatball could really roll out the door? Why or why not?

4. Why do you think the meatball turned to mush?

Predicting/Purpose Setting

Have children read pages 14–21 and note in their journals silly things that happen. Use the questions on T236 for discussion.

LITTLE BIG BOOK **PLUS**

It rolled into the garden

10

And then my poor meatball

12

Informal Assessment

If children's responses indicate that they are understanding the selection, you may wish to have them read the rest of the story cooperatively or independently.

Quick REFERENCE

Phonics/Decoding Review

Have children find the word *meatball* on page 12. Ask what letter the word begins with. Have children find another word that begins with the same sound and letter on page 13. *(mush)*

Concepts of Print

Point out that this selection is based on a song and that this is why the lines are written like the lines of a song or poem. Each new line begins with a capital letter, even though it may not be the beginning of a new sentence.

And <u>under</u> a bush,

11

Was no<u>th</u>ing but mu<u>sh</u>.

13

High-Frequency Words
under

Have volunteers find the word *under* on page 11. Ask a volunteer to name the word that means the opposite of *under*. (*over*) Have a volunteer use each word in a sentence about something in the picture.

MEETING INDIVIDUAL NEEDS

Students Acquiring English

If children seem confused about what *nothing but mush* means, have them look at the meatball pictured on page 12 and compare it to the meatball on page 11. Explain that the meatball was flattened out. Demonstrate how a flattened meatball might look by flattening a small ball of clay.

MINILESSON

Phonics/Decoding
Digraphs *sh, th*

Teach/Model

TESTED SKILL

Ask a volunteer to read aloud pages 10–13. Then write these words in a chart on the board, underlining as shown.

bu<u>sh</u>	<u>th</u>en
mu<u>sh</u>	no<u>th</u>ing

Have children listen for the sound for *sh* as they say *bush* and *mush*. Explain that two letters can stand for one sound. Ask what letters stand for the end sound in *bush*. (*sh*)

Follow a similar procedure for *th* in *then* and *nothing*. Point out the slight variation (voiced and unvoiced) in pronunciation.

Ask children to name other words that contain *sh* and *th*. Add them to the chart, and ask a volunteer to underline the letters *sh* or *th*.

Practice/Apply

Write these silly sentences on the board, and help children read them:

- The sheep wash their dishes in a bathtub.

- The sharks brush their teeth with seashells.

Have each child choose one sentence, copy it onto a piece of drawing paper, and illustrate it.

SKILL FINDER

Phonics and Spelling, pp. T244, T245, T352, T353

Minilessons, pp. T287, T327

Interact
with
Literature

LITTLE BIG BOOK **PLUS**

14

Reading Strategies

▶ **Evaluate**

Model for children how to use the Evaluate strategy while reading.

Think Aloud

The story says that the meatball grew into a tree. And the picture shows spaghetti growing on the branches. I know this could never happen in real life. I think this story is really silly but lots of fun to read.

Reading Strategies

▶ **Think About Words**

Ask children how they could figure out the word *grew* on page 17.

- **What makes sense** The story says *It_____into a tree.* The word must tell something the meatball did.

- **Picture clues** The picture shows a tree with round things that look like meatballs. I think the meatball turned into a tree.

- **Sounds for letters** How does the word begin? (with *gr*) What word begins with *gr* and tells how the meatball turned into a tree? (*grew*)

Have children reread pages 16–17 to see if *grew* makes sense here.

And early next summer

16

MEETING INDIVIDUAL NEEDS **Challenge**

Point out that the author said that the tree grew *early next summer.* Encourage children to guess how big a *real* tree would get in the first growing season. Display a growth chart from an encyclopedia or other source.

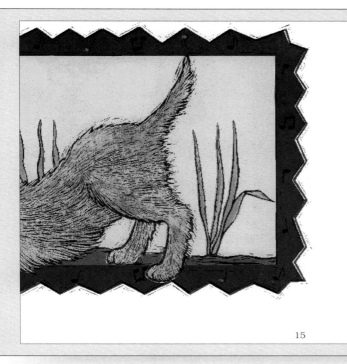

15

It grew into a <u>tree</u>,

17

Comprehension

Cause and Effect

TESTED SKILL

Teach/Model

Ask children what happens if they go outside when it's raining. (They get wet.) Explain that something that makes something else happen is called a *cause*. The rain would cause them to get wet. Mention that good readers look for causes as they read.

Explain that one way to figure out the cause of something is to ask yourself *why* it happened. Go back to pages 4–5 and model how to identify cause-effect relationships.

Think Aloud

I see that the meatball fell, so I ask myself why. Both the words and the pictures tell me that the boy's sneeze caused it to fall.

Draw a chart on the board and discuss the first entry in each column.

Cause	Effect
The boy sneezed.	The meatball fell.
	The spaghetti tree grew.

Practice/Apply

Return to page 17 and call attention to the tree. Then ask children to help you complete the chart by telling what caused a spaghetti tree to grow. Encourage them to use the pictures to find the cause.

SKILL FINDER

Full lesson/Reteaching, pp. T242–T243; Themes 6, 8

Minilesson, p. T335

High-Frequency Words
tree

Have children find the word *tree*. Discuss the initial consonant cluster. Then ask them to use the word in a sentence.

Students Acquiring English
MEETING INDIVIDUAL NEEDS

Pronoun Referent You may need to explain that *it* on page 17 refers to the meatball.

Science Link

Ask children to name fruits that really do grow on trees. (apples, lemons, bananas, coconuts, pears, cherries) Discuss the silliness of a spaghetti tree.

2

Interact
with
Literature

Guided Reading

Comprehension/Critical Thinking

Have children share their journal entries for this part of the story. Talk about the silliness of a meatball growing into a tree. Then ask these questions:

1. What did the dog do with the meatball? (He buried it.) How do you know? (from the picture on pages 14–15)

2. What happened to the meatball then? (It grew into a tree covered with meatballs.)

3. Is it possible for a meatball to grow into a tree? Why not?

Predicting/Purpose Setting

Ask children to list some things they want to find out as they read to the end of the selection. Then suggest that they decide how much they liked the story and rate it in their journals, using the scale shown.

1	2	3	4
No good	Good	Very good	Great!

Informal Assessment

Use pages 18–25 to informally assess children's oral reading fluency. See the Oral Reading Checklist in the *Teacher's Assessment Handbook* for criteria.

LITTLE BIG BOOK PLUS

All covered with meatballs

18

As big as could be.

20

QuickREFERENCE

High-Frequency Words
as, big, could, be

Have children read page 20. Encourage them to use this phrase in sentences. (For example, *The elephant was as big as could be.*)

Challenge

Invite volunteers to describe how the artist would have to revise the picture of the meatballs growing on the tree if the text were changed to read *As small as could be* or *As flat as could be.*

Phonics/Decoding Review

Review the sound for *c,* as in *covered* and *could,* and the sound for *b,* as in *big* and *be.*

19

21

Comprehension

Sequence

Teach/Model

Ask a volunteer to pantomime these steps for assembling a plate of spaghetti:

1. Put cooked spaghetti on a plate.
2. Pour sauce on top.
3. Sprinkle on some cheese.
4. Eat it up!

Next have the child pantomime the same steps in this order; 3, 4, 2, 4, 1. Ask children if *they* would prepare dinner that way and why or why not. (steps out of order; don't make sense) Invite them to name other things they usually do in a certain order, such as follow the school-day schedule.

Put the following chart on the board. Then reread pages 2–5 of the story, and help children identify the beginning event.

Beginning	The meatball falls off the spaghetti.
Middle	
End	

Practice/Apply

Have children complete the chart. Help them identify the events.

Middle	• The meatball rolls out the door and into the garden. • It grows into a spaghetti-and-meatball tree.
End	Storyteller's advice: Don't sneeze when eating spaghetti.

SKILL FINDER

Full lesson/Reteaching, pp. T350–T351; Themes 2, 6, 9

Minilesson, p. T333

Interact
with
Literature

 ## Guided Reading

Comprehension/Critical Thinking

Ask children to share their ratings of the story. Encourage them to give reasons for their feelings about it. Then ask these questions:

1. What happened to the meatball after the dog buried it in the garden?
   (It grew into a tree.)

2. What grew on the tree? (meatballs and spaghetti)

3. Where do you think the meatball shown on page 22 came from?

Reading Strategies

▶ **Evaluate**

Ask children if they think what the storyteller says about not sneezing is good advice.

Self-Assessment

Ask children where they stopped in the story to be sure they understood what they read. Discuss these questions:
- Did I look at the pictures for help?
- Did I read on, keeping in mind that the story is meant to be silly?

LITTLE BIG BOOK
PLUS

So if you eat spaghetti

22

Hold on to your meatball

24

 Quick**REFERENCE**

High-Frequency Words
your

Read aloud page 24, omitting *your*. Have a volunteer point out and say the word you omitted. Then ask volunteers to use the word in sentences.

Extra Support

Rereading Encourage small groups to read the story chorally.

Multi-Age Classrooms Older children can guide the reading and help younger children with word identification by using language patterns, letter sounds, and picture clues.

All covered with cheese,

23

And don't ever sneeze!

25

Comprehension

Inferences: Drawing Conclusions

Teach/Model

Remind children that writers often let readers figure out some things about a story on their own. Reread pages 22–25 and ask children why they think the girl and the boy are giving this advice. Then model for children how readers figure out things the author doesn't say word for word.

Think Aloud

I remember what happened at the beginning of the story: The boy's sneeze caused the girl's meatball to roll out the door and into the garden, where it grew into a spaghetti-and-meatball tree. Now I think the girl and the boy are telling the readers of this silly story to hold on to their food and not to sneeze when they eat spaghetti so that the same thing won't happen to them.

Invite children to respond to the conclusion you modeled. Encourage them to form their own.

Practice/Apply

Ask children why they think the dog in the story buried the meatball. Encourage children to use their experiences with dogs to help them draw conclusions.

SKILL FINDER Full lesson/Reteaching, Themes 2, 7, 9

Health Link

Share these facts about sneezing:

- Holding back a sneeze can hurt one's ears.
- People cover their faces when they sneeze to keep germs from spreading.

Phonics/Decoding Review

Ask children to identify the beginning sound in the word *your* on page 24. Then have them turn to page 22 and find a word that begins with the same sound. *(you)*

2

Interact *with* Literature

Responding

Responding Activities

Retelling *On Top of Spaghetti*

Materials
- modeling clay
- paper plates
- precut lengths of yarn

Have children make meatballs from modeling clay. Then give each child a paper plate and lengths of yarn to serve as spaghetti. Ask them to place their meatballs on top of the yarn, and retell the story. Tell children that they can give their meatballs a little push to help get them rolling but that the meatballs must remain on their desktops for safety reasons.

Challenge Children who have memorized the story may enjoy reciting it while others act it out with their props.

Make a Dream Tree

Who wouldn't like a meatball-and-spaghetti tree? Help children make a "dream tree" of their favorite foods.

- Ask children what foods they wish would grow on trees. List them on the board.

- Make a large tree trunk and branches from construction paper for the bulletin board.

- Have children decorate the branches with pictures and labels of the foods they have named.

Materials
- construction paper
- old magazines
- scissors
- art supplies

Informal Assessment

Use the Comprehension Check or the Guided Reading questions to assess children's general understanding of the selection.

Additional Support:
- Have children sing the song "On Top of Spaghetti" on page 26 of the Big Book Plus.
- Take a picture walk through the story. Ask volunteers to summarize what is happening as you turn the pages.

More Responding Activities

Home Connection

Suggest that children work with their families to draw their own illustrations for *On Top of Spaghetti.* Display the Sentence Strips one at a time in a pocket chart and ask each child to copy the the text onto pieces of drawing paper. Children can take home their pages, work with family members to illustrate each scene, and then combine the pages into a book. Ask children to bring in their books to share with the class.

Materials

- crayons or colored markers
- drawing paper
- Sentence Strips

On top of spaghetti

All covered with cheese,

On top of spaghetti   All covered with cheese,

Literature Discussion
Cooperative Learning

Divide the class into small groups to talk about the selection. Allow them to discuss anything they want to about the story. Then ask each group to pick a spokesperson to share some of the things they talked about.

What a Mess!

- Ask if children have ever had a problem with food spilling or falling onto the floor. Discuss what caused the problem and how such problems might be avoided.

- Ask children to draw and write about a time when they had a food problem. How did they solve their problem? Or didn't they?

Children As Authors

On Top of Spaghetti is part of a rich oral tradition of songs and rhymes composed by children for themselves. Ask children to tell about other songs, stories, or jump-rope rhymes that they have made up or heard from other children. They also might enjoy hearing selections from *The Lore and Language of School Children* by Iona and Peter Opie.

Challenge Have children choose another traditional song to illustrate.

Portfolio Opportunity

As a writing sample, save children's work from the writing activity on this page.

Instruct
and
Integrate

Comprehension

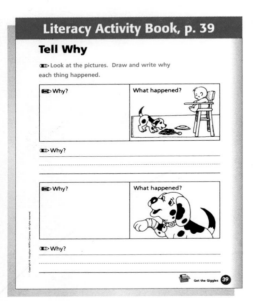

Transparency 4–1

Cause and Effect

Why?	What Happened?
	The ball rolled across the floor.
	The meatball rolled off the table.
	A tree all covered with meatballs grew in the garden.

TRANSPARENCY 4–1
TEACHERS BOOK PAGE T242

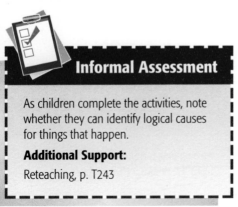

Literacy Activity Book, p. 39

Tell Why

☞ Look at the pictures. Draw and write why each thing happened.

☞ Why?	What happened?
☞ Why? _____

☞ Why?	What happened?
☞ Why? _____

Get the Giggles 39

Informal Assessment

As children complete the activities, note whether they can identify logical causes for things that happen.

Additional Support:
Reteaching, p. T243

INTERACTIVE LEARNING

TESTED SKILL

Cause and Effect
LAB, p. 39

Teach/Model
Display Transparency 4–1 and read aloud the chart headings. Then invite a volunteer to come to the front of the class and gently kick a ball across the floor. Read the first sentence in the *What Happened?* column, and have children tell why the ball rolled. (It was kicked.) Record the answer in the *Why?* column.

Explain that good readers also think about why things happen in stories, because it makes them easier to remember and more fun to read. Read the next sentence in the *What Happened?* column. Then display pages 4 and 5 of the Big Book Plus as you help children recall why the girl lost the meatball. Record the cause in the *Why?* column. (The boy sneezed.)

Next, read the last sentence in the second column and model for children how a good reader might figure out what event caused the tree to grow.

Think Aloud

A real tree would grow because someone planted the right kind of seed. But in this silly, make-believe story there's a spaghetti-and-meatball tree! I wonder what kind of seed the author thought would grow into *that*? I remember that the dog buried the meatball, almost as if planting it. I'll guess that the buried meatball caused the make-believe tree to grow.

Practice/Apply
Help children fold a sheet of drawing paper to make eight boxes. Ask them to hold their papers vertically and draw pictures of the following items in the right-hand boxes:

- a chair falling over
- a dog barking at a door
- a cat climbing a tree
- a glass of milk spilling

Now ask children to draw pictures in the left-hand boxes to show what might have caused each event to happen.

Have children complete *Literacy Activity Book* page 39.

SKILL FINDER ▸ Minilessons, pp. T235, T335

More Practice Activities

What Would You Do?

Ask children to draw pictures showing what the following situations might cause them to do next:

- You want to get a new toy.
- You want to find out more about dinosaurs.
- You want to become friends with the new boy or girl next door.

Then have children share their drawings with the class and tell what they would do. For example, "To learn more about dinosaurs, I will read books about them."

Physical Changes

Invite children to explore what causes water to evaporate. Have them watch as you follow the procedure shown.

- Have children predict what will happen to the water in each cup. After three hours, invite them to check the water level in both cups.

- **What happened?** (The water level in the cup in the warmer place should be lower than the water in the other cup.)

- **Why?** (The warmth caused one cup of water to dry up faster than the other.)

Physical Change Experiment

Materials: water, two identical clear plastic cups, permanent marker

Procedure:

- Put equal amounts of water in the two cups and mark the levels on each.
- Put one cup near a radiator or in a window that gets direct sun.
- Put the other cup in a cool, shady place.

What Caused It to Happen?

Ask small groups to brainstorm and record lists of possible causes for each of the following events: a flat bicycle tire, a hole in your sock, a missing button on a coat, a jammed zipper, a lost lunch box.

Invite each group to share their lists with the class.

Reteaching   ## Cause and Effect

Read the following fable. Ask children to listen for what happens and why.

Once a dog found a nice big bone. He decided to take the bone home and bury it. On the way, the dog passed by a pond. He looked into the water, and he saw another dog. Of course, what he saw was his own reflection, but the dog didn't know that. The bone in the water looked bigger and better than his own. So the dog opened his mouth to snatch it away from the other dog. Out fell his own bone, into the pond, where it sank to the bottom.

Go back through the fable, letting children tell you what caused the dog to lose his bone and why.

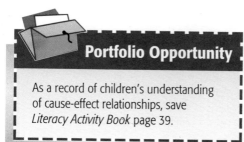

Portfolio Opportunity

As a record of children's understanding of cause-effect relationships, save *Literacy Activity Book* page 39.

Instruct and Integrate

Phonics and Spelling

Portfolio Opportunity

Save *Literacy Activity Book* pages 40–43 as a record of children's ability to identify words with the digraphs *sh* and *th*.

INTERACTIVE LEARNING

Digraph *sh*

TESTED SKILL

LAB, pp. 40, 41

- Print the following on the board: *Sh, sh, sh!* Tell children this is what a mother might say if she hears her children slurping their spaghetti! Identify the /sh/ sound and have children name the two letters that stand for it.

- Tell children that the /*sh*/ sound can be heard at the beginning of words like *shine* and *sheep,* in the middle of words like *sloshy* and *washes,* and at the end of words like *bush* and *mush*.

- On the board, write the following words: *sad, sheet, dogs, shirt, wishing, shop, sorry, push, miss, dashing,* and *hush.* Give each child an index card on which you've written *sh.* As you read the words in random order, children should hold up their cards if they hear the /*sh*/ sound and repeat the word after you. As they repeat words, circle them.

- Have children choose three of the circled words, write them, and illustrate them. Then ask volunteers to use the words in oral sentences.

- Have children complete *Literacy Activity Book* pages 40, 41.

SKILL FINDER Minilessons, pp. T233, T287, T327

More Practice Activities

Rhyme Time

Remind children that the meatball in the story rolled under a bush and turned to mush. (Pronounce *mush* so that the words rhyme.) Write the following words on the board: *he, not, came, my, out, back, but, make.*

Have children read each word, write a rhyming word that begins with *sh,* and use the new word in an oral sentence.

Let's Fish

Make big and little fish shapes out of construction paper. Then write the following words on the shapes: *fish, shark, shed, ship, shop, wish, wash, dish.* Put the words in the bowl. Have children take turns fishing for a word, reading it, and using it in a sentence.

Materials
- construction paper
- large plastic jar or bowl

INTERACTIVE LEARNING

Digraph *th*

LAB, pp. 42, 43

- Have a volunteer read Sentence Strips 6–9 aloud. Point to the words *the* and *then.* Remind children that two letters together sometimes stand for one sound. Invite them to say *the* and *then* and listen for the sound *th.* Explain that the */th/* sound can be heard at the beginning, middle, or end of words. Write the chart below on the board and read the words.

Beginning	Middle	End
then	no*th*ing	wi*th*

- Next, pass out self-stick notes with these words written on them: *the, think, that, weather, mother, father, cloth, mouth, moth.* With your help, each child can read a word aloud while the others listen for the */th/* sound and call on a classmate to tell where the words should be posted on the chart.

SKILL FINDER Minilessons, pp. T287, T233, T327

- Have pairs take turns choosing a word, reading it, and using it in a sentence. Then have children complete *Literacy Activity Book* pages 42, 43.

More Practice Activities

Listen Up!

Distribute index cards on which you've written *sh* or *th.* Tell children to listen carefully as you say some words. If the word begins like *sheep,* children with the *sh* cards should hold them up. If the word begins like *thin,* children with the *th* cards should hold them up. Say these words: *thumb, shirt, thank, sharp, show, thump, sheet, third.* Repeat the activity for final *sh* and *th,* using these words: *dash, cloth, push, wash, mouth, moth, path.*

Word Wall

Divide a Word Wall into two sections labeled *TH* and *SH*. As children come across words with either digraph, they can add them to the wall.

Where IS My Baby?

WATCH ME READ

Where IS My Baby?
by Deborah Eaton

This story includes words with the digraphs *sh* and *th* for decoding practice.

Literacy Activity Book, p. 42

Spaghetti Dinner!

Literacy Activity Book, p. 43

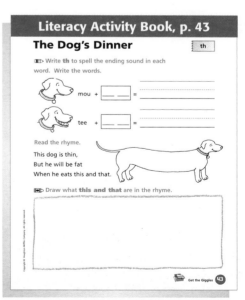

The Dog's Dinner

Instruct *and* Integrate

Phonics/Decoding

INTERACTIVE LEARNING

Think About Words

Teach/Model

Use a self-stick note to cover the word *floor* on page 7 of *On Top of Spaghetti*. Reread the page with children, saying *blank* for *floor*. Then uncover the word, and have children tell how they could figure it out if they did not recognize it right away.

Model how a good reader uses many clues to figure out a new word.

Think Aloud

What Makes Sense First I'll read the sentence, which begins on page 6 … I know the word tells where the meatball went when it rolled off the table.

Letter Sounds Now I'll look at the letters in the word. I see *fl* at the beginning. I know the sounds for *fl*. I also see *r* at the end, and I know the sound for *r*.

Picture Clues The picture shows the meatball under the table and on the floor. I think the word must be *floor*. I'll read the sentence again to be sure *floor* makes sense.

Display Sentence Strips 6–9.

> It rolled off the table
>
> And onto the floor,
>
> And then my poor meatball,
>
> It rolled out the door.

Cover *door* and read the lines, saying *blank* for *door*. Ask a volunteer to uncover the word, read the lines, and tell what clues he or she used to figure out *door*. (Examples: sentence meaning; sound for *d*; rhymes with *floor*; picture clues)

Practice/Apply

Have volunteers choose a verse from the story, read it or sing it for the group, and explain how they figured out any unfamiliar words.

Informal Assessment

Note children's ability to apply the Think About Words strategy as they read aloud from library books or the WATCH ME READ Books for this theme.

MINILESSON

Using Context for Decoding

Teach/Model   Remind children that it's important to think about what makes sense as they try to figure out new words. Display pages 10–11 of the Big Book Plus. Read all but the last word *(bush)* on page 11, having children supply it. Model how to use context to figure out the word.

Think Aloud

I know from the line on page 10 that the meatball rolled into the garden. This word must name something found in a garden. The word begins with the sound for *b* and ends with the sound for *sh*. *Bush* makes sense and has the right sounds. And I see a bush in the picture on page 11.

Have children tell how they knew the word wasn't *tree*. (wrong sounds) Ask how they knew the word wasn't *bash*. (*Bash* does not make sense.)

Practice/Apply   Have children read pages 16–17 and tell how the picture and the meaning of the sentence could help them figure out *summer*. Ask how they know the word isn't *swimmer*.

MINILESSON

Word Meaning from Context

Teach/Model   Have children reread pages 12–13 with you. Ask if they knew what the word *mush* meant before they read the story for the first time. Discuss how they could figure out the word's meaning from the sentence and the part of the picture that appears on page 12. Point out that even if they did not know exactly what the word meant, they could still understand the story because they know it describes what the meatball looked like at this point in the story.

Practice/Apply   Have children turn to page 28 and read the title of the activity: "Make Pasta Art!" Ask how the picture on the page could help them figure out the meaning of the word *pasta*, if they didn't know what the word meant.

3

Instruct *and* Integrate

Vocabulary

WATCH ME READ

Where IS My Baby?
by Deborah Eaton

This story provides practice and application for the following skills:

- **High-Frequency Words:** *as, be, big, could, tree, under, when, your*
- **Phonics/Decoding Skills:** Digraphs *sh, th*
- **Cumulative Review:** Previously taught decoding skills and High-Frequency Words

Literacy Activity Book, p. 44

The Meatball Tree

➤ Finish the poem. Draw a picture of your ending.

On your tree, I could see
Three nice meatballs as big as could be.
So when I go walking under your tree,

I will _____

_____

➤ Draw or write your ending.

44 Get the Giggles

Informal Assessment

As children read aloud the WATCH ME READ Book or complete other activities on this page, note the ease with which they recognize the High-Frequency Words.

High-Frequency Words

TESTED SKILL

High-Frequency Words: *as, be, big, could, tree, under, when, your*

Our Word Tree

Remind children that the author of *On Top of Spaghetti* made up a meatball tree. Invite them to create a word tree for the reading center.

Place the branch in the bucket, using the sand to stabilize it. Distribute leaf shapes to eight volunteers. Display the word cards. Have children copy the words onto the leaves, read them and use them in sentences, and then hang them on the tree. Children can borrow leaves when they need help writing these words.

As you proceed through the theme, add other High-Frequency Words. Periodically, have children read all the words that have been put on the tree.

Materials

- leafless tree branch with twigs
- bucket filled with sand
- leaf shapes cut from green paper
- hole punch
- string
- High-Frequency Word cards

The Meatball Tree

LAB, p. 44

Review the High-Frequency Words with children. Together, read the directions on *Literacy Activity Book* page 44. Have children complete the page and share their work with a partner.

Spaghetti Words

On construction paper, sketch a large platter with a few meatballs. Have children form the High-Frequency Words from alphabet pasta or letter cards and glue them on the platter. Display their work on the Word Wall.

Word Matches

Display the Sentence Strips in a pocket chart. Invite children to read the lines chorally. Then cover the words *as, be, big, could,* and *tree.* Distribute cards for the same words. Have children take turns identifying their words, using them to replace blanks, and rereading the lines.

Materials

- Sentence Strips 14–17

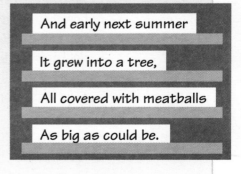

And early next summer

It grew into a tree,

All covered with meatballs

As big as could be.

MINILESSON

Vocabulary Skill
Rhyming Words
LAB, p. 45

Teach/Model Read aloud the second sentence of *On Top of Spaghetti,* pointing to *floor* and *door.* Model how to identify rhyming words.

Think Aloud

I know that rhyming words end with the same sounds. *Floor* and *door* end with the same sounds and also end with the same letters, *-oor.*

Explain that rhyming words always end with the same sounds and that they often, but not always, end with the same letters.

Practice/Apply
- Continue reading, pausing to let children supply the second rhyming word in each verse. Write the rhyming pairs on the chalkboard. *(cheese–sneezed, floor–door, bush–mush, tree–be, cheese–sneeze)*

- Help children reread each pair of words, compare the ending sound and spellings, and suggest other words that rhyme with them. Point out that *cheese* and *sneezed* are near rhymes, rather than full rhymes.

- Have children complete *Literacy Activity Book* page 45.

MINILESSON

Vocabulary Expansion
Foods That Go Together

Teach/Model Write the words *spaghetti and meatballs* on the chalkboard. Read the words, and point out that certain foods go especially well together. Ask children to name other pairs of foods that go well together, and record their ideas on the chalkboard.

Practice/Apply Have each child draw and label a pair of foods that go well together. Bind all the pages to make a book of food pairs.

Portfolio Opportunity

- Children must read the High-Frequency Words to complete *Literacy Activity Book* page 44. You might want to save the page as a record.

- Save *Literacy Activity Book* page 45 to show children's ability to identify rhyming words.

Language and Writing

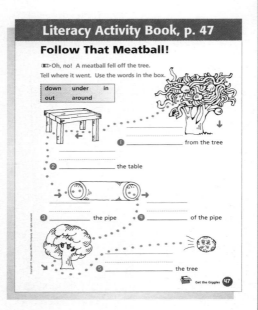

Literacy Activity Book, p. 47

Follow That Meatball!

Oh, no! A meatball fell off the tree.
Tell where it went. Use the words in the box.

| down | under | in |
| out | around | |

1. _____ from the tree
2. _____ the table
3. _____ the pipe 4. _____ of the pipe
5. _____ the tree

Get the Giggles **47**

MINILESSON

Writing to Tell Where

LAB, p. 47

- Reread *On Top of Spaghetti*. Then have children tell you each place the meatball went after somebody sneezed.

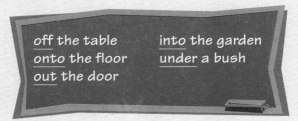

off the table   into the garden
onto the floor   under a bush
out the door

- Give each child a small manipulative, such as a bead or a marble, and a cup. Give children directions, using position words, and have them follow the directions. For instance, you might say, "Put the bead in the cup" or "Put the cup over the bead."

- Encourage volunteers to come up with new directions to give their classmates. Write their responses on the board.

- Have children complete *Literacy Activity Book* page 47 for practice in writing to tell where.

Practice Activities

Word Wall

Make a Word Wall of *Words That Tell Where*. Have children brainstorm position words and sentences using the words. Children can draw a small picture next to each sentence to illustrate the word's meaning.

Under
The cat is under the bed.

On
My hat is on my head.

Writing Directions

Invite children to create an activity course in your classroom or in a large area such as the gym. Help children write labels to post along the course, telling other children what to do next. For instance, labels might say, "Read a book under the table," "Write your name on the chart," and "Put your hand in the bag."

Informal Assessment

Check children's understanding of position words. If a child is having difficulty understanding their meaning, repeat the cup-and-bead activity with him or her individually to determine the specific source of confusion.

More Practice Activities

Giving Directions

Oral Language Development Have partners take turns telling each other how to get from one part of the classroom to another. Encourage them to use words like *up, down, in, out, left, right*, and *over*. Or have children hide something special for you or another adult. They can then give directions for the person to follow to the surprise.

Position Words
Cooperative Learning

Grammar Connection Create flash cards with position words on them. Have children work in small groups. Distribute one flash card to each group, and have them brainstorm sentences using the word on the card. Encourage groups to act out their sentences for their classmates.

Speech Balloons

Have children draw favorite scenes from *On Top of Spaghetti* and write in speech balloons what they think one of the characters in that scene is saying. Ask children to draw a line under any position words that they use.

Act It Out

Students Acquiring English Use a simple prop, such as a ball, to help children act out the position words. Have them place the ball in different places in the room. Help them describe the position of the ball after they have placed it. Repeat the position word each time to reinforce its meaning.

Children can use The Learning Company's new elementary writing center to write, illustrate, and publish their work to share with others.

Portfolio Opportunity

- Save *Literacy Activity Book* page 47 to demonstrate children's ability to write position words.

- Save children's written responses to activities on these pages as samples of their writing development.

3

Instruct *and* **Integrate**

Communication Activities

Audio Tape
for Get the Giggles: *On Top of Spaghetti*

Tell children to pay special attention to the rhyming words as the narrator reads.

Listening and Speaking

Sing and Play

Materials
- xylophone
- cymbals
- drum

Have children play a variety of simple musical instruments as they sing "On Top of Spaghetti." You may wish to help them orchestrate the song to reflect the words:

- *When somebody sneezed:* Crash cymbals.

- *It rolled off the table:* Drag the hammer down the keys of a xylophone.

- *Was nothing but mush:* Bang the drum.

- *And early next summer/It grew into a tree:* Beat the drum louder and faster with each word.

- *As big as could be:* Crash the cymbals after the line is sung.

Viewing

Art in Motion

Ask children to look at pages 4, 5, 6, 7, and 9 to see how Katherine Tillotson showed movement in her pictures. Help them identify the lines that show the meatball rolling or bouncing and the lines that show the air moving when the boy sneezes. Point out examples of this technique in other picture books and comic strips. Then encourage children to use it as they create their own comic strips.

Viewing from Different Angles

Display page 7 of the Big Book Plus for children and point out how the girl is standing as she watches her meatball roll. Ask them how they think the meatball looks to her from this position. Invite pairs to take turns looking at an object in the classroom, such as a ball, from different angles and describe what they see.

Independent Reading & Writing

Student-Selected Reading

Felt Boards

Keep a felt board in the classroom. Children can draw characters from their favorite stories, cut them out, and glue felt to the back. They can retell their favorite stories, using the felt characters they have created.

Read-Aloud Visitors

Invite parent or grandparent volunteers to come to class regularly to listen to children read aloud. Set up a special time to coach volunteers on how to help children if they get "stuck." Have children prepare for the occasions by selecting the books they would like to read aloud.

Books for Independent Reading

Encourage children to choose their own books. They might choose one of the following titles.

Hooray for Snail! by John Stadler

Where IS My Baby? by Deborah Eaton

On Top of Spaghetti illustrated by Katherine Tillotson

Have children reread this selection silently or aloud to a partner.

See the Bibliography on pages T212–T213 for more theme-related books for independent reading.

Ideas for Independent Writing

Encourage children to write on self-selected topics. For those who need help getting started, suggest one of the following activities:

- a **list** of places the meatball might travel
- a **recipe** for a favorite food
- a **health poster** about sneezing

Student-Selected Writing

Spelling Resources

Remind children that they can look around the room for the spelling of words. Call their attention to charts, Word Walls, books, and other resources. Make a point of praising children who use these resources to help themselves.

Publishing Center

Work with other teachers to create a Publishing Center in your school. Invite parent volunteers to help staff the center. Classes can sign up for certain days of the week when they can go to the Publishing Center to get help putting their writing into its final form.

Portfolio Opportunity

Save examples of the writing children do independently on self-selected topics.

Cross-Curricular Activities

Math

Pasta Patterns

Call children's attention to the different patterns on the borders of the story pages. Then let children use different types of pasta to make a pattern on their desktops. Encourage each child to explain his or her pattern to the class. You might ask:

- What makes your design a pattern?

- Can you show the part of your pattern that happens over and over again? (the pattern stem)

Have children change seats with a partner. Ask them to identify their partner's pattern stem and continue the pattern.

Materials
- different types of pasta

Art

Pasta Frames

Discuss with children how the borders on the story pages are similar to picture frames. Then invite children to make pasta picture frames using some of the patterns they created in the math activity.

Students Acquiring English As you verbally give directions for this activity, demonstrate how to make the frame, holding up each object and stating its name.

- Provide children with cardboard sheets that have been precut into frames.

- Have them arrange and glue their pasta in a pattern on the frames. Let children paint their frames after the glue has set.

- Ask children to choose their favorite part of the story, draw pictures of it, and glue it to their frames.

Materials
- pasta of different shapes and sizes
- cardboard
- glue
- paint
- drawing paper
- crayons or markers

Choices for Science

Some Food Really Grows on Trees

In *On Top of Spaghetti,* meatballs grow on a tree. Children will enjoy discovering that many things really do grow on trees and bushes.

- Ask children to name foods that grow on trees or bushes.

- Write their responses on chart paper and post the list in the science center.

- In the science center, make available nature magazines, picture books, and/or encyclopedias that contain photos of trees and bushes that bear fruit. Invite visitors to the center to look through these reference materials to find out what foods really grow on trees and bushes. Have them draw and label pictures of their findings and display them on a bulletin board.

Fruit that Grows on Trees

lemons   apples   figs   oranges

Why Spaghetti Gets Soft When It's Cooked

- Distribute magnifying glasses and pieces of uncooked spaghetti to children.

- Ask them to look closely at the spaghetti noodles with the magnifying glasses to find tiny little specks.

- Explain that these are called starch granules. When spaghetti is cooked, these granules soak up the hot water, and they swell up and get soft. This makes the spaghetti get softer and larger, too!

- Now distribute some boiled strands of spaghetti to children and have them compare the size differences. Challenge volunteers to review why the cooked spaghetti is larger.

Book List

Science

A Book of Fruit
by Barbara Hirsch Lember

How Do Apples Grow?
by Betsy Maestro

Apple Tree
by Barrie Watts

Materials
- magnifying glasses
- uncooked spaghetti
- cooked spaghetti

LITTLE BIG BOOK PLUS

Introduce the Literature

Prior Knowledge

Play or hum the music to the song and see who recognizes it. Ask children to share any versions of the song they know.

Interact with Literature

Performing the Song

Audio Tape for Get the Giggles: *On Top of Spaghetti*

After children read the lyrics, you can hold a sing-along. Just play the song on the Audio Tape.

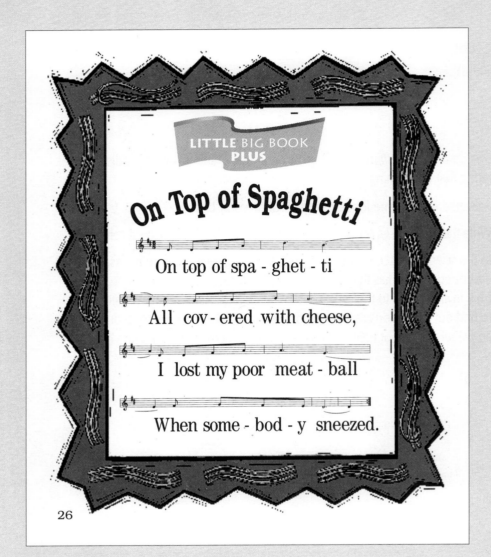

Instruct and Integrate

Writing

Song Lyrics Children may enjoy writing new lyrics for this song, individually or in small groups. You might offer these examples:

- On top of my taco, all covered with cheese, I lost my poor pepper when somebody sneezed.
- On top of my sundae, all covered with sauce, I lost my red cherry when somebody coughed.

Aaaah . . . Choo!
What Happens When You Sneeze?

First . . .
Something tickles your nose. It may be dirt or dust. This makes you take in air through your mouth.

Next . . .
Air blasts out your mouth and nose. Out comes whatever was tickling your nose.

27

Introduce *the* Literature

Prior Knowledge

Discuss with children about times when people sneeze. Ask them if people sneeze only when they are sick. Talk about other times when people sneeze.

Interact *with* Literature

Using Diagrams

Read the text aloud. Explain to children that diagrams can help readers understand what they are reading. Discuss the two parts of sneezing shown by the diagrams on the page. You may want to point out how the arrows are used to show the direction of air. Ask children where else they have seen arrows showing direction. (Highway signs and juice cartons are two possibilities.)

Health

I Have a Cold! In pairs, have children role-play having a cold and helping to take care of someone with a cold. Then, as a class, discuss all the ways we help ourselves stay well and get better.

LITTLE BIG BOOK PLUS

Introduce the Literature

Building Background

Display a variety of pasta with various shapes such as wheels, elbows, and bow ties. Have the class describe each shape.

Interact with Literature

Following Instructions

Have a volunteer read the materials list aloud while the class collects and distributes the items.

Brainstorming

Invite children to think of different things that they could make with the pasta. Encourage creative silliness. For example, they could use pasta wheels for earrings. Write their ideas on the board.

Make Pasta Art!

What You'll Need

different kinds of pasta, glue, string, paint, paper plates, paper

28

Instruct and Integrate

Art

Pasta Art Children can use the class ideas on the board, the pictures on the page, or their own ideas to create pasta art. Set up an area in the classroom to display their work.

What's Silly?

Turn the page to find out.

1 What's silly here?

2 Now what's silly?

29

Building Background

Rearrange the classroom so that something is silly when children arrive, such as an upside-down calendar or a chair in the wastebasket. Then ask children to tell you what silly sights they see in the classroom.

Observing Details

Read the first page aloud. Children can write their answers, then check them by reading the answers on the next page.

Art

Making Silly Pictures Children can have fun making their own silly pictures. Have them print *What's Silly?* at the top of each page.

1 The ketchup and comb!

2 The flowers and spaghetti!

30

What's Silly?

Creative Movement

Playing What's Silly Now? Children practice identifying and remembering details in the following game.

- Three children leave the room together.

- When they return, they have made some silly changes. Perhaps one has a hat on; another has lost one shoe; the third has a jacket turned upside down.

- Children in the room look for what's silly.

- Then the three leave and return with everything back in place.

- Children must tell what was silly.

Playing "Silly Mirrors" Here's another chance for children to identify silly details. Follow these steps:

- Explain that the class has "the sillies."

- To get rid of them, you must pass a silly face all the way around the room.

- Have the first child make a silly face.

- The second child mirrors it.

- Then he or she turns to the next child and makes another silly face, and so on, all the way around the room.

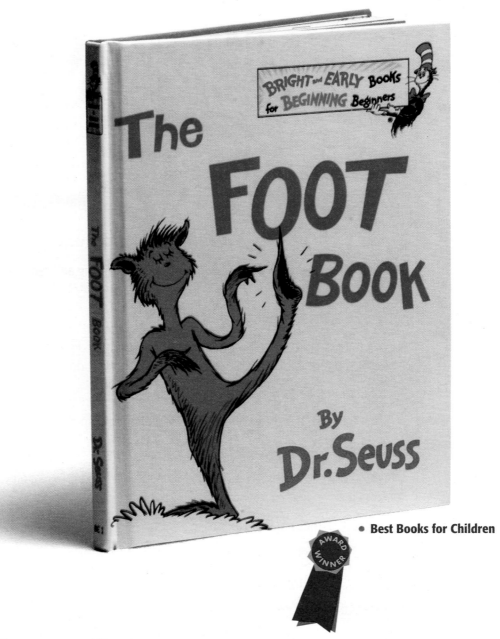

ANTHOLOGY
SELECTION:
The Foot Book

by Theodor Seuss
Geisel (Dr. Seuss)

Other Books by the Author

Green Eggs and Ham

The Cat in the Hat

Horton Hatches an Egg

Horton Hears a Who!

If I Ran the Circus

● **Best Books for Children**

Selection Summary

Can you guess how many different types of feet there are? In this rhyming selection, you won't believe all the feet you'll encounter. There are wet feet, dry feet, trick feet, sick feet, slow feet, quick feet, and fuzzy fur feet. There are clown feet, pig feet, and even twenty-four feet. With every page you turn, you'll find more and more silly feet to make you giggle!

Lesson Planning Guide

	Skill/Strategy Instruction	Meeting Individual Needs	Lesson Resources
1 **Introduce** *the* **Literature** *Pacing: 1 day*	**Preparing to Read and Write** Warm-up, T264 Prior Knowledge/Background, T264 **Key Words**, T265 • left • right **High-Frequency Words**, T265 • at • back • come • her • house • how • more • over	**Other Choices for Building Background**, T265 **Students Acquiring English**, T265	**Poster** Warm-up, 4B **Transparency** Selection Vocabulary, 4–2 *Literacy Activity Book* Selection Vocabulary, p. 48
2 **Interact** *with* **Literature** *Pacing: 1–3 days*	**Reading Strategies** Self-Question, T268, T272 Evaluate, T268, T280, T292 Monitor, T270 Think About Words, T274 **Minilessons** ✓ Fantasy and Realism, T283 Categorize/Classify, T285 Digraphs: *sh, th,* T287 ✓ Digraph: *ch,* T289 **Responding**, T296	**Choices for Reading**, T268 **Guided Reading**, T268, T272, T278, T284, T290, T294 **Students Acquiring English**, T271, T280 **Extra Support**, T277, T294 **Challenge**, T285 **Responding Choices**, T297	**Reading-Writing Workshop** Writing About Something Silly, T316–T317 *Literacy Activity Book* Comprehension Check, p. 49 The Learning Company's new elementary writing center software
3 **Instruct** *and* **Integrate** *Pacing: 1–3 days*	✓ **Comprehension** Fantasy and Realism, T298–T299 ✓ **Phonics and Spelling** Initial Digraph *ch,* T300 Final Digraph *ch,* T301 **Vocabulary** ✓ High-Frequency Words, T302 Antonyms, T303 Alliteration, T303 **Language and Writing** Writing to Describe a Person, Animal, or Thing, T304–T305 **Communication Activities**, T306 **Independent Reading & Writing**, T307 **Cross-Curricular Activities**, T308–T310	**Activity Choices/Reteaching** Fantasy and Realism, T299 **Activity Choices** Initial Digraph *ch,* T300 Final Digraph *ch,* T301 **Activity Choices** High-Frequency Words, T302 **Activity Choices** Language and Writing, T304–T305	**Reading-Writing Workshop** Writing About Something Silly, T316–T317 **Poster** Communications, 4C **Transparency** Comprehension, 4–3 *Literacy Activity Book* Comprehension Skill, p. 50 Phonics and Spelling, pp. 51–54 High-Frequency Words, p. 55 Vocabulary Skill, p. 56 Language and Writing, p. 57 **Audio Tape** for Get the Giggles: *The Foot Book* The Learning Company's new elementary writing center software

✓ *Indicates Tested Skills. See page T217 for assessment options.*

Introduce *the* Literature

Preparing to Read and Write

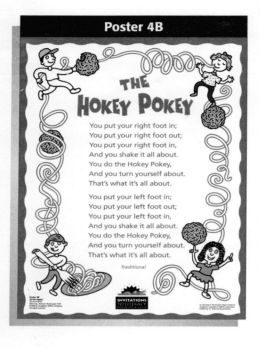

Poster 4B

INTERACTIVE LEARNING

Warm-up

Singing a Song

- Read aloud the lyrics to "The Hokey Pokey" on Poster 4B. (See page H6 for music.)

- Read the lyrics again, inviting children to chime in on words they know.

- Invite each child to identify his or her right foot and left foot. Suggest that children dance the Hokey Pokey as you sing or read the lyrics. Pay special attention to which foot they put in and out of the circle.

- Add a new verse to the song by covering the word *foot* on the poster with self-stick notes marked *hand*. Invite children to sing and dance to the new verse as they put first their right and then their left hands in and out of the circle.

- Encourage children to suggest additional left and right body parts they might place in and out of the circle (leg, arm, hip, ear). Make self-stick notes with the names of these body parts to place on the poster.

Prior Knowledge/Building Background

Key Concept
Left and right

- Ask children to share any methods they use for remembering left and right. For example, children may answer, "I have a freckle on my left hand" or "I throw a ball with my right hand."

- Have children identify their left hand and their right hand.

- After children have correctly identified left and right, play a simple game of Simon Says. Use the words *left* and *right* in each of the directions. For example, "Simon says, 'Raise your left hand'; Simon says, 'Hop on your right foot.'"

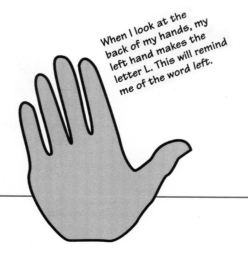

When I look at the back of my hands, my left hand makes the letter L. This will remind me of the word left.

Other Choices for Building Background

Selection Vocabulary

Key Words: *left, right*

High-Frequency Words: *at, back, come, her, house, how, more, over*

Tell children that they are going to draw a silly picture while they practice reading some words that are in *The Foot Book*. Display Transparency 4–2 and have children follow along as you read the directions to "Come See My House." Reread each line, pausing to have children identify the underlined words. Then have them follow the directions to draw a picture.

After children have drawn their own pictures, have them join you as you read through the directions once more, drawing your own picture at the bottom of the transparency. Have volunteers tell you what to draw next and where to draw it based on the directions. Encourage children to compare their pictures to the one you drew.

Vocabulary Practice Have children complete *Literacy Activity Book* page 48.

Left Foot, Right Foot
Cooperative Learning

Have children work with partners to trace the outlines of each other's feet. Then have children label the feet with the words *left* and *right*. Encourage discussion of the drawings. You might ask these questions:

- Who has small feet? Big feet?
- Who has "her" feet? "His" feet?
- Who has slow feet? Quick feet?

Opposites

Students Acquiring English Tell children that many words in *The Foot Book*, such as *left* and *right*, are opposites. Help children name opposites they may know and list their suggestions on the board. Then ask them to help make a class set of opposite-word flash cards. Have each child pick one pair of opposite words and label the front and back of an index card with the words. Ask them to make small drawings on the card to illustrate each word.

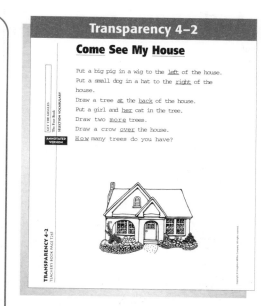

Transparency 4–2

Come See My House

Put a big pig in a wig to the <u>left</u> of the house.
Put a small dog in a hat to the <u>right</u> of the house.
Draw a tree <u>at</u> the <u>back</u> of the house.
Put a girl and <u>her</u> cat in the tree.
Draw two <u>more</u> trees.
Draw a crow <u>over</u> the house.
<u>How</u> many trees do you have?

Literacy Activity Book, p. 48

Come to Pat's House

Follow the path to Pat's house. Use the directions.

1 Walk to the tree.
2 Then go left.
3 Jump over the plants.
4 Walk up to the big cat.
5 Put a **1** on her back.
6 Then go right.
7 Go to one more cat.
8 Put a **2** on her back.
9 Do you see Pat's house?
   A tree is at the back of her house.

10 How many cats do you see?

48 Get the Giggles

Story Opposites

left/right   wet/dry
front/back   up/down
morning/night   high/low
slow/quick   small/big

Interact
with
Literature

More About the Author-Illustrator

Theodor Seuss Geisel ("Dr. Seuss")

Theodor Seuss Geisel, beloved as "Dr. Seuss," wrote and illustrated more than forty books which have altogether sold over two hundred million copies. Famous for his wonderful nonsense, Dr. Seuss always said that his goal was to convince children that reading was fun. His unforgettable characters, such as the Cat in the Hat, have become a part of American tradition, appearing in movies, on television, and even in Macy's Thanksgiving Day parade in New York City.

Theodor Seuss Geisel wrote his first children's book on a ship, when he began to put words to the rhythm of the ship's engine. The result was *And to Think That I Saw It on Mulberry Street*. Now a classic, the book was rejected more than twenty-five times before it was finally published! Since then, his books have won numerous awards, including a special Pulitzer Prize.

After his death in 1991, his wife discovered an unpublished manuscript. The happy result was the publication of one more Dr. Seuss book, *Daisy-Head Maisie*.

Meet Dr. Seuss

Dr. Seuss's real name was Theodor Seuss Geisel. He wanted children to have fun reading, so he used easy words and funny rhymes in his stories.

122

Dr. Seuss started drawing
animals when he was a child.
He visited the zoo his father
ran and drew all the animals.
Of course, he drew them his
own silly way!

123

Interact
with
Literature

Reading Strategies

▶ **Self-Question**
Evaluate

Discussion Review some of the things good readers do before, during, and after reading. Elicit suggestions such as make predictions, ask yourself questions, and think about what you liked or didn't like about the story.

Ask children what they would do to think of questions for this story. (read the title, look at the pictures, think about what they know from real life) Also, encourage them to share questions they might ask themselves during and after reading to decide, or evaluate, how they feel about the story.

Predicting/Purpose Setting

Have children suggest questions about what might happen in the story and record them for later use. Encourage children to read to find the answers.

124

Choices for Reading

Teacher Read Aloud	Shared Reading	Guided Reading	Cooperative Reading	Independent Reading
Have children pose questions about the story. As you read the story aloud, encourage them to listen for answers. Stop periodically for discussion and for children to pose new questions.	After children ask questions about the story, invite them to chime in with you as you read it aloud. Encourage children to share their feelings about the story, discussing whether or not they liked it or thought it was funny.	Have children ask questions about the story and read pages 125–129 to find if any of their questions are answered. Follow up with the Guided Reading questions on page T272.	Have partners read the story together, alternating pages of text. Encourage them to stop periodically to share their feelings about the story and to pose any additional questions they may have about it.	After children establish their purpose-setting questions, have them read to find the answers. Encourage children to share their reactions to the story.

Left foot
Left foot

Right foot
Right

QuickREFERENCE

Vocabulary

Repetition Ask children to name the words that are repeated on the page. *(left, foot, right)* Have them count how many times each word appears. Have children hold up first their left foot, then their right foot.

 Journal

Suggest that children write their purpose-setting questions in their journals. Children can refer back to these questions as they read.

Interact *with* Literature

Reading Strategies

▶ **Monitor**

As children read the story, encourage them to ask themselves these questions: Is there something I don't understand? Is something confusing me? If so, suggest they reread the text and look at the illustrations.

For example, children may be confused by the text and the illustrations on page 127 when they see that the last character is labeled *right* although he is in basically the same position as the others. Paying careful attention to the illustration will show that the words *left foot* are under the first three characters' left feet while the word *right* is under the right foot of the last character.

Feet in the morning

Feet at night

126

QuickREFERENCE

High-Frequency Words
at

Print the word *at* on the board and have children read it. Have them find the word on the page. Note the final consonant *t,* reminding children that this letter stands for the sound they hear at the end of *eat* and *out*.

Science Link

Reread page 126 with children. Ask them to discuss the difference between morning (day) and night. Encourage them to compare and contrast the daytime and nighttime sky.

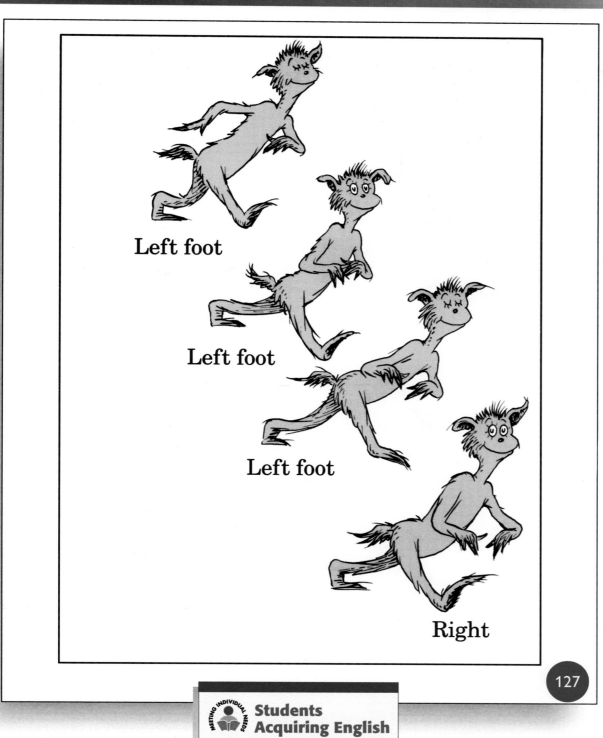

Left foot

Left foot

Left foot

Right

127

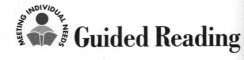

Interact with Literature

 Guided Reading

Comprehension/Critical Thinking

Discuss whether any of the children's questions about the story have been answered yet. Then ask:

1. What is this story about? (feet)

2. What kinds of feet have you seen? Are any of them opposites? (left/right, morning/night, wet/dry, high/low)

3. Where have you seen some of the feet? (in bed, in a lake, on a hill)

4. How do you think the character in the story feels about feet?

5. Is this a serious story about feet or a funny one?

Predicting/Purpose Setting

Ask children to think about other types of feet they might meet or where those feet might be. Record their responses, then have them read pages 130–135.

Reading Strategies

▶ **Self-Question**

Ask children to pose new questions about the story such as: Are there other characters in the story? Will there be more opposites? If children have difficulty thinking of questions, ask them to name the opposites they have already read about. Then have them suggest more opposites and help them record any new questions they have.

Wet foot

Dry foot

128

QuickREFERENCE

 Journal

Encourage children to write or draw their ideas about other feet that might appear in the story. Suggest that children match their feet ideas to the feet that do appear in the story.

High foot

Low foot

129

Vocabulary

Opposites Have children identify the opposites on pages 128–129. Ask them to name other things that may be wet, dry, high, or low.

Interact with Literature

Reading Strategies

▶ **Think About Words**

Ask children how they could figure out the word *black* on page 131 if they did not recognize it.

- **What makes sense** The words just before this word name the red feet. I know from the pattern of the story that this word will probably also name a color.

- **Familiar word parts** When I look at the word, I see that it ends with the same letters as *back /ack/*. So the word might rhyme with *back*. *Black* is a color and rhymes with *back*.

- **Sounds for letters** I see that this word begins with the cluster *bl*. I can think of two colors that begin with the cluster *bl: black* and *blue*.

- **Picture clues** Finally, I look at the picture. The picture shows a character with black feet. So the word must be *black*, not *blue*.

Have volunteers read the phrases aloud and discuss whether or not the word *black* makes sense.

Front feet

130

Back feet

Red feet

Black feet

131

High-Frequency Words
back

Have children find the word *back*. Then have them point to the back feet in the picture. Note the initial *b* and the ending phonogram *ack*. Ask children to find another word that ends with *ack*. (*black*)

Vocabulary

Rhyming Words Encourage children to look for rhyming words not only at the end of lines but buried within the text, such as *back* and *black* on page 131, and *dry* and *high* on pages 129–130.

Left foot

Right foot

Feet

Feet

Feet

132

How many, many
feet you meet.

133

Anthology p. 133

QuickREFERENCE

High-Frequency Words
how

Have children find and read the word *how*. Mention that in this sentence the word *how* does not ask a question; it begins a sentence that shows surprise and feeling.

MEETING INDIVIDUAL NEEDS

Extra Support

If children have difficulty understanding the structure of the sentence on page 133, help them brainstorm other sentences beginning with *how* that don't ask questions, such as *How wonderful* or *How good it is to see you.*

Interact *with* Literature

Guided Reading

Comprehension/Critical Thinking

Invite children to compare their ideas about the feet they would meet to the feet that appeared in the story. Then discuss the following:

1. What new opposites did you read?
(front/back, slow/quick)

2. What rhyming words did you read?
(back/black, quick/trick/sick)

3. How do the characters feel about having trick feet or quick feet? Why do you say that?

4. How does the character with sick feet feel? How do you know?

Predicting/Purpose Setting

Encourage children to pose new questions based on what they have read up to this point. Have them read pages 136–141 to find out if any of their questions are answered. Use the questions on T284 for discussion.

Slow feet

Quick feet

134

Informal Assessment

If children's responses demonstrate an understanding of the story, have them continue reading independently or cooperatively.

Quick**REFERENCE**

Phonics/Decoding Review

Have children look at the word *quick*. Ask them what letter it begins with. *(q)* Remind them that when they see *q* at the beginning of a word, it will be followed by *u*. Have them think of other words that begin with *q*.

Vocabulary

Word Meaning Have children name the opposites on page 134. *(slow, quick)* Ask if children can name a word that means the same as *quick*. *(fast)* Have children pantomime how to run in place slowly and quickly.

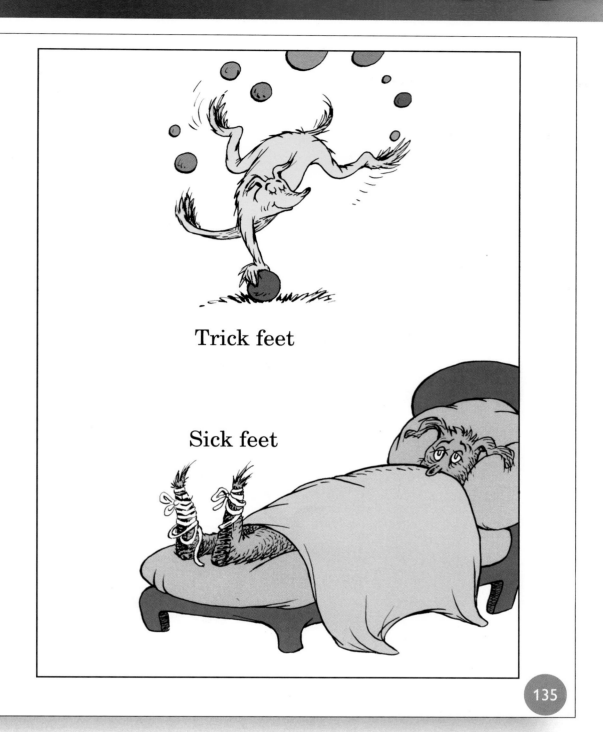

Trick feet

Sick feet

Visual Literacy

Have children look at the illustrations of slow feet and quick feet. Discuss how the illustrations help them understand the words. Have them notice the aspects of the pictures that the artist added to indicate quick and slow.

Vocabulary

Rhyming Words Have children find and compare the words *quick, trick,* and *sick*. Children should note that all three words end with *-ick* but begin with different consonants. Invite children to use the words in oral sentences.

Interact
with
Literature

Reading Strategies

▶ **Evaluate**

Remind children that while they are reading they should stop every so often to think about whether or not they agree with what they read. Ask children if they agree with the way in which the author shows up feet and down feet. Encourage them to suggest other ways in which up feet and down feet might have been drawn.

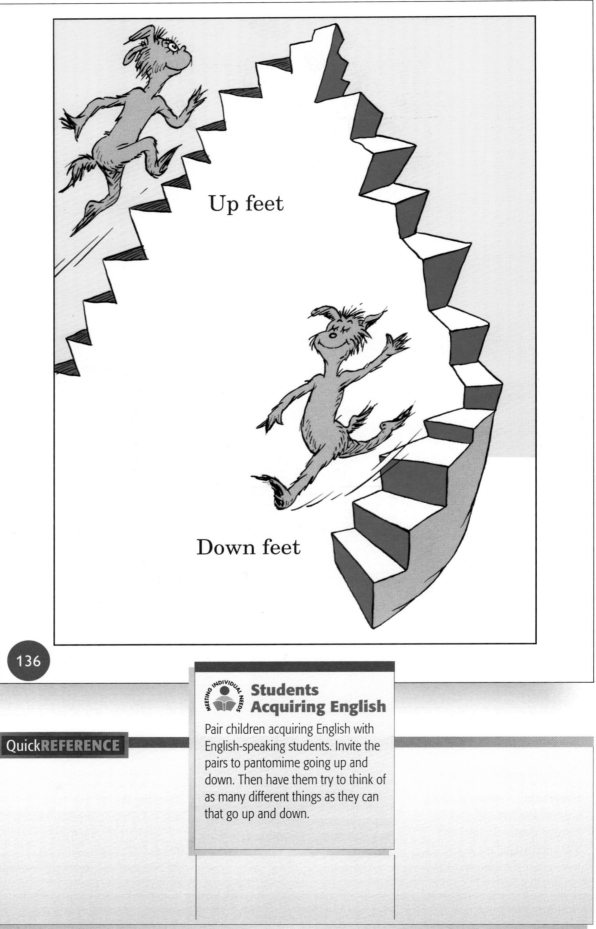

Up feet

Down feet

136

QuickREFERENCE

Students Acquiring English

Pair children acquiring English with English-speaking students. Invite the pairs to pantomime going up and down. Then have them try to think of as many different things as they can that go up and down.

Here come clown feet.

High-Frequency Words

come

Have children identify the word *come* on page 137. Call on volunteers to use the word in an oral sentence.

Phonics/Decoding Review

Note the word *clown* with children and identify the *cl* cluster. Encourage children to be on the lookout for other two-letter clusters in the story, including *bl, dr, sl, fr, sm*.

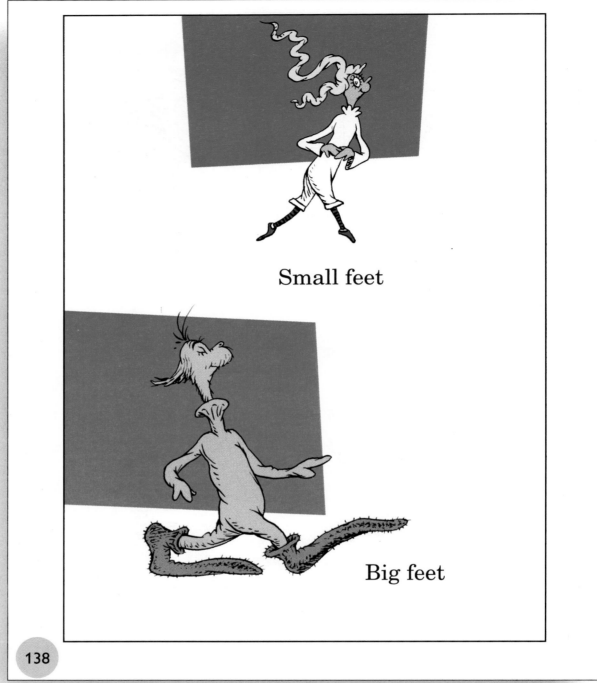

Small feet

Big feet

138

Math Link

Have children use the words *big* and *small* to compare various objects in the classroom.

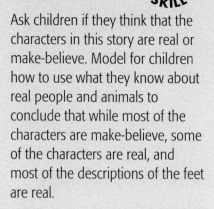

Here come pig feet.

Science Link

Discuss the pig's feet with children. Ask if they know what pigs' feet are called. (hooves) Encourage children to name other animals that have hooves, such as horses, goats, and sheep.

Comprehension

Fantasy and Realism

TESTED SKILL

Teach/Model

Ask children if they think that the characters in this story are real or make-believe. Model for children how to use what they know about real people and animals to conclude that while most of the characters are make-believe, some of the characters are real, and most of the descriptions of the feet are real.

Have children look at the words and illustrations on pages 138–139.

Think Aloud

When I read the words, I know that real people can have big feet or small feet and that there are real pig feet. And when I look at the picture of the pig, it looks like pictures of real pigs I've seen. But when I look at the pictures of the characters with big feet and small feet, they do not look like any real people or animals I have ever seen. These are make-believe characters, and they help make the story funny.

Practice/Apply

Have children look at the characters on pages 140–141 and ask them which characters are real (the boy and the girl) and which are make-believe.

SKILL FINDER

Full lesson/Reteaching, pp. T298–T299; Themes 6, 10

Minilesson, p. T329

Interact *with* Literature

Guided Reading

Comprehension/Critical Thinking

Ask children if any of their questions were answered. Then discuss the following questions:

1. Are there such things as clown feet? Pig feet? Fuzzy fur feet?

2. Which pair of feet did you think was the funniest? Why?

Predicting/Purpose Setting

Encourage children to set their own purposes for reading pages 142–147. Use the questions on T290 for discussion.

His feet

Her feet

140

QuickREFERENCE

High-Frequency Words
her

Have children find the word *her* on the page, and point to the character it refers to. (the girl) Explain that another way to say *the girl's feet* is to say *her feet.*

Fuzzy fur feet

Comprehension
Categorize/ Classify

Teach/Model

Ask children what all the sentences in this story are about. (feet) Have them notice how the author labeled all of the different types of feet in the story. Remind children that by labeling or grouping things together, they can show how they are alike.

Have children look at the characters on pages 140–141 and ask them which characters are real. (the boy and the girl) Then ask them to suggest one heading, or category, that describes all the other characters on pages 140–141. (make-believe) Explain that when categories are created, they should include all the different objects. Then ask children to think of categories they might create based on the characters' feet. (examples: *his feet, her feet, silly feet*)

Practice/Apply

Encourage children to think of other ways the characters and their feet might be grouped. Some groupings children might come up with include

- make-believe and realistic characters

- furry and nonfurry creatures

- big and little creatures

- colors

SKILL FINDER Full lesson/Reteaching, Theme 2

Challenge

MEETING INDIVIDUAL NEEDS

Encourage children to think of different sounds that the different feet in the story might make. For example, *fuzzy fur feet* might make the sound *flop, flop, flop* or *fzz, fzz, fzz.*

Vocabulary

Alliteration Ask children to name the words on page 141 that begin with the same sound. *(fuzzy fur feet)* What letter does each word begin with? *(f)* Then reread the phrase aloud and ask children if they like the way the phrase sounds.

In the <u>house</u>,
and on the street,

142

Informal Assessment

Oral Reading Use pages 138–143 to informally assess children's oral reading fluency. See the Oral Reading Checklist in the *Teacher's Assessment Handbook* for criteria.

QuickREFERENCE

High-Frequency Words
house

Have children find the word *house*, noting the beginning consonant *h*. Ask children if they can find another word on pages 142–143 that begins with the same sound as *house*.
(how)

Vocabulary

Synonyms Point out the word *street*. Ask children if they can name other words that mean the same or almost the same thing as *street*.
(road, avenue, lane)

how many, many
feet you meet.

143

Phonics/Decoding

Digraphs: sh, th

REVIEW & MAINTAIN

Teach/Model

Have children find the word *the* on page 142. Write the word on the board and underline the initial *th*. Recall with children that sometimes two consonant letters come together to make a new sound. Then display the following phrases:

<u>th</u>ick feet	<u>sh</u>ort feet
<u>th</u>in feet	<u>sh</u>aggy feet
clo<u>th</u> feet	fi<u>sh</u> feet
mo<u>th</u> feet	di<u>sh</u> feet

Read the phrases and have volunteers underline the digraphs *th* or *sh* in each. Then ask children to look at pages 142–143 and identify the thin, thick, short, and shaggy feet.

Practice/Apply

Have children listen for the sound for *th* or *sh* at the beginning or end of the words you read.

- **th:** *thumb, thorn, bath, those, teeth, thump, both*

- **sh:** *sheep, wish, brush, shadow, bush, shiny, sharp, fresh*

List the words on the board and read them with children. Suggest that they choose several of the words and use them to write about some funny feet.

SKILL FINDER

Phonics and Spelling, pp. T244, T245, T352, T353

Minilessons, pp. T233, T327

Up in the air feet

144

Over a chair feet
- - - - - - -

145

Phonics/Decoding

Digraph: *ch*

Teach/Model

TESTED SKILL

Have children read the phrase on page 145. Have them say the word *chair,* listening for the beginning sound. Print *chair* on the board, underline the *ch,* and remind children that two letters together sometimes stand for one sound. Invite children to name other words that begin with the same sound as *chair* and list their suggestions on the board. Responses may include the following:

chick	check
cherry	chin
child	cheese
chop	chirp

Mention that the /ch/ sound can also be heard in the middle and at the end of words. Ask children to listen as you read the following words to tell if the /ch/ sound is heard in the middle or at the end:

sandwich	teacher
grouch	beach
speeches	coach

Practice/Apply

Help children read the words listed on the board. Encourage them to draw and label two or three of the words.

SKILL FINDER

Phonics and Spelling, pp. T300, T301, T352, T353

Minilesson, p. T327

QuickREFERENCE

High-Frequency Words
over

Have children read the first word on page 145. Ask them to name a word that means the opposite of *over.* (*under*) Call on volunteers to demonstrate stepping over a chair and crawling under a chair.

Interact *with* Literature

Guided Reading

Comprehension/Critical Thinking

Ask children if any of their purpose-setting questions were answered. Then discuss the following:

1. Where did you see feet? (in the air, over a chair, in the house, in the street)

2. Which of the characters are the most realistic? Which could only be make-believe?

Predicting/Purpose Setting

Have children set their own purposes for reading. Then ask them to read to the end of the story.

More and more feet

146

QuickREFERENCE

High-Frequency Words

more

Have children read the first word on page 146. Ask them to find the other *more* on the page. Point out that the first *more* begins with a capital letter because it is at the beginning of a line.

Twenty-four feet

147

Math Link

Ask children to count the number of feet that appear on each animal on page 147. (6, 8, and 10 feet) Then have them count all of the feet together. Help them realize that by adding or counting all of the feet, they get a total of 24 feet.

Science Link

Point out that people have two feet and many animals have four feet. Ask children to name any creatures they can think of that have more than four feet. Children's responses may include ants, caterpillars, octopuses, and spiders.

Interact
with
Literature

Reading Strategies

▶ **Evaluate**

Encourage children to stop and think about how they are feeling about the story. These are questions they might consider:

- Do I like this story? Is it funny? Why or why not?

- How does the story make me feel?

Here come
more and more . . . .

148

QuickREFERENCE

Concepts of Print

Points of Ellipsis Call attention to the points of ellipsis and explain that writers sometimes use these marks to show that a sentence is not yet finished. Have children reread the sentence beginning on page 148 and ending on page 149.

. . . . and **more** feet!

149

Concepts of Print

Special Type Have children notice the size of the word *more.* Explain that authors sometimes make one word larger than another so the word or ideas stand out. Ask children why the author might have made the word *more* larger.

Interact with Literature

 Guided Reading

Comprehension/Critical Thinking

Have children review the list of questions they asked before and during reading. Discuss which of their questions were answered in the story and which were not. Then discuss the following:

1. Was this story about just a few feet or many different feet? (many)

2. Did all of the characters in the book have left and right feet? (yes)

3. Why do you think the author used make-believe characters in this story?

4. Do you think the story would have been as funny if only real characters were used? Why or why not?

5. Do you think *The Foot Book* was a good title for this story? Why or why not? Can you think of a better title?

Left foot.   Right foot.

Feet. Feet. Feet.

150

Self-Assessment

Ask children how asking themselves questions before, during, and after reading helped them understand and enjoy this story. Encourage them to tell what other things they did to help them understand the story and to help them decide how they feel about the story.

QuickREFERENCE

 Extra Support

Rereading Have individuals rehearse and reread a favorite page to the class.

Multi-Age Classrooms Older children may enjoy assisting younger ones by helping them to identify unfamiliar words using meaning clues, rhyme and letter sounds, and picture clues.

Oh, how many
feet you meet!

151

Anthology p. 151

Concepts of Print

Exclamation Mark Point out the exclamation mark on page 151. Elicit or explain that when children see this mark at the end of a sentence, they should read the words with feeling. Call on several volunteers to read the sentence aloud.

Journal

Encourage children to refer back to the questions they wrote in their journals at the beginning and throughout the story. Were their questions answered? Did their questions help them focus on the story?

Interact
with
Literature

Responding Activities

✎ Personal Response

Recall with children that the author told about many make-believe and many realistic kinds of feet in the story. Have children tell about which pair of feet they liked best in the story and why. Then encourage them to draw and label pictures of their own feet and a pair of make-believe feet they'd like to have.

Anthology Activity

Have children work in groups to count the total number of feet in their class. Encourage them to use their own counting strategies. If necessary, suggest that each group member tally one type of feet (desk feet, chair feet, people feet, and so on) and then work with the rest of the group to count the total number.

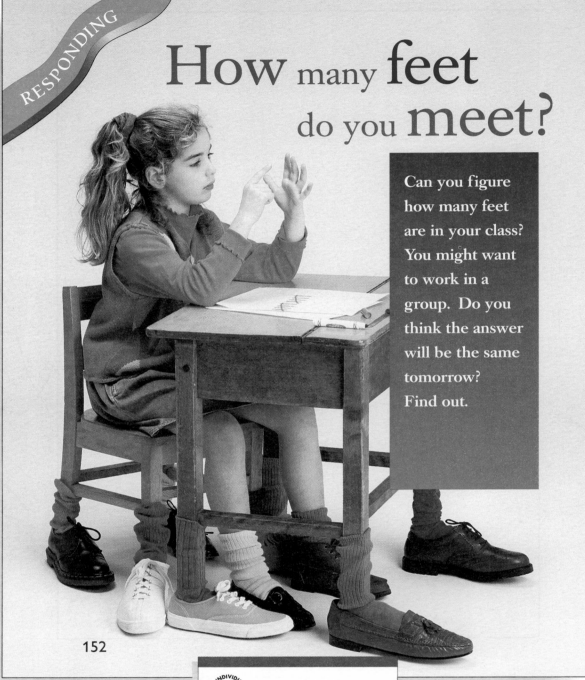

RESPONDING

How many feet do you meet?

Can you figure how many feet are in your class? You might want to work in a group. Do you think the answer will be the same tomorrow? Find out.

152

✎ Informal Assessment

Use the Comprehension Check or the Literature Discussion to informally assess children's understanding of the story.

Additional Support:
• Use the Guided Reading questions to review the story.

QuickREFERENCE

🏠 **Home Connection**

Children may enjoy working with family members to think of ways in which they can describe the feet found in their homes: baby feet, chair feet, long feet, short feet, Mom feet, Dad feet, and so on.

MEETING INDIVIDUAL NEEDS
Challenge

Have children count the number of feet in another classroom or site. Have them make a list of each type of feet in the classroom and then tally the total. How does the number of feet in the other classroom compare to the number in their own?

More Responding Activities

How Many, Many Feet You Meet

Students Acquiring English Have children look through old magazines to find and cut out pictures of different kinds of feet and shoes. Encourage children to create a bulletin board display of their findings and label the feet with phrases like those found in the story.

Literature Discussion
Cooperative Learning

Invite children who have read other Dr. Seuss books to form a discussion circle. Provide the following prompts:

- How is *The Foot Book* like other Dr. Seuss stories you have read? How is it different?

- How do the rhyming words and silly pictures help you enjoy his stories?

Shared Writing: *A Class Story*

Recall that *The Foot Book* was a silly story about one topic—feet. Invite children to work together to write a silly story about a single topic of their choice, for example, noses, animal tails, or hair.

- Encourage children to brainstorm possible topics, and list their suggestions on the board. Conduct an informal vote to choose one topic.

- Then have children brainstorm words or phrases that relate to the topic, and record their suggestions in a word web on the board.

- Invite children to contribute sentences to the class story, and record their suggestions on the board. Recall with them that many of the phrases in *The Foot Book* show opposites together. Suggest that children organize some of their phrases in a similar manner.

- Have partners work together to illustrate a page of the book. Help children print the appropriate phrases at the bottom of each drawing.

- Bind the pages into a book for the classroom library. You may want to make copies for children to take home and share with their families.

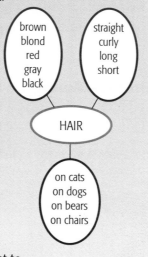

brown
blond
red
gray
black

straight
curly
long
short

HAIR

on cats
on dogs
on bears
on chairs

Comprehension Check

To determine children's understanding of the story, use these questions and/or *Literacy Activity Book* page 49.

1. Look at the different feet in the story. Which kind of feet might real people or real animals have?

2. Which kind of feet could only make-believe people or animals have?

3. How does the author use silly feet to help you learn about opposites and rhyming words?

Literacy Activity Book, p. 49

Funny Feet

Write the word from the box that goes with the picture.

| big | back | left | pig | small | wet |

Color the pictures.

Get the Giggles 49

Portfolio Opportunity

- As a record of selection comprehension, save *Literacy Activity Book* page 49.

- As a writing sample, save children's Personal Response.

3

Instruct *and* Integrate

Comprehension

Literacy Activity Book, p. 50

That's Fantastic!

Circle the books that are make-believe.

The Walking Fish · My Three Fish · I Have Two Cats · The Fast Cats

Draw your own book cover. Write a title.

Check one:
☐ Real
☐ Make-believe

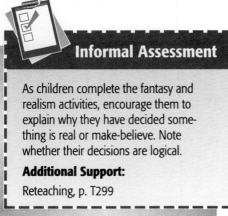

Informal Assessment

As children complete the fantasy and realism activities, encourage them to explain why they have decided something is real or make-believe. Note whether their decisions are logical.

Additional Support:
Reteaching, p. T299

INTERACTIVE LEARNING

TESTED SKILL

Fantasy and Realism
LAB, p. 50

Teach/Model

Tell children that story authors sometimes write about things that could happen in real life, and sometimes about make-believe things that could never happen. Invite them to page through *The Foot Book,* read the text under some of the illustrations, and discuss whether or not the characters (and their feet) are real or make-believe. Lead children to see that including make-believe things in a story can make it fun to read.

Materials
- index cards with the letters *R, M*
- pencils or markers

Give each child two index cards, one labeled *R,* the other labeled *M.* Then read the sentences on Transparency 4–3, and discuss whether each is about something real or make-believe. As you read, have children hold up either the *R* or the *M* to show whether they think the sentence tells about a real or make-believe event.

Think Aloud

In the first sentence, the storyteller says that his cat is nice. I know that most pet owners do think their cats are very nice. So I'll hold up my card with an *R* for *real.* In the second sentence, the storyteller says that his cat bakes him a cake. I know that cats can't bake! I'll hold up my card with an *M* for *make-believe.*

Continue with the remaining sentences, discussing them as needed. Then help children to conclude that this is a make-believe story because some of the events in it could never happen.

Practice/Apply

- Have partners choose another story they have read and decide whether it is real or make-believe. Ask them to share their findings with the class and name the clues that helped them decide.

- Have children complete *Literacy Activity Book* page 50.

SKILL FINDER Minilessons, pp. T283, T329

More Practice Activities

Real and Make-Believe Feet

Write phrases to describe real and make-believe feet on sentence strips. Then put the headings *Real* and *Make-Believe* in a pocket chart. Distribute the strips to volunteers. Help them read the strips and place them under the correct heading.

Students Acquiring English Children may enjoy illustrating the phrases to help show real and make-believe feet.

REAL
small baby feet
fat cat feet
duck's wet webbed feet
big pig feet
run and jump feet

MAKE-BELIEVE
spots and dots on people feet
flying frog feet
hogs that jog feet
walking fish feet
pigs in wigs feet

What's the Story?

Invite children to choose their favorite make-believe book title from *Literacy Activity Book* page 50, or have them create their own book title. Encourage them to describe what kind of things might happen in this story. Children acquiring English might act out some of the events as they describe them.

Challenge Some children may want to write and illustrate a make-believe story about one of the book titles. Encourage them to share their stories with the class.

Finding Real and Make-Believe in a Story

Invite children to make a chart to record real and make-believe things in *On Top of Spaghetti.* You might also want to use another theme-related story. (See the Bibliography on pages T212–T213.)

Real Things	Make-Believe Things
• spaghetti with cheese	• meatball rolling out the door
• meatball	• meatball rolling under a bush
• boy and girl	• meatball growing into a tree

Reteaching **Fantasy and Realism**

Gather together several books from the classroom library; include both realistic and make-believe titles and cover art. Display the books and invite children to read the titles, examine the art, and discuss each book in turn.

• Have children predict from the cover and title whether the book tells about real or make-believe events. Have them share clues they used.

• Have children sort the books according to real and make-believe events.

Portfolio Opportunity

Save *Literacy Activity Book* page 50 as a record of children's understanding of fantasy and realism.

3 Instruct *and* Integrate

Phonics and Spelling

Literacy Activity Book, p. 51

Follow the Footprints

How did the boy find the chest?

Color the pictures whose names begin like [flag].
Draw footprints to show the boy's path.

Write the two letters that spell the sound [flag] begins with. _____

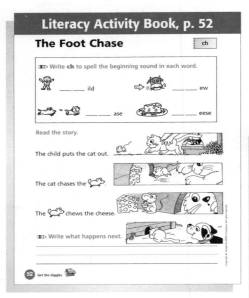

Literacy Activity Book, p. 52

The Foot Chase

Write **ch** to spell the beginning sound in each word.

Read the story.

The child puts the cat out.

The cat chases the [dog].

The [dog] chews the cheese.

Write what happens next.

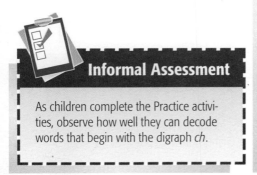

Informal Assessment

As children complete the Practice activities, observe how well they can decode words that begin with the digraph *ch*.

✓ Initial Digraph *ch*

LAB, pp. 51, 52

Display page 144 of *The Foot Book* and read the phrase together. Write *air* on the board and read it aloud. Then read the phrase on page 145. Write *chair* on the board and have children compare the words.

Invite children to pronounce *chair* several times, listening for the beginning sound. Remind them that two letters together can sometimes stand for one sound. Ask them what two letters they think spell the beginning sound in *chair*. (*ch*) Have them pronounce /ch/ and name some other words that begin with the sound.

Write the words *at, eat, in* on the board and have children read them. Then say the words *chat, cheat,* and *chin,* and ask what sound children hear at the beginning of each one. Ask volunteers to change the words on the board to *chat, cheat,* and *chin.*

- Have children complete *Literacy Activity Book* pages 51, 52.

SKILL FINDER → Minilessons, pp. T289, T327

More Practice Activities

Chain Champs

Challenge children to see who can make the longest paper chain with words beginning with *ch*. When children have completed their chains, count the words correctly spelled to see who are the Chain Champs. Then attach all the chains end to end and hang the long chain on the Word Wall.

Change It!
Cooperative Learning

Distribute cards with the words *cat, more, plant, sick, time, walk,* and *will.* Invite pairs of children to place a self-stick note with the letters *ch* over the beginning consonant or cluster in each word to make new words. Have partners read the new words aloud and illustrate two of them. (*chat, chore, chant, chick, chime, chalk, chill*)

INTERACTIVE LEARNING

Final Digraph *ch*
LAB, pp. 53, 54

Have children turn to page 145 of the story, read the phrase aloud, and name the item the story character is going over. (chair) Write *chair* on the board and have a volunteer underline the letters that stand for the beginning sound. Next ask children if they can think of a special type of chair that has no back. (bench) Write *bench* on the chalkboard. Invite children to pronounce *bench* several times and listen for the ending sound. Ask them what letters spell the /ch/ sound in *bench*.

Think Aloud

I hear the same sound at the end of *bench* as at the beginning of *chair*. I know that the two letters *ch* at the beginning of *chair* spell the /ch/ sound. So I think that the two letters *ch* spell the /ch/ sound at the end of *bench*.

Write each of the following words on the board, underlining as shown, and say the word. Have a volunteer place a self-stick note with the letters *ch* over the underlined letter, read the new word, and use it in a sentence.

rea<u>d</u> (reach)	bea<u>t</u> (beach)	mu<u>d</u> (much)
coa<u>t</u> (coach)	ea<u>t</u> (each)	ar<u>t</u> (arch)

SKILL FINDER Minilessons, pp. T289, T327

- Have children complete *Literacy Activity Book* pages 53, 54.

More Practice Activities

Word Wall for *ch*

Invite children to help you begin a Word Wall chart for *ch* words. As children read or look through stories, have them watch for words that begin or end with *ch*. Start two lists, one for initial *ch* and one for final *ch*.

Students Acquiring English Encourage children to contribute words by finding and cutting out appropriate pictures in old magazines. They can work with partners to add labels.

Fox and Chick

WATCH ME READ
Fox and Chick
by Cass Hollander

This story includes words with the digraph *ch*.

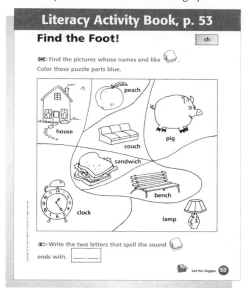

Literacy Activity Book, p. 53

Find the Foot!   ch

Literacy Activity Book, p. 54

Where Are the Feet?   ch

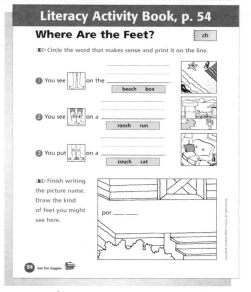

Portfolio Opportunity

As a record of children's ability to decode words with the digraph *ch*, save *Literacy Activity Book* pages 51–54.

3

Instruct and Integrate

Vocabulary

Fox and Chick

WATCH ME READ

Fox and Chick
by Cass Hollander

This story provides practice and application for the following skills:

- **High-Frequency Words:** *at, back, come, her, house, how, more, over*
- **Phonics/Decoding Skills:** Digraph *ch*
- **Cumulative Review:** Previously taught decoding skills and High-Frequency Words

Literacy Activity Book, p. 55

My Pig Is So Small . . .

Informal Assessment

As children read aloud *Fox and Chick* or complete other activities on this page, observe how easily they recognize the High-Frequency Words.

High-Frequency Words

TESTED SKILL

High-Frequency Words: *at, back, come, her, house, how, more, over*

The Foot Bulletin Board

Make sets of sentence strips such as the ones shown here, and give one to each child. Have children read their sentence strip to a partner and add an illustration on art paper. Then display the pictures and the sentence strips on a long bulletin board and invite children to read the new silly story!

Challenge Some children may wish to copy several of the strips on writing paper, add pictures, and bind the pages together to make their own foot books.

I see feet at a tree.

I see back feet on a dog.

Here come cat feet.

I see her feet.

I see feet in a house.

My Pig Is So Small...

LAB, p. 55

Review the High-Frequency Words with children. Together, read the directions on *Literacy Activity Book* page 55. Have children complete the page and share their work with a partner.

Left and Right

Have pairs of children play Left and Right as follows:

- Provide one partner with a set of left-foot word cards and the other with a matching set of right-foot word cards.

- To play, the first child chooses a card and reads it aloud. The partner searches through his or her word cards to find the match and reads it aloud.

- Each partner then uses the word in a sentence.

- Partners take turns reading word cards and making sentences until all the feet have been paired.

Students Acquiring English Pair children with readers proficient in English. Have the English speaker read a word and display it for his or her partner to find the match. As children acquiring English become comfortable with the words, have them switch roles.

Opposite Feet
Cooperative Learning

Have children work together to name an opposite for each word card—*back, come, her, more,* and *over.* Then invite them to draw pictures of feet that illustrate the opposites and label them.

Materials

- a set of left and right foot-shaped word cards with the High-Frequency Words

---

M I N I L E S S O N

Vocabulary Skill
Antonyms

LAB, p. 56

Teach/Model

Have children read page 125 aloud. Begin two columns on the chalkboard with the words *Left* and *Right*. Ask whether anyone knows what this pair of words is called. *(opposites)* Explain that *opposites* are words whose meanings are completely different.

Point out that *The Foot Book* contains many opposites. Reread the story with children, helping them find the following opposites and adding them to the chart: *wet/dry, high/low, front/back, slow/quick, up/down, small/big.*

Practice/Apply

Have children read aloud pages 142–145. Ask: What is the opposite of *in*? *(out)* What is the opposite of *up*? *(down)* What is the opposite of *over*? *(under)*

- Ask children to name some other opposites, such as hot/cold, new/old, or day/night Ask volunteers to use these word pairs in sentences.

- Have children complete *Literacy Activity Book* page 56.

Literacy Activity Book, p. 56

Left Foot, Right Foot

☞ Read the sentence. Write the opposite of the underlined word.

❶ I see <u>small</u> feet.　　I see _____ feet.

❷ Feet are <u>in</u> socks.　　Feet are _____ of socks.

❸ Feet go <u>down</u> the hill.　　Feet go _____ the hill.

❹ Feet are <u>wet</u>.　　Feet are _____.

☞ Draw these feet.　　☞ Now draw these feet.

56 Get the Giggles

M I N I L E S S O N

Vocabulary Expansion
Alliteration

Teach/Model

Read aloud page 141, encouraging children to chime in with you. Ask why they think the author put the words *fuzzy fur feet* together. Point out that words with the same beginning sound are fun to say and hear. Help children find other examples of alliteration in the story, such as these:

> How <u>m</u>any, <u>m</u>any feet you <u>m</u>eet. *(page 133)*
> <u>Tw</u>enty-four feet *(page 147)*
> Here come <u>m</u>ore and <u>m</u>ore . . . and <u>m</u>ore feet! *(pages 148–149)*

Practice/Apply

Have children practice saying some alliterative tongue twisters and naming the words that begin with the same sound.

> She sells seashells from the seashore.
> Peter Piper picked a peck of pickled peppers.

Portfolio Opportunity

- Children's responses to *Literacy Activity Book* page 55 will show how well they read the High-Frequency Words.

- Save *Literacy Activity Book* page 56 as a record of children's ability to identify antonyms.

3

Instruct *and* Integrate

Language and Writing

Literacy Activity Book, p. 57

What Am I?

✂ Cut along the dotted lines.
Paste the pictures in the boxes.

✏ Color the picture.
✏ Write about your picture.
Use words that tell about size and color.

What am I? _____

Get the Giggles **57**

MINILESSON

Writing to Describe a Person, Animal, or Thing

LAB, p. 57

- Have children look at the illustration on page 141 of *The Foot Book*. Invite them to come up with a fun name for this creature. Then write the beginning of a description of him on the board.

> This is our friend _____.
> He has two fuzzy, furry feet.

- Ask children to add to the description. Encourage them to tell you about the creature's size, shape, and color.

- Have children complete *Literacy Activity Book* page 57 for practice in writing to describe.

Practice Activities

Crazy-Creature Posters

- Have children paint or draw a silly creature on a large sheet of paper.

- Encourage them to label their drawings with describing words that tell about its size, shape, and color.

- Post the silly creatures around the room.

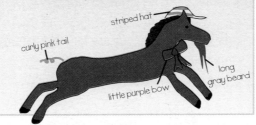

striped hat

curly pink tail

little purple bow

long gray beard

Plan a Skit

Cooperative Learning

Have small groups work together to answer this question: What's so great about feet? Encourage groups to write down their ideas. Then give them a chance to act them out in front of the class. When each group has presented its skit, discuss the ways in which the skits were the same or different.

Informal Assessment

Check children's understanding of using describing words to tell about a person, animal, or thing.

More Practice Activities

I'm Thinking of Someone Who...

Oral Language Development Have children play this game in pairs:

- One child thinks of a person everyone in the class knows, such as a teacher, an aide, a secretary, or a member of the class. The child says, "I'm thinking of someone who has [a physical attribute such as long brown hair]."

- The other child makes a guess. If the guess is incorrect, the first child provides another clue. The game continues until the identity of the person is discovered. The children then switch roles.

Using *foot/feet, tooth/teeth*

Grammar Connection Have children look at page 150 in *The Foot Book*. Ask them why the author used the word *foot* at the top of the page and the word *feet* at the bottom. (*Foot* is for one foot; *feet* is for more than one.) Write the words *tooth* and *teeth* on the board. Ask volunteers to use each word in a sentence. Invite children to compare *tooth* and *foot* and *teeth* and *feet*. Ask them what they notice about the letters in the middle of the words. (The two *o*'s become two *e*'s to mean more than one.) Have children make up silly sentences, using the words *foot, feet, tooth,* and *teeth*.

Children can use The Learning Company's new elementary writing center to write, illustrate, and publish their work to share with others.

Describing Duos

- Have children brainstorm describing words, such as colors, shapes, and sizes. Record their ideas on the board. Then have each child write one of the words on an index card.

- Turn all of the cards face down on a table. Children take turns flipping two cards over and coming up with an object, real or silly, that the pair of cards describes. For example, if the two cards say *long* and *yellow*, the player might suggest a banana.

Silly Foot Book

 MEETING INDIVIDUAL NEEDS

Challenge Have children write their own riddles, tongue twisters, or jokes about feet or shoes. Children can illustrate their work and bind the pages to make a book to share with the rest of the class.

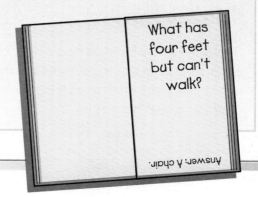

What has four feet but can't walk?

Answer: A chair.

Portfolio Opportunity

- Save *Literacy Activity Book* page 57 as a sample of children's ability to use describing words.

- Save children's written responses to activities on these pages as samples of their writing development.

Instruct and Integrate

Communication Activities

Listening and Speaking

Audio Tape
for Get the Giggles: *The Foot Book*

Suggest that children pay special attention to rhyming words and opposites as the narrator reads.

Be Kind to Your Feet

Invite children to discuss things they can do "to be kind to their feet." Record their responses on chart paper.

Be Kind to Your Feet

Clip your toenails.

Wear dry socks and shoes.

Make sure your shoes fit.

Tips for Having a Discussion
- Take turns speaking.
- Make sure someone has finished speaking before sharing your ideas.
- Make sure everyone has a chance to say something.

Poster 4C

ANIMAL TRACKS

Tying Shoes
Cooperative Learning

Invite children to work with partners to "teach" each other how to tie shoes. Children should take turns being the teacher and the student, with the student following along as the teacher demonstrates and explains how to tie his or her shoes.

Extra Support If there are children in the class who cannot tie their own shoes, pair them with children who can for a practical teaching experience.

Viewing

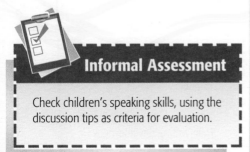

Informal Assessment

Check children's speaking skills, using the discussion tips as criteria for evaluation.

Animal Tracks

Display the animal tracks on Poster 4C for children to observe and talk about. Have them look at the animals on the poster and encourage them to speculate about which animals made each set of tracks. Then have them draw lines to match animals to their tracks.

Independent Reading & Writing

Student-Selected Reading

Favorite Books

Encourage children to bring a favorite book from home to share with the class. Have children discuss the book and tell what makes it one of their favorites. Keep a running list of children's favorites and arrange, if possible, to get multiple copies for the classroom or school library.

Too Difficult?

What do you do if children are interested in reading a book that appears too difficult for them to read independently? It's a good idea to let them try the book anyway. Suggest that they may want to read the book with a partner or with a family member at home.

Books for Independent Reading

Encourage children to choose their own books. They might choose one of the following titles.

Hooray for Snail!
by John Stadler

Fox and Chick
by Cass Hollander

The Foot Book
by Dr. Seuss

Have children reread this selection silently or aloud to a partner.

See the Bibliography on pages T212–T213 for more theme-related books for independent reading.

Ideas for Independent Writing

Encourage children to write on self-selected topics. For those who need help getting started, suggest one of the following activities:

- a **mural** of footprints with rhyming words on them
- a **description** of a favorite pair of shoes
- a **book** about hands

Student-Selected Writing

High-Frequency Words

You may want to use the last page of the children's journals to record the correct spelling of High-Frequency Words or tape an index card with these words on children's desks. Children can refer to these as they are writing.

at

come

house

Conference Help

A parent, teacher's aide, or other adult may be available to help with writing conferences. Establish guidelines that will help this person work with the children effectively. For example, explain your approach to issues such as discussing content first, skills later. Model the kind of questions and procedures you use during conferences. Be sure that children understand that the adults are there to assist them but not to do the writing for them.

Portfolio Opportunity

Save examples of the writing children do independently on self-selected topics.

Cross-Curricular Activities

Choices for Math

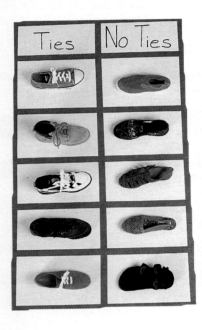

Graphing Shoes

Shoes with bumpy soles, shoes with smooth soles. Shoes with laces, shoes without. Extend *The Foot Book* as your class sorts and graphs shoes.

- Ask each child to take off one shoe and place it in a pile in the front of the class.

- Have children look at the shoes. Ask them: How are the shoes alike? How are they different? Then have the class brainstorm ways that the shoes can be sorted into two groups. Choose two categories for graphing and place labels on a floor graph.

- Invite each child to take his or her shoe from the pile and place it on the graph.

- Ask children if they can tell which group has more shoes without counting. Have them describe how the graph helps them.

Materials
- children's shoes
- masking tape

Measuring with a Foot

Children can use their feet to measure objects and distances.

- Place two chairs at different distances from your desk. Ask children to predict which chair is closer to your desk. Then ask them how they might use their feet to measure the distance from the chair to the desk.

- Invite two children to stand by the chairs. Have each child walk off the distance—heel to toe—from the chair to your desk while other children count.

- Next, ask children to guess how many footsteps long your desk or the bookcase is. Let a child walk off the distance heel to toe while other children count. Encourage children to measure the length of objects in the classroom.

- Then ask students how they could use their feet to measure a chair leg or the height of the bookcase. If no one thinks of it, suggest that children trace their feet on a piece of paper, cut out the tracing, and use it to measure the lengths. Encourage children to measure several different objects in the room.

Materials
- construction paper
- scissors
- crayons or markers

Science

Neat Animal Feet

Challenge Recall with children that some of the feet in *The Foot Book* belonged to real animals. Explain that different animals have special types of feet to help them.

- Have children browse through a variety of books and magazines about different animals, and ask them to look at the feet.

- Help children make a chart of the different types of animal feet and the names of animals with those feet. You might add pictures of the different types of animal feet to the column headings.

- Invite volunteers to tell how the different animals use their feet to help them. Record their responses in the chart.

Types of feet	Animals	How their feet help them
Paws with claws	cats beavers	cats climb trees beavers dig their homes both protect themselves
Webbed feet	ducks frogs	help them swim
Hooves	horses cows	help them walk and run on rocks and sand
Talons	eagles	help them catch their dinner

Social Studies

Special Shoes for Special Jobs

- Ask children if they have a pair of shoes that they wear only at certain times or for a specific activity. Have them explain when and why they wear different shoes.

- Explain that, for some jobs, people need to wear special shoes to keep their feet safe or to help them with their jobs. Ask children if they know people who wear special shoes for their jobs. What do they do?

- Display pictures of the kinds of footwear used for different professions, and discuss with children what they are used for. Have them explain why each type of shoe might be useful for that profession.

- Then ask what kind of special shoes you might need if you were a nurse, an athlete, a deep-sea diver, a dancer, a construction worker, or a telephone repair person. If children are unfamiliar with these occupations, briefly describe what they entail and then elicit children's responses.

Book List

Science

What Neat Feet!
by Hana Machotka

Feet!
by Peter Parnall

Social Studies

Whose Shoe?
by Margaret Miller

Shoes
by Elizabeth Winthrop

Hard top to keep toes safe from falling objects.

Bumpy soles to walk over dirt and rocks.

Webbed toes to help swim fast.

Elastic to hold the flipper on your foot.

Instruct *and* Integrate

Cross-Curricular Activities *(continued)*

Art

Making Silly Feet and Shoes

Invite children to get the giggles as they design their own silly feet or shoes.

Students Acquiring English Provide a rich experience for children acquiring English by describing the steps as you demonstrate them.

Materials
- tag board
- elastic
- stapler
- pencils
- markers, pastels, or crayons

1 Have pairs trace the front half of each other's feet on tag board.

2 Have each child draw silly feet or shoe shapes on the tag board that are slightly larger than the tracing of their feet and cut them out.

3 Invite children to decorate their silly feet. Staple a strip of elastic to the feet shapes so that they can wear them!

Music

Be Kind to Your Web-Footed Friends

(sung to the tune of "Stars and Stripes Forever")

Be kind to your web-footed friends,
For a duck may be somebody's mother.
They live all alone in the swamp
where the weather's so cold and damp.
You may think that this is the end.
Well—it is!

New Verses for a Silly Song

Cooperative Learning

Teach children the words to the silly song "Be Kind to Your Web-Footed Friends." Then have children work with partners to write new verses to the song. Their verses may include animals with paws, hoofs, claws, or two feet. Invite volunteers to sing their new verse to the class.

Knock, Knock!

WHO'S THERE?

153

Building Background

Begin by telling a knock-knock joke of your own. For example:

Knock knock. Who's there?
Boo. Boo who?
Oh, please don't cry.

Explain that knock-knock jokes always follow the same pattern. Ask the class to talk about their experiences with knock-knock and other types of jokes.

Discussion

Read the jokes aloud. Ask children how the picture clues help them make sense of the jokes. Discuss which words switch their meanings or their sounds in the punch lines. (beets/ beats; Ken/Can; ketchup/catch up)

List the words on the board and have children discuss the differences in meaning. Ask them why they think these changes make the jokes funny.

Students Acquiring English
Children may need help with the idioms *beats me* and *catch up.* Explain that *beats me* is the same as saying *I don't know.* Then act out the two sayings for them.

Reading the Jokes
Cooperative Learning

Have pairs of children read the knock-knock jokes. Have them take turns telling or answering the joke.

Students Acquiring English Pair children acquiring English with native speakers to read the knock-knock jokes. Have them pantomime the actions in the joke as they tell them.

Language Arts

Homophone Riddles Draw a picture of a beet on the chalkboard and ask this question:

- When is a beet not a beet?

- When it's a *beat* in music.

Ask children if they can think of any words that sound alike but have different meanings. List their responses on the board and brainstorm possible riddles. You might use this example:

- When is a pear not a pear?

- When it's a pair of shoes.

Other homophones you might suggest are *ant/aunt; eight/ate; cent/scent; clothes/close; flower/flour; knot/not.*

Writing

Knock-Knock Jokes Children may enjoy writing their own knock-knock jokes. Provide children with the basic form for knock-knock jokes. You may want to choose a theme for the jokes, such as food or animals. Then invite pairs of children to act out their knock-knock jokes together.

Knock knock

Who's there?

Beets

Beets who?

Beets me, I just forgot my name!

Knock knock

Who's there?

Ken

Ken who?

Ken I come in? I'm freezing out here!

154

Listening and Speaking

Sound Words Invite children to help you create a "Noisy" bulletin board. Write the words *knock, knock* on an index card and tack the card to the bulletin board. Have children draw or cut out pictures from magazines that illustrate the *knock, knock* sound and add these to the board. Encourage them to add other sound words, such as *quack* and *toot,* along with pictures. As each new word is added, have them read and perform all the sounds.

Knock knock
Who's there?
Ketchup
Ketchup who?
Ketchup with me and I'll tell you.

155

Instruct and Integrate

Art

Funny Pictures Invite children to draw funny things they'd like to see outside their front door.

Materials
- construction paper
- scissors
- crayons or markers

Have children draw a door and door frame on colored construction paper. Have them cut the door so that it will swing open and then paste the edges of the door frame onto white construction paper. Invite them to draw something funny on the white construction paper that they'd like to see when they answer their front door. Encourage them to share their doors with the class.

Instruct and Integrate

Social Studies

Role-Playing Encourage children to role-play knocking on and answering the door. Ask children to imagine how they would behave in various situations, such as knocking on a classroom door, knocking on a bedroom door, or answering the door at home. Then have them role-play each scenario as they knock on and answer the classroom door. Afterwards, talk about appropriate and safe behavior.

Introduce the Literature

Prior Knowledge

Ask children if they have ever seen clouds that were shaped like animals or objects. Talk about the kinds of things they have seen in cloud formations. Explain that, while we know they are really clouds, it's fun to look for and imagine pictures in them.

Interact with Literature

Find the Faces

Read the title question aloud, and discuss the use of a question mark. Have children look for the faces in each picture. Then read the picture captions aloud, as volunteers trace the funny faces with their fingers. Ask children if they agree that these are funny faces in funny places.

Can you find the Funny Faces in Funny Places?

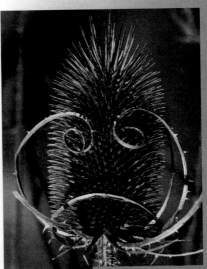

Weed

156

Instruct and Integrate

Science

Going on a Funny-Faces Hunt Encourage children to scout out things in nature that look like faces. They might find faces in leaves, tree trunks with knots, or even interesting rocks. You may want to bring along rice paper and charcoal for making rubbings.

Flower

Caterpillar

Moth

Beetle

157

Art

Making Funny Faces Have children work together to create funny faces.

> **Materials**
> - construction paper folded into thirds horizontally
> - crayons or markers

Distribute a folded sheet of construction paper to groups of three children. The first child draws eyes and hair on the top section of the paper, folds the picture under, and passes the paper along. The next child draws a nose and ears on the second section, folds the picture under, and passes the paper along. The last child draws a mouth and chin on the bottom section of the paper. Then have children unfold the paper and enjoy the funny faces!

 ★★★ **Multicultural Link**

Appreciating Diversity Once you begin watching, you will see interesting faces everywhere. Start a bulletin board entitled *Love Those Faces.* Encourage children to bring in photos or pictures from magazines and newspapers to show faces they enjoy. Add your own pictures to provide a diversity of faces. Discuss what they find interesting about each face.

  Challenge

Creating New Names Some plants and animals have wonderfully descriptive names, such as *porcupines* and *weeping willows.* Ask children to use their imaginations to rename the living things on this page with names that really describe what they look like.

Reading-Writing Workshop

Writing About Something Silly

Connecting to *The Foot Book*

Invite children to look back at *The Foot Book* and tell what parts of the book were funny or made them giggle. Explain that this kind of writing is called *humor.*

Discussing the Student Models

Tell children that Erik and Thuy drew pictures of something that made them giggle. Invite children to look at the pictures as you read aloud the captions. Discuss what Erik and Thuy wrote about.

Prewriting

Choose a Topic Encourage children to work with a partner to brainstorm something silly they could write about. Invite them to act out what they will draw. If children need help thinking of a topic, make some suggestions, such as a funny animal, a funny person, a silly song, or a humorous adventure.

Plan the Writing Once children have chosen a topic, help them plan what they want to include in their drawings. You may want to have individual conferences with children to help them focus on what they will tell about.

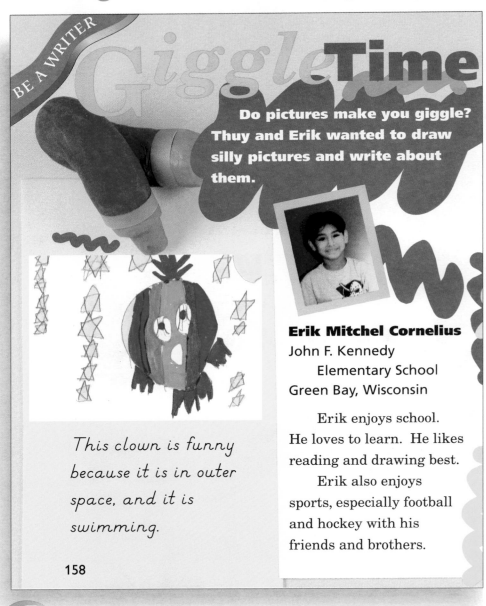

BE A WRITER

GiggleTime

Do pictures make you giggle? Thuy and Erik wanted to draw silly pictures and write about them.

This clown is funny because it is in outer space, and it is swimming.

Erik Mitchel Cornelius
John F. Kennedy Elementary School
Green Bay, Wisconsin

Erik enjoys school. He loves to learn. He likes reading and drawing best.

Erik also enjoys sports, especially football and hockey with his friends and brothers.

158

SKILL FINDER

RESOURCES FOR INSTRUCTION

Theme Resources	Theme Resources
Writing	*Grammar*
● Writing to Tell Where, pp. T250–T251	● Position Words, p. T251
● Writing to Describe a Person, Animal, or Thing, pp. T304–T305	● Using *foot/feet, tooth/teeth,* p. T305
● Writing Names for People, pp. T356–T357	● Special Names for People, p. T357

The cat was growing hair.
The sun was growing hair.
The birds, the butterflies,
and the flowers were growing
hair too.

Thuy Huynh
Navy Point Elementary School
Pensacola, Florida

Thuy is a very good student. She likes math, and she is good in reading, writing, and drawing. Thuy wants to be a firewoman when she grows up. **159**

Drafting

Have children sketch their pictures of something silly. As children draw, move around the room to give help as needed. If children are having trouble starting, prompt them by asking questions such as these: What is it about this idea that makes you giggle? How would you like to show that?

Revising

Tell children they are going to be editors. Have them work in small groups to discuss each other's work. Ask children to share their work with the group and to tell what is silly. Have the writer ask the other children questions such as these: What do you like best about my drawing? Is there anything I should add? Children can then add to their drawings, based on their writing conferences.

Publishing and Sharing

When children have finished their drawings, help those who want to dictate sentences about what they have drawn. Display children's work on a bulletin board under the heading *Silly Things That Make Us Giggle*.

Children can use The Learning Company's new elementary writing center to write, illustrate, and publish their work to share with others.

Building Background

Ask children to tell about some of the different poems they have read. Point out that some poems use beautiful language, while others can be funny.

Discussion

Read the poems aloud together. Then discuss the following questions:

- What happened to the woman in the first poem? Why do you think that?

- Where is the cat in the second poem? How do you know?

- How are these two poems alike?

POEMS AND DRAWINGS
by Shel Silverstein

SNAP!

She was opening up her umbrella,
She thought it was going to rain,
When we all heard a snap
Like the clap of a trap
And we never have seen her again.

160

  Writing

Challenge Ask children to write their own poems about looking for something or someone. Have them first decide a funny place for the missing person or object to be before they begin writing. The hiding place should be a surprise at the end of the poem. Children also may enjoy writing in cooperative pairs.

THE LOST CAT

We can't find the cat,
We don't know where she's at,
Oh, where did she go?
Does anyone know?
Let's ask this walking hat.

161

Background: FYI

In addition to being an author of children's books, Shel Silverstein is also a cartoonist, songwriter, folk-singer, and reporter. You may be familiar with his song, "A Boy Named Sue," which Silverstein wrote and country singer Johnny Cash recorded. In the words of Silverstein, "I want to go every-where, look and listen to everything. You can go crazy with some of the wonderful stuff there is in life."

Books by Shel Silverstein

- *The Giving Tree*
- *A Light in the Attic*
- *Where the Sidewalk Ends*
- *Who Wants a Cheap Rhinoceros?*
- *The Missing Piece Meets the Big O*

Instruct
and
Integrate

Vocabulary

Finding Rhymes Divide the class into teams to play a rhyming game. Write a word on the board that's easy to rhyme, for example, *cat, me,* or *pig*. Ask teams to think of as many rhyming words as they can in a given amount of time. Then have a spokesperson from each team read the list of rhymes. The team with the most rhyming words wins.

ANTHOLOGY

SELECTION:

The Lady with the Alligator Purse

- **Library of Congress Children's Books of the Year**
- **Best Books for Children**
- **Kentucky Bluegrass Award**
- **IRA/CBC Children's Choice**

by Nadine Bernard Westcott

Other Books by the Author

Peanut Butter and Jelly: A Play Rhyme

There's a Hole in the Bucket

I Know an Old Lady Who Swallowed a Fly

Skip to My Lou

Getting Up

Going to Bed

Selection Summary

What silly things happen when Miss Lucy puts her baby, Tiny Tim, in the bathtub to see if he can swim? He drinks all the water, eats all the soap, and even tries to eat the tub! Miss Lucy needs help, and she calls the doctor, the nurse, and the lady with the alligator purse. The doctor thinks Tiny Tim has the mumps, and the nurse thinks he has measles. The lady with the alligator purse thinks it's all nonsense and gives him pizza, and everything turns out fine.

Lesson Planning Guide

	Skill/Strategy Instruction	Meeting Individual Needs	Lesson Resources
1 — **Introduce** *the* **Literature** — *Pacing: 1 day*	**Preparing to Read and Write** Warm-up, T322 Prior Knowledge/Background, T322 **Key Words,** T323 • alligator • nonsense • purse **High-Frequency Words,** T323 • down • had • him • his • if • she	**Other Choices for Building Background,** T323 **Students Acquiring English,** T323 **Extra Support,** T323	**Poster** Warm-up/Building Background, 4D **Transparency** Selection Vocabulary, 4–4 *Literacy Activity Book* Selection Vocabulary, p. 59
2 — **Interact** *with* **Literature** — *Pacing: 1–3 days*	**Reading Strategies** Predict/Infer, T324, T334 Summarize, T324, T340 Think About Words, T326 Evaluate, T330 Monitor, T332 **Minilessons** ✔ Digraphs *sh, th, ch,* T327 Fantasy and Realism, T329 Clusters with *r, s,* T331 ✔ Sequence, T333 Cause and Effect, T335 **Responding,** T348	**Choices for Reading,** T324 **Guided Reading,** T324, T330, T336, T340, T346 **Students Acquiring English,** T334, T345 **Extra Support,** T332, T346 **Challenge,** T335 **Responding Choices,** T349	**Reading-Writing Workshop** Writing About Something Silly, T316–T317 *Literacy Activity Book* Comprehension Check, p. 60 The Learning Company's new elementary writing center software
3 — **Instruct** *and* **Integrate** — *Pacing: 1–3 days*	✔ **Comprehension** Sequence, T350–T351 ✔ **Phonics and Spelling** Initial Digraphs Review, T352 Final Digraphs Review, T353 **Vocabulary** ✔ High-Frequency Words, T354 Contractions with *not,* T355 Career Words, T355 **Language and Writing** Names for People, T356–T357 **Communication Activities,** T358 **Independent Reading & Writing,** T359 **Cross-Curricular Activities,** T360–T362	**Activity Choices/Reteaching** Sequence, T351 **Activity Choices** Initial Digraphs Review, T352 Final Digraphs Review, T353 **Activity Choices** High-Frequency Words, T354 **Activity Choices** Language and Writing, T356–T357	**Reading-Writing Workshop** Writing About Something Silly, T316–T317 **Poster** Comprehension, 4E *Literacy Activity Book* Comprehension Skill, p. 61 Phonics and Spelling, pp. 63–66 High-Frequency Words, p. 67 Vocabulary Skill, p. 68 Language and Writing, p. 69 **Audio Tape** for Get the Giggles: *The Lady with the Alligator Purse* The Learning Company's new elementary writing center software

✔ *Indicates Tested Skills. See page T217 for assessment options.*

Introduce *the* Literature

Preparing to Read and Write

Poster 4D

A hippo yawned
And I looked inside
And saw three monkeys
Taking a ride.
Then one of them yawned
And I looked inside
And there were three bumble bees
Taking a ride.
Then one of them yawned
And I looked inside
And there were three little fleas
Taking a ride.
Then one of them yawned
And I looked inside
And there were three hippos
Taking a ride.

by Arnold Spilka

INTERACTIVE LEARNING

Warm-up

Sharing Poetry

- Read aloud the poem on Poster 4D, emphasizing the name of each animal as it is mentioned.

- Read the poem again, helping children identify the language patterns, the repeating phrases, and the rhyming words.

- Have children form a circle and pantomime the actions as you read the poem once more. One child can be the narrator looking in the animals' mouths, three children can be hippos, three can be monkeys, and so on. Designate one child from each group to yawn.

Prior Knowledge/Building Background

Key Concept
What's real and what's nonsense

- Read the first line of the poem on Poster 4D.

- Invite children who know what a hippo is to tell about it. Ask if they think it's possible for a hippo to yawn.

- Then read the next three lines of the poem and ask children if they think it's possible for three monkeys to take a ride inside a hippo's mouth.

- Explain to the children that most of the poem about the hippo is *nonsense*—something silly that the poet made up just for fun.

- Put the following chart on the board, and help children add to it.

Real	Nonsense
Hippo yawning	Monkeys riding in hippo's mouth
Monkey yawning	Bees riding in monkey's mouth

Selection Vocabulary

Key Words: *alligator, nonsense, purse*

High-Frequency Words: *down, had, him, his, if, she*

Display Transparency 4–4 and read the question aloud, pointing to the alligator purse. Then give children these word clues:

- a word that begins with *d* and means the opposite of *up* (*down*)
- a word that begins with *n* and means the opposite of *sense* (*nonsense*)
- a word that you'd use instead of *he* in a sentence about a girl (*she*)
- a word that you'd use instead of *her* in a sentence about a boy (*him*)
- a word that you'd use instead of *hers* in a sentence about a boy (*his*)

As children guess each word, write them inside the purse. Then have them brainstorm endings for the sentence at the bottom of the transparency.

Vocabulary Practice Have children complete *Literacy Activity Book* page 59.

Transparency 4–4

What's in the alligator purse?

If I had an alligator purse, I would _____

Literacy Activity Book, p. 59

Where's the Baby?

Circle a word to finish each sentence. Color the pictures.

1. "Where is my baby?" said Mrs. ____. dog Alligator
2. Mrs. Alligator called for ____. him his
3. She put down her ____. purse nonsense
4. "Here I am!" said Baby ____. all Alligator
5. "You ____ me with you all the time!" if had

Where was the baby?

Get the Giggles **59**

Picture Walk

Students Acquiring English Have children look at the illustrations on pages 163–171. Invite them to point to and name objects they recognize in the pictures. If they aren't familiar with names, have them ask for help.

Read pages 163–171 to children, pointing to the different characters and objects mentioned. Then ask them if they can guess what will happen after Miss Lucy calls the doctor, the nurse, and the lady with the alligator purse.

Doctors and Nurses

Extra Support Have children tell about times they have been to see the doctor. Ask them if they visited the doctor for a checkup or because they were sick. Did they meet a nurse at the doctor's office? What did he or she do? Help children understand that much of the time doctors and nurses try to keep people from getting sick. However, when people do get sick or hurt, doctors and nurses can help them get better. Encourage children to draw a picture of their doctor or nurse.

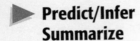

Interact *with* Literature

Reading Strategies

▶ **Predict/Infer**
   Summarize

Student Application Talk with children about how good readers make predictions about a story and stop to think about what has happened so far.

Encourage children to tell how they might make predictions and summarize while reading the selection. Elicit that they should first look at the pictures to predict what might happen. As they read, stop now and then to check their predictions and make new ones. They should also stop to tell the important parts of the story.

Predicting/Purpose Setting

Suggest that children tell what they think might happen to Tiny Tim. Have them record their predictions in their journals and then read to find out if their predictions match the story.

162

Choices for Reading

Teacher Read Aloud

Read aloud pages 163–169 as children look at the pictures. Encourage them to predict what might happen to Tiny Tim. As you read the rest of the story, stop periodically for children to summarize and make new predictions.

Shared Reading

After children have made predictions about what will happen in the story, read the story aloud as they follow along in their books. Invite them to chime in on familiar parts.

Guided Reading

Record children's predictions about what Tiny Tim might do. Then have them read pages 163–169. Use the questions on page T330 to check their comprehension.

Cooperative Reading

Have partners share predictions about the story and then read together, with each child reading aloud one two-page spread. Encourage partners to stop periodically to tell what has happened so far. Check their comprehension after pages 169, 175, 179, and 184.

Independent Reading

Help children establish a purpose for reading, for example, to make predictions and to look for the most important parts of the story. They might note their purposes in their journals. Suggest children read silently and refer back to their purposes.

Miss Lucy <u>had</u> a baby,
<u>His</u> name was Tiny Tim,

163

Interact *with* Literature

Reading Strategies

► **Think About Words**

Ask children how they could figure out the last word on page 165. (*swim*) Discuss the following strategies:

- **What makes sense** In the story, Miss Lucy put Tiny Tim in the tub to see if he could *do* something. This word must be an action word, something someone can do in water, maybe *swim* or *splash*.

- **Sounds for letters** How does the word begin? (with *sw*) How does it end? (with *m*)

- **Picture clues** The picture on pages 164–165 shows Tiny Tim trying to swim. The word is probably *swim*.

Have children read the sentence aloud and discuss whether or not the word *swim* makes sense here.

164

QuickREFERENCE

Environmental Print

Point out the labels on the bubble bath, shampoo, and soap in the picture. Talk about the importance of being able to read such labels.

Health Link

Discuss the importance of keeping one's body clean by taking baths and washing. Point out the toothbrush and the toothpaste in the part of the picture that appears on page 164. Ask how these help keep our bodies clean.

She put <u>him</u> in the bathtub
To see <u>if</u> he could swim.

165

MINILESSON

Phonics/Decoding

Digraphs: sh, th, ch

TESTED SKILL

Teach/Model

Ask a volunteer to read aloud the words on page 165. Then write these words on the board, underlining as shown.

<u>sh</u>e	<u>th</u>ink
bru<u>sh</u>	ba<u>th</u>

Have children listen for the sound for *sh* as they say *she* and *brush*. Review that *sh* stands for a sound that is different from the sound for *s* or for *h* alone. Follow a similar procedure for *think* and *bath*.

Point out the checked pattern of the floor in the picture. Then write these words on the board as shown.

<u>ch</u>eck

ea<u>ch</u>

Help children read the words and identify the letters that stand for the /ch/ sound.

Practice/Apply

Write these words on the board and read them aloud: *chair, cheek, child, chin, sheet, shirt, shoe, thumb, teeth.* Have children work with partners to try to find these objects in the picture on pages 180–181.

SKILL FINDER
Phonics and Spelling, pp. T244, T300, T352

Minilessons, pp. T233, T287, T289

High-Frequency Words

she, him, if

Have children find *she, him,* and *if* on page 165. Point out that *she* means Miss Lucy, and *him* means Tiny Tim. Ask children to look at the picture to see *if* Tiny Tim is swimming.

Interact
with
Literature

He drank up all the water,
He ate up all the soap,

166

167

Comprehension

Fantasy and Realism

REVIEW & MAINTAIN

Teach/Model

Make a chart with the headings *Real Life* and *Make-Believe*. Then reread pages 165–166 with children. Ask if they think it is possible to put a baby in a bathtub. Help children understand that this is a real event (done with little water and close supervision), and record it under *Real Life.*

Then ask children if they think someone could drink all the water in a bathtub in one sitting. Elicit that this would not be possible. Ask if they think that it's likely that a little baby would eat a whole bar of soap and then blow bubbles. Record both items under *Make-Believe.*

Have children discuss if the story is real or make-believe. Lead them to conclude that since the story has some events that could never happen in real life, it is a fantasy.

Practice/Apply

Have children reread the story and complete the chart shown.

Real Life	Make-Believe
• Putting baby in tub	• Drinking a tub full of water
	• Eating up all the soap

SKILL FINDER

Full lesson/Reteaching, pp. T298–T299; Themes 6, 10

Minilesson, p. T283

The Lady with the Alligator Purse

THEME: **GET THE GIGGLES**

Interact *with* Literature

Reading Strategies

▶ **Evaluate**

Invite discussion about the silliness of the story. Review that it is a nonsense story. Have children explain what they think is silly about the story. Ask them if they like stories that are silly. Do children agree or disagree that this is a good story for the theme Get the Giggles?

Guided Reading

Comprehension/Critical Thinking

Compare children's predictions about what would happen to Tiny Tim with the events in the story. Then ask:

1. Why did Miss Lucy put Tiny Tim in the bathtub? (to find out if he could swim) Should a *real* adult do that?

2. Was Tiny Tim able to swim? How do you know? (The picture on pages 164–165 shows him swimming.)

3. What did Tiny Tim do? (drank the water in the tub, ate the soap, tried to eat the tub)

4. How do you know that this is a very silly story?

Predicting/Purpose Setting

Ask children what silly things might happen next. Then have them read pages 170–175 to find out. Use the questions on page T336 to check their comprehension.

168

QuickREFERENCE

High-Frequency Words
down

Ask children to find the word *down* on page 169. Ask them to name a word that means the opposite of *down*. (up) Then ask them to name words that rhyme with *down* such as *brown, clown, town.*

He tried to eat the bathtub,
But it wouldn't go <u>down</u> his throat.

169

Phonics/Decoding

Clusters with *r, s*

Teach/Model

REVIEW & MAINTAIN

Reread the sentence on page 169. Write these words on the board:

try   cry   dry

Have children read the words and then have volunteers underline the letters that stand for the beginning sounds. Follow a similar procedure for these words:

swim   skin
slim   spin

Practice/Apply

Write these words on the board, and help children read them:

scale	frog
sky	brush
slipper	drain
snake	cream
sponge	glass
stool	tray

Ask how many of these words children can find in the pictures on pages 168–169. Which ones name things that you might find in your bathroom? Have each child choose a word to copy and illustrate.

SKILL FINDER

Full lesson/Reteaching, pp. T76, T136, T190

Minilessons, pp. T65, T67, T107, T123, T181

Interact
with
Literature

Reading Strategies

▶ **Monitor**

After children have read pages 163–171, ask them why they think Miss Lucy called a doctor and a nurse. If they have difficulty explaining, have them reread the pages to find out. Encourage children to tell what they did as they read to help themselves. Did they use picture clues? Did they use what they know about real-life and nonsense?

170

Informal Assessment

Oral Reading Use page 171 to informally assess children's oral reading fluency. See the Oral Reading Checklist in the *Teacher's Assessment Handbook* for criteria.

QuickREFERENCE

Phonics/Decoding Review

Ask what Miss Lucy is doing in the picture on page 170. (talking, calling) Write *talk* and *call* on the board. Remind children of the ending *-ing*. Have volunteers write *ing* at the end of each word.

Extra Support

Multiple-Meaning Words Ask what Miss Lucy is doing in the picture on pages 170–171. Point out that *called* means "got in touch by telephone." Ask children to suggest another meaning for *called*. (spoke loudly)

Miss Lucy called the doctor,

Miss Lucy called the nurse,

Miss Lucy called the lady
With the alligator purse.

171

Comprehension

Sequence

TESTED SKILL

Teach/Model

Reread page 171 with children. Then display the following chart.

Miss Lucy called…	In came…
1. doctor	1.
2. nurse	2.
3. lady with the alligator purse	3.

Think Aloud

On page 171, Miss Lucy calls the doctor first, then she calls the nurse, and finally she calls the lady with the alligator purse. I think that this is the order in which she called the people. The events in stories are usually told in the order in which they happened.

Have children read page 172, and add the people's names to the chart to show the order in which they came.

Practice/Apply

Have children add a third column to the chart, headed *Out went. . . .* Have them reread pages 183–184 to decide on the order in which the people went out, and add these names to the chart.

SKILL FINDER

Full lesson/Reteaching, pp. T350–T351; Themes 2, 6, 9

Minilesson, p. T237

Health Link

Ask children what doctors and nurses do. Help them understand that doctors try to keep people healthy and help people get better when they are sick.

★★★ Multicultural Link

In some cultures, women are more likely to be doctors than men are. You may want to ask children from various cultures to tell who the doctors are and whether or not there are nurses.

Interact
with
Literature

Reading Strategies

▶ **Predict/Infer**

Invite children to predict what will happen next in the story. What will the doctor, the nurse, and the lady with the alligator purse do? What might they say to Tiny Tim? Do children think that Tiny Tim will get better?

In came the doctor,
In came the nurse,
In came the lady
With the alligator purse.

172

Self-Assessment

Remind children that good readers check to see if they understand what they are reading and look for important things to remember. Ask children what they have been doing to help themselves understand the story.

- Have I been asking myself questions about the story and looking for answers?
- Have I thought about what the important things to remember in the story are?

QuickREFERENCE

Visual Literacy

Call attention to the body language that Miss Lucy and the girl are using in the picture on pages 172–173. Ask why they are pointing to Tiny Tim's room. Ask why the girl might be waving her left arm. (Her gesture means to hurry.)

Students Acquiring English

Syntax On the board, write these sentences: *In came the doctor. The doctor came in.* Discuss that the lines have the same meaning. Then help children reorder the words in the sentence *In came the nurse.*

173

Comprehension

Cause and Effect

Teach/Model

REVIEW & MAINTAIN

Point out that sometimes events in a story are related and one event is the cause of another. Make a chart as shown and then reread page 165. Discuss with children what Miss Lucy did with Tiny Tim, and enter their responses under *Effect.* Then ask why she put him in the tub, and record children's responses under *Cause.* Help children understand that the cause led to what happened next.

Cause	Effect
(why it happened)	(what happened)
Miss Lucy wanted to see if Tiny Tim could swim.	She put him in the bathtub.

Practice/Apply

Have children reread page 173 and look at the illustrations. Ask them what happened. (The doctor, the nurse, and the lady all came in.) Then have them reread pages 170–171 and ask them what caused them all to come. (Miss Lucy called them.) Record the events in the appropriate columns on the chart. Repeat the procedure for the events on pages 174–179.

SKILL FINDER

Full lesson/Reteaching, pp. T242–T243; Themes 6, 8

Minilesson, p. T235

Challenge

MEETING INDIVIDUAL NEEDS

Synonyms Ask children to look at the illustration and to suggest other words that tell what the doctor, the nurse, and the lady did. Elicit such synonyms for *came* such as *raced, ran,* and *dashed.*

Interact
with
Literature

Guided Reading

Comprehension/Critical Thinking

Compare children's predictions about what silly things would happen with the events in the story. Then discuss these questions:

1. What did Miss Lucy do after Tiny Tim tried to eat the bathtub? (called the doctor, the nurse, and the lady with the alligator purse)

2. Why did Miss Lucy call the doctor and the nurse? (She thought they could help Tiny Tim get well.)

3. What did the doctor think was wrong with Tiny Tim? (He had the mumps.)

4. What did the nurse think was wrong? (Tiny Tim had the measles.)

5. Did the lady with the alligator purse agree with either of them? How do you know? (No. She said *"Nonsense!"*)

6. Why do you think Miss Lucy called the lady with the alligator purse?

Predicting/Purpose Setting

Ask children to predict whether or not the lady with the alligator purse does something silly in the next few pages. Then have them read pages 176–179 of the story to find out what happens.

Informal Assessment

If children's responses indicate that they are understanding the story, have them finish reading it cooperatively or independently.

"Mumps," said the doctor,

174

QuickREFERENCE

Vocabulary

Explain that mumps is a disease that causes the glands at the back of a person's jaw to swell and feel sore. Measles is also a disease; it causes a high fever and a rash. Ask children if they have ever had either of these diseases.

Phonics/Decoding Review

Explain that *mumps* and *measles* are special because they always have a final *s*. Recall with children how to make words plural. Have volunteers add an *-s* or *-es* to *nurse*, *doctor*, and *coach*.

"Measles," said the nurse,

"<u>Nonsense!</u>" said the lady
With the alligator purse.

175

Concepts of Print

Quotation Marks Point out the quotation marks around the words *mumps* and *measles*. Explain that these marks show the exact words someone says. Ask a volunteer to read aloud what the lady with the alligator purse said. *(Nonsense!)*

Health Link

Point out the thermometer in Tiny Tim's mouth. Explain that it is used to take a person's temperature. For most people, normal temperature is 98.6° F. A temperature above that may mean that a person has a fever and is sick.

"Penicillin," said the doctor,

176

QuickREFERENCE

Vocabulary

Explain that *penicillin* can sometimes help sick people get better. Penicillin may be taken orally or in the form of a shot. *Castor oil* is also a medicine; it is made from the seeds of a plant. Castor oil is taken orally and has an unpleasant taste.

"Castor oil," said the nurse,

177

Interact *with* Literature

 Guided Reading

Discuss the silliness of giving pizza to a sick baby. Then ask these questions:

1. What did the doctor, the nurse, and the lady with the alligator purse prescribe to make Tiny Tim get better? (medicine, pizza)

2. How do you think Tiny Tim felt about the pizza? (very happy) How do you know?

3. How did the other people around Tiny Tim's bed feel?

4. Do you think Tiny Tim was really sick? Why or why not?

Predicting/Purpose Setting

Ask children to read to the end of the story, looking for the most important things to remember.

Reading Strategies

▶ **Summarize**

Invite children to tell, in their own words, what has happened thus far in the story. Ask them what parts of the story to include in their summary. Elicit that they should include the names of the main characters and only the most important things that have happened. You may want to remind children that in a nonsense story some things may not make sense. If children disagree on the main events, invite them to page through the story and reread parts they missed.

178

"Pizza!" said the lady
With the alligator purse.

179

★★★ Multicultural Link

Explain that *pizza* means "pie" in Italian. Pizza originated in Naples, a city in Italy. According to legend, it was invented by a baker at the royal court. Today, pizza is enjoyed by people all over the world.

Math Link

The lady seems to be taking big boxes of pizza from her alligator purse. Discuss concepts of size with children. Elicit that it would be impossible to fit boxes of pizza inside a purse. Point out that this is another element of nonsense in the story.

180

QuickREFERENCE

 Journal

Ask children to write a sentence or two about the picture on pages 180–181. They might tell what the people and animals are all doing and how everyone seems to be feeling. They might also write what Tiny Tim is thinking.

181

Math Link

Have children count the pizza boxes in the picture on pages 180–181. (There are twelve.) Have them count how many people (and animals) are eating pizza. Ask if there are more or fewer boxes of pizza than there are eaters. (There are three more.)

182

Out went the doctor,
Out went the nurse,

183

Anthology p. 183

QuickREFERENCE

Students Acquiring English

MEETING INDIVIDUAL NEEDS

Syntax Review the use of inverted word order in the sentence on page 172. Ask children how the lines on page 183 would normally be said. *(The doctor went out; the nurse went out.)*

Interact *with* Literature

Guided Reading

Comprehension/Critical Thinking

Discuss with children how the story ended. Help them understand that it's nonsense to eat as much pizza as the characters in this story have eaten. Everyone would be sick! Then discuss the answers to these questions with children:

1. Who helped Tiny Tim get well? (the lady with the alligator purse)

2. How did she do it? (by giving him lots of pizza)

3. Do you think Tiny Tim liked this "cure"? How do you know?

Out went the lady
With the alligator purse.

184

Self-Assessment

Encourage children to tell about the things they did to sum up the story and to tell what they thought about it.

- Did they think about who was in the story and what happened?
- Did they think about how the story ended?
- Did they try to decide what kind of story this was—silly or serious?

QuickREFERENCE

Extra Support

Rereading Have small groups reread the verses for the various scenes in the selection. Invite each group to choose a favorite scene to read to the whole class.

Multi-Age Classrooms Younger children may enjoy rereading pages 163–169 with a more experienced reader.

Nadine
Bernard
Westcott

likes to make her readers laugh. She writes silly stories that show lots of funny things going on at the same time. She often puts cats in her stories. She draws them with silly faces or doing something silly. Can you find a cat in this story?

185

More About the Author-Illustrator

Nadine Bernard Westcott

Nadine Bernard Westcott started drawing at a very young age, and she remembers sketching on paper place mats at a local restaurant where she ate with her family. Upon entering college, she intended to become a teacher but changed her major to fine arts when she realized that she was spending more time on art than on the subjects she was supposed to be studying!

After college, she worked for a greeting-card company. Later she moved to Vermont, married, had a daughter, and started her own greeting-card business. In her spare time, she began to create children's books. Though her work was not published right away, she kept trying. Finally her talent for creating humorous stories was recognized in 1981, when *I Know an Old Lady Who Swallowed a Fly* was named a Children's Choice book. Other works by Nadine Bernard Westcott include *Skip to My Lou, Getting Up,* and *Going to Bed.*

Interact *with* Literature

Responding Activities

✏ Personal Response

Ask children to think about nonsense things that happened in the story. Have them pick one thing and write or draw about it.

Anthology Activity

Have children work with partners; one child can play Miss Lucy, and the other can play either the doctor, nurse, or the lady with the alligator purse. Encourage children to think about what Miss Lucy would tell the characters and how they might respond. Then have them role-play making telephone calls, taking turns being Miss Lucy.

Give Them a Call!

Use string and two cups to make telephones. Work with a friend.

Now act out the phone calls made in the story.

186

Informal Assessment

Use the Comprehension Check, the Literature Discussion, or the Guided Reading questions to assess children's general understanding of the story.

Additional Support:

- Reread any confusing sections aloud to help children understand the story.
- Have pairs of children go through the story, taking turns explaining what is happening in each scene.

QuickREFERENCE

 Students Acquiring English

You may want to pair children whose first language is English with children acquiring English. Have partners discuss what they will say before they make their phone calls.

 Home Connection

Have children draw a picture of their favorite part of the story to share with their family. Then encourage them to tell family members the story about the lady with the alligator purse.

More Responding Activities

Be the Lady with the Alligator Purse

Students Acquiring English Invite five volunteers to play the parts of Miss Lucy, Tiny Tim, the doctor, the nurse, and the lady with the alligator purse. Have children perform their parts as you read the story aloud.

Sense and Nonsense Chart

Help children make a chart of real things and nonsense things that happened in *The Lady with the Alligator Purse* or one of the other selections in this theme. Have them look through the illustrations to find events that *could* happen in real life and those that are silly and would probably *never* happen.

Real Things	Nonsense Things
• Miss Lucy had a baby.	• Miss Lucy put Tiny Tim in the bathtub to swim.
• Miss Lucy called the doctor.	• Tiny Tim drank all the water in the bathtub.
• Miss Lucy called the nurse.	• Tiny Tim ate up all the soap.

The Way *I* Heard It Was . . .

Tell children that, because this story has been told orally for a long time, there are many different versions of it. Have children suggest alternative words for what the doctor, the nurse, and the lady with the alligator purse said when they saw Tiny Tim. Record their sentences on the board, and invite them to read the story using the new verses.

Literature Discussion
Cooperative Learning

Divide the class into groups of three or four children. Provide the following prompts about this story and other stories in the theme:

- Which part of this story did you think was the silliest? Why?

- Imagine that you are Tiny Tim. What would you like the lady with the alligator purse to bring you? Why?

- Which story in this theme did you like the best? Why?

- How are all of the stories in this theme alike? How are they different?

Comprehension Check

To assess children's understanding of the story, use these questions and/or *Literacy Activity Book* page 60.

1. What made Tiny Tim sick? (drinking water and eating soap)

2. Who did Miss Lucy call to help Tiny Tim? (doctor, nurse, lady with the alligator purse)

3. What helped him get better?

4. Could the things that happened in this story happen in real life?

Portfolio Opportunity

- For a record of selection comprehension, save *Literacy Activity Book* page 60.

- For a writing sample, save children's Personal Response.

Comprehension

Instruct and Integrate

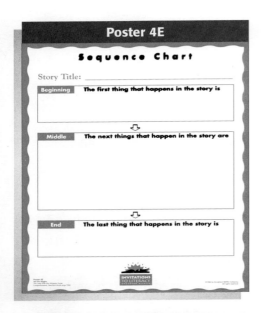

Poster 4E

Sequence Chart

Story Title: _____

Beginning	The first thing that happens in the story is
Middle	The next things that happen in the story are
End	The last thing that happens in the story is

Literacy Activity Book, p. 61

What Happens Next?

Cut out and paste the pictures in order.

Beginning	Middle	End

Write a story about the pictures.

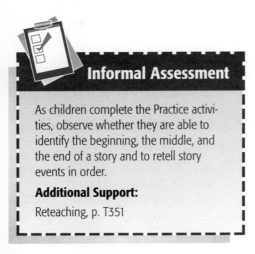

Informal Assessment

As children complete the Practice activities, observe whether they are able to identify the beginning, the middle, and the end of a story and to retell story events in order.

Additional Support:

Reteaching, p. T351

Sequence

LAB, p. 61

Teach/Model

Write headings for the sections of a story across the chalkboard as shown. Then ask a volunteer to pantomime and describe the steps Miss Lucy might follow to give Tiny Tim a bath. After each step, write the child's description below the appropriate heading. Include order words the child uses, such as *first, next, then, last*.

Beginning	Middle	End
First, run the bath water.	Next, undress the baby. Then scrub, scrub, scrub!	Last, dry the baby with a towel.

Explain that each story has a beginning, a middle, and an end, and that events happen in a logical order. Help children complete Poster 4E so that it shows the sequence of events in *The Lady with the Alligator Purse*.

- Read aloud pages 163–165 of the story, and ask children to tell what happens at the beginning. List children's responses in the chart.

- Next, reread the end of the story on pages 183–184, and have children tell you how to complete the part of the chart labeled *End*.

- Explain that all the events between the beginning and the end make up the *middle* of the story. Have children name some of the story events to list in the *Middle* section of the chart.

- Reread the chart with children to verify that the order of events makes sense. Point out the usefulness of words like *first, next, then,* and *last.*

Practice/Apply

- Have small groups identify the beginning, the middle, and the end of another story they have heard or read recently. (Have them choose something other than *The Foot Book* or *On Top of Spaghetti.*) If necessary, reread the story first to refresh their memories.

- Have children complete *Literacy Activity Book* page 61.

SKILL FINDER Minilessons, pp. T237, T333

More Practice Activities

Get Ready to Eat

Recall that the lady with the alligator purse brought pizza for everyone to share. Ask children to tell about things *they* do before, during, and after a meal. (Examples: washing hands, setting the table, eating dinner, clearing the table) Have children draw pictures to show three or more things they do at meal time and number them to show the usual order. Then ask them to dictate sentences that tell about their pictures, encouraging them to use the words *first, next, then,* and *finally*.

Challenge Some children may enjoy writing their own sentences. Display the order words for children's reference. Encourage them to use temporary/invented spellings for other words.

It's a Dog's Life

Tell children to imagine that Miss Lucy put the dog in the bathtub to see if it could swim. Challenge them to draw and write about what might happen. Remind them to tell the events in order. Then invite children to share their new stories.

What Part Am I?
Cooperative Learning

Have children work in pairs. One partner chooses and reads aloud a sentence from *The Lady with the Alligator Purse*. The other partner listens and determines which part of the story (beginning, middle, or end) it is from.

Remind children that each verse ends with a period. Explain that they may have to read more than one page before they come to the end of the verse.

Reteaching

End

> Hold on to your meatball

Middle

> It rolled out the door.

Beginning

> I lost my poor meatball

Reteaching **Sequence**

Reread *On Top of Spaghetti* with children. Then choose Sentence Strips from the beginning, the middle, and the end of the story and help children put them in order. You might want to have children draw pictures to go with the Sentence Strips and put them in order as well.

Portfolio Opportunity

- As a record of children's ability to identify sequence of events, save *Literacy Activity Book* page 61.
- You may want to save children's responses to Get Ready to Eat.

Phonics and Spelling

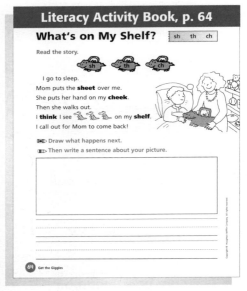

INTERACTIVE LEARNING

TESTED SKILL

Initial Digraph Review
LAB, pp. 63, 64

Write the following story sentences on the board, underlining as shown:

> <u>She</u> put him in the bathtub to <u>see</u> if he could swim.
> He tried to eat the bathtub, but it wouldn't go down his throat.

Ask children to read the first sentence aloud and note the beginning sounds in the underlined words. Ask which of the two words begins with the /sh/ sound. (*she*) Remind children that sometimes two letters stand for one sound. Ask them what letters spell /sh/.

Then have them read the second sentence, listening for the words with the /th/ sound. Have a volunteer underline the letters that stand for this sound each time they appear and identify the words. Then ask children where they hear the sound for *th* in *bathtub*. (middle of the word)

Finally, ask children what other two letters together stand for one sound like *sh* and *th*. (*ch*) Have them think of words that begin with /ch/.

Have children complete *Literacy Activity Book* pages 63, 64.

SKILL FINDER Minilessons, pp. T233, T287, T289, T327

More Practice Activities

Three Cheers!
Cooperative Learning

Invite children to work in small groups to make up cheers using words that begin with *ch, sh,* and *th.* For example:

> *Cheer for the champs.*
> *Charge, charge, charge.*

You might want to have children refer to the Word Wall to help them recall words with digraphs.

Riddle Time
Cooperative Learning

Challenge pairs of children to make up riddles for words that begin with *sh, ch,* and *th*, for example: *I am an animal that says BAAA. What am I?* (a sheep) Have children share their favorite riddles with the class.

Challenge Have children write their riddles on index cards and put the answers on the back.

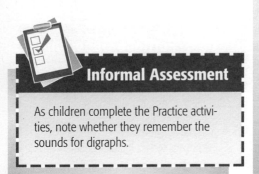

Informal Assessment

As children complete the Practice activities, note whether they remember the sounds for digraphs.

INTERACTIVE LEARNING

Final Digraphs Review

LAB, pp. 65, 66

Write *the lady with the alligator purse* on the chalkboard. Read the phrase aloud, asking children to raise their hands when they hear the /th/ at the end of a word. Invite a volunteer to underline the word that ends with /th/. *(with)*

Recall with children that words can also *end* with the /sh/ and /ch/ sounds. Write this sentence on the board: *I will teach you to wash your face.* Read the sentence and ask children to raise their hands when they hear the /sh/ at the end of a word. Then have a volunteer underline the word that ends with /sh/. Repeat, having children listen for the /ch/.

Have children complete *Literacy Activity Book* pages 65, 66.

SKILL FINDER ▶ Minilessons, pp. T233, T287, T289, T327

Hank and Lin

WATCH ME READ

Hank and Lin
by Stu Goodwin

This story includes words with the digraphs *sh, ch,* and *th* for decoding practice.

Literacy Activity Book, p. 65

Splash in the Bath | sh th ch |

▶ Write **sh, th,** or **ch** to spell the ending sound in each word. Write the words.

1. spla + ___ ___ = ____
2. ba + ___ ___ = ____
3. lun + ___ ___ = ____
4. tee + ___ ___ = ____
5. bea + ___ ___ = ____

Get the Giggles 65

More Practice Activities

Word Sort

MEETING INDIVIDUAL NEEDS

Students Acquiring English
List these words on the board and read them: *tooth, path, beach, peach, lunch, dish, bush, brush.* With children, take turns pantomiming or drawing pictures on the board to convey each word's meaning. Then have each child choose one word and illustrate it on art paper. Children can label their pictures and sort them for display on a bulletin board with sections for *-ch, -sh,* and *-th.*

Rhyme Time

Cooperative Learning

Write the words *ash, brush, dish, bath, teach* on the board. Have pairs of children brainstorm as many rhyming words as they can in a set amount of time. Then have them share their words with the class.

Challenge Have partners write a short poem using the rhyming words.

Literacy Activity Book, p. 66

Bath Time! | sh th ch |

Read the story.

| sh | th | ch |

I go to the **beach**. Then I come back.
I jump into a **bath** to **wash** off the sand.
I **splash** and I drip!

▶ Write about when you take a bath.

_____

66 Get the Giggles

3

Instruct and Integrate

Vocabulary

Hank and Lin
by Stu Goodwin

This story provides practice with the following skills:

- **High-Frequency Words:** *down, had, him, his, if, she*

- **Phonics/Decoding Skills:** Digraphs *ch, sh, th*

- **Cumulative Review:** Previously taught decoding skills and High-Frequency Words

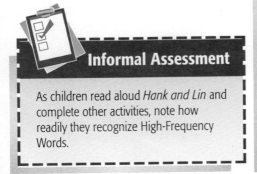

Literacy Activity Book, p. 67

Miss Lucy and Friends

Write the words to complete the rhyme.

| She | His |
| him | had |

Miss Lucy had a big dog.

_____ house was on a hill.
When she called, he ran down.

Miss Lucy called _____ Bill.

Miss Lucy had a fat cat.

_____ called the fat cat Kit.
And if she said, "Come here, Kit."
Kit came to eat a bit.

Miss Lucy _____ a small fish.
She put it on the wall.
"Where is my fish?" Miss Lucy said.
"It is not here at all."

What do you think happened to the fish?

Get the Giggles **67**

Informal Assessment

As children read aloud *Hank and Lin* and complete other activities, note how readily they recognize High-Frequency Words.

 High-Frequency Words: *down, had, him, his, if, she*

Which Word Is Hiding?

Write the following sentences on chart paper. Use self-stick notes to cover the words *had, his, she, him,* and *if*.

> Miss Lucy had a baby,
> His name was Tiny Tim,
> She put him in the bathtub
> To see if he could swim.

- Distribute High-Frequency Word cards to six children and ask them to stand.

- Read each sentence aloud, saying *blank* for each covered word. When you say *blank*, the child with the word that makes sense should come forward, remove the note, and check to see that the words match.

- When all notes have been removed, have children read the lines with you.

- Ask the child with the remaining word card to read his or her word. *(down)* Then ask children who have been standing if they can guess what you would like them to do next. (sit down)

Miss Lucy and Friends

LAB, p. 67

Review the High-Frequency Words with children. Together, read the directions on *Literacy Activity Book* page 67. Have children complete the page and share their work with a partner.

Word Rhymes

Cooperative Learning

Divide the class into groups of three, and give each group the word cards for *down, him,* and *had*. Group members should work together to list as many rhyming words as they can for each word within a set period of time. When time is up, children from each group can share their words.

Rhyme Innovation

Display these lines:

> Miss Lucy had a _____,
> His name was _____,
> She put him in a _____
> To see if he could _____.

Have children copy the sentence frames and complete them to make their own silly sentences. Encourage them to exchange papers and read or sing each other's verses.

M I N I L E S S O N

Vocabulary Skill
Contractions with *not*

LAB, p. 68

Teach/Model   Read aloud page 169 of the story with children. Then write the word *wouldn't* on the board. Ask whether anyone knows another way to say *wouldn't*. *(would not)* Write *would not* on the board. Point out that people sometimes use the shorter form because it is easier to say. Ask children which letter is dropped when the apostrophe is added. *(o)*

Practice/Apply   Write these other expressions with *not* on the board and ask children whether they know a shorter way to say each of them. Have volunteers write the contractions on the board and use them in oral sentences.

could not   was not
is not   have not

Have children complete *Literacy Activity Book* page 68.

M I N I L E S S O N

Vocabulary Expansion
Career Words

Teach/Model   Have children reread page 171, and ask them whom Miss Lucy called when Tiny Tim swallowed the soap and water in the bathtub. Point out that *doctor* and *nurse* are two names for people who help others get well. Have children discuss these jobs. Help them understand that both men and women can be doctors or nurses.

Practice/Apply   Have children brainstorm other occupations and record their responses in a word web on chart paper. Encourage them to talk about what each career entails. Then have them find pictures of people at work, mount them on construction paper, and label them using the sentence *I am a(n)____.* Display the web and the pictures on a bulletin board.

Literacy Activity Book, p. 68

He Couldn't Eat the Bathtub!

Draw a picture and finish the sentence. Make the underlined words shorter.

Example: Tiny Tim could not ____.
Tiny Tim couldn't eat the bathtub.

❶ Tiny Tim would not ____.
Tiny Tim

❷ Miss Lucy was not ____.
Miss Lucy

❸ The lady is not ____.
The lady

68   Get the Giggles

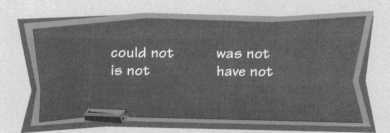

Portfolio Opportunity

- Children's responses to *Literacy Activity Book* page 67 will show how well they read the High-Frequency Words.

- Save *Literacy Activity Book* page 68 as a record of children's ability to form contractions.

Instruct and Integrate

Language and Writing

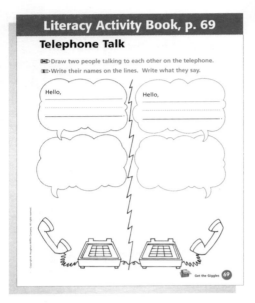

MINILESSON

Writing Names for People

LAB, p. 69

- Write these sentences from the story on the board.

- Read aloud the first two sentences. Point out that *Miss Lucy* and *Tiny Tim* start with capital letters. Ask children to tell you why these words begin with capital letters. (They are people's names.)

- Then read aloud the last sentence. Ask children why *doctor* is not capitalized. (It is not a person's name.)

- Write these sentence frames on the board, and ask children to complete them with people's names.

> Our teacher's name is _____.
>
> Our librarian's name is _____.
>
> Our principal's name is _____.

- Have children complete *Literacy Activity Book* page 69 for practice in writing names for people.

> Miss Lucy had a baby.
> His name was Tiny Tim.
> In came the doctor.

Practice Activities

Call for the Doctor!

Set up a telephone center with toy phones and sheets of paper. Write a sample phone message, and post it in the phone center. Have pairs of children take turns role-playing a phone call:

- One child calls and asks to speak with another person in the class.

- The child answering the phone tells the caller that the person is not available and offers to take a message.

- After the receiver writes the message, pin it on the message board. Remind children to use capital letters when writing the name of the person the message is for, the person who called, and their own name.

Informal Assessment

Check children's understanding of using capital letters to begin people's names.

More Practice Activities

Introducing People

Oral Language Development Have children imagine they are the ones to open the door to each new visitor in the story and they are in charge of introducing the people to each other. Model making an introduction by saying, "Hello, Doctor. I'd like you to meet Miss Lucy and Tiny Tim." Then ask children to take turns introducing the nurse and the lady with the alligator purse to the other characters.

Exclusive Interviews

Oral Language Development Have children brainstorm a list of questions for Miss Lucy, Tiny Tim, or the lady with the alligator purse. Then have volunteers role-play each of the characters. Children can take turns posing their questions to those being interviewed.

Names for People

Grammar Connection Write the following words on the board.

> doctor
> nurse
> lady with the alligator purse

Ask children to create names for each of these story characters. Write the names on the board, and point out the capital letters for each person's name. Then have children think of other professions, such as pizza maker, police officer, basketball player, and singer. Write children's responses on the board, and ask them to brainstorm names of people for each profession. As you write the names on the board, remind children that people's names begin with capital letters.

Children can use The Learning Company's new elementary writing center to write, illustrate, and publish their work to share with others.

Family Names

MEETING INDIVIDUAL NEEDS

Students Acquiring English Have children write the names of people in their families. Write these sentence frames on the board, and have children complete the sentences with names of people in their family:

My mother [or father] has a child. His [or her] name is _____.

My uncle [or aunt] has a sister [or brother]. Her [or his] name is _____.

Write down children's responses, and then have them copy the sentences.

Portfolio Opportunity

- Save *Literacy Activity Book* page 69 as a sample of children's ability to write names for people.

- Save children's written responses to activities on these pages as a sample of their writing development.

3

Instruct *and* Integrate

Communication Activities

Audio Tape
for Get the Giggles: *The Lady with the Alligator Purse*

Tell children to listen for rhyming words. You may also want to have them lightly clap their hands or tap their feet to help them feel the rhythm of the verse.

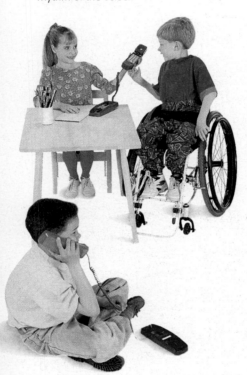

Informal Assessment

As children role-play telephone conversations, note their ability to place and answer phone calls.

Listening and Speaking

How to Eat Pizza

Have children notice all the different ways the characters on pages 180–181 eat their pizza. Then have them notice the mess. Ask each child to think of a rule that would be wise to follow while eating pizza. Point out that since this theme is Get the Giggles, their rules can be silly. Encourage them to take turns sharing their rules.

Telephone Time
Cooperative Learning

Have groups of two to three children role-play making telephone calls. Before children make their calls, have them brainstorm who they want to call and what they want to talk about.

Remind children that it is important to introduce themselves when they call someone on the phone, because the person on the other end of the phone can't see them and might not recognize their voice. However, they should not give their names to strangers who call them.

Tips for Making a Phone Call
- Always be polite.
- Say "Hello" and introduce yourself.
- Ask for the person you want to speak to.
- Say what you would like to say.
- Say "Good-bye" when you are done.

Viewing

Animals Get into the Act

Have children find the dog, the cat, and the frog in the picture on pages 164–165. Then have children choose one of the animals to "follow" through the rest of the story. Does the animal appear in every scene? What is the animal doing? Is it something silly? Children who choose the frog might try to guess where the frog could be hiding in pictures that do not show the frog.

Independent Reading & Writing

Student-Selected Reading

Book Swap

Have a book swap. Write a letter to parents or guardians asking them to send to school books that their children are ready to trade for another. Display all books on a table, and let each child choose a new book to take home.

Book Banners

Invite children to make banners for their favorite books. On a large sheet of paper, have each child write the title of a book and the author's name. Children can illustrate their banners with scenes from the books. Hang the banners around the room.

Student-Selected Writing

Don't Wait

Don't wait until children are writing sentences before having them publish their work. They may want to publish pictures with captions or labels. Share books by Richard Scarry as examples of this form of writing. Publishing provides tremendous motivation for a child at any developmental stage.

Webs

Many children like to use webs to plan their writing. Teach children to write a word for their topic in the center of a page and draw a circle around it. Then show them how to draw lines from the large circle and make smaller circles. Have them write their ideas about the topic in the outer circles.

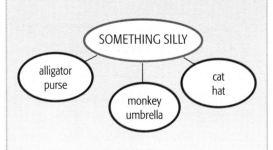

Books for Independent Reading

Encourage children to choose their own books. They might choose one of the following titles.

Hooray for Snail!
by John Stadler

Hank and Lin
by Stu Goodwin

The Lady with the Alligator Purse
by Nadine Bernard Westcott

Have children reread this selection silently or aloud to a partner.

See the Bibliography on pages T212–T213 for more theme-related books for independent reading.

Ideas for Independent Writing

Encourage children to write on self-selected topics. For those who need help getting started, suggest one of the following activities:

- an **illustrated retelling** of a favorite rhyme
- a **description** of a silly animal accessory
- a **different ending** to *The Lady with the Alligator Purse*

Portfolio Opportunity

Save examples of the writing children do independently on self-selected topics.

3

Instruct *and* Integrate

Cross-Curricular Activities

Math

Equal Parts

Cooperative Learning

Recall with children that the lady with the alligator purse gave Tiny Tim pizza to make him feel better. Explain that children are going to figure out how to share pizza evenly.

- Demonstrate making a pizza out of clay. Then ask children how you might share the pizza with three other people.

- Cut the pizza into four obviously unequal pieces and ask children if they think this is a fair way to share it. Discuss why it is not fair, having children think in terms of pieces that are equal in size.

- Distribute materials to groups of different sizes (two to four members) and invite each group to make a model of the pizza with their choice of "toppings." The pizza can be round or rectangular.

- Then have each group use the ruler or another piece of cardboard to cut the pizza into equal portions. Encourage children to share their results with the class, explaining how they know that each group member got an equal part.

Materials
- modeling clay in several colors
- cardboard
- rulers

Social Studies

Interviews with Workers

MEETING INDIVIDUAL NEEDS

Challenge Have children name the people whom Miss Lucy called. Invite volunteers to talk about what doctors and nurses do.

Ask children to think about what they would like to do when they grow up. Suggest that they find out more about each occupation by interviewing someone who has that job or who knows about it. Help children prepare questions to ask. Then have them share their findings.

Materials
- construction paper
- crayons

Name: Elisa Nelson
Job: Firefighter
Who I talked to: Ms. Fries
What the person does: Puts out fires

Science

Floating and Sinking

Cooperative Learning

Recall with children why Miss Lucy put Tiny Tim in the bathtub. (to see if he could swim) Then ask children if they know how to swim or float. Explain that they will do an experiment to see what floats and what doesn't.

- Display several small objects. Survey children as to which objects they think will float and which ones they think won't. Tally and record their responses in a chart.

- Have children work in groups of four. Give each group a container of water and several small objects. Have them try floating each object in a container of water.

- Invite children to discuss the results.

Materials

- large fish tank or deep, clear bowl filled with water
- objects that float or sink

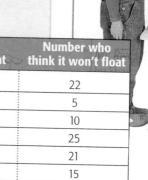

Object	Number who think it will float	Number who think it won't float
banana	3	22
candle	20	5
coconut	15	10
coins	0	25
eraser	4	21
modeling clay	10	15

Health

Staying Healthy

Have children recall why Miss Lucy called the doctor, the nurse, and the lady with the alligator purse. Then ask children to recall what each character said was wrong with Tiny Tim and what they prescribed to make him better. (mumps—penicillin; measles—castor oil, pizza)

- Encourage children to talk about times they have been sick and what they did to get well.

- Discuss with children what they can do to help them stay healthy, and list their ideas on the board.

- Have children draw a picture of one of the ideas. Then create a bulletin board with all of the pictures.

Ways We Stay Healthy

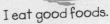

I eat good foods.

I jump rope to stay healthy.

I go to sleep early every night.

I wash my hands before I eat.

3 Instruct and Integrate

Cross-Curricular Activities (continued)

Creative Movement

"Miss Lucy Had a Baby"

Materials
- jump rope

Tell children that *The Lady with the Alligator Purse* is an adaptation of an old jump rope chant. (See page H7 for the tune.)

Assign the parts of Miss Lucy, Tiny Tim, the doctor, the nurse, and the lady with the alligator purse to children. Start with one jumper, Miss Lucy. Have children chant or sing the lyrics while jumping rope. As Tiny Tim, the doctor, the nurse, and the lady with the alligator purse are introduced, have them join "Miss Lucy" jumping rope. As the last verse is recited, have them jump out of the rope.

Art

Animal Purses

Materials
- half-gallon carton
- liquid detergent
- tempera paint
- construction paper
- precut tag-board animal shapes
- glue or paste
- scissors

Invite children to make their own animal purses. First:

- Cut the children's cartons down to a height of about four inches.
- Add a few drops of liquid detergent to the tempera paint.

Have children follow these steps:

1 Paint the sides of the carton.

2 Cut 2" x 18" strips from construction paper. Glue the strips to the sides of the carton to make the handle.

3 Trace and cut out two copies of an animal shape from a sheet of construction paper. Glue the shapes to the carton, one on each side.

Bath Time for Calvin

by Bill Watterson

187

Introduce the Literature

Prior Knowledge

Take an informal survey of the class, asking how many children like bath time and how many do not. Then discuss how children feel about bath time and why they feel that way.

Interact with Literature

Reading the Cartoon

Read the cartoon together, then have children take the parts of Calvin and his mother. Ask children if they think Calvin likes taking baths. Have them explain their answers. Then discuss why it's funny that Calvin is lying in the empty tub.

Instruct and Integrate

  Writing

Making a Comic Strip Talk about times when children might disagree with their parents. Some examples are meal times, getting dressed in the morning, and bedtime. Have children create their own comic strips depicting family times. Have them draw each cartoon box on a separate sheet of paper, then line them up together. Save their work as a part of the Ongoing Project, Our Class Funnies (page T218).

Building Background

Ask if anyone knows what the word *evidence* means. Discuss times when children have left evidence to show parents what they've been doing. Examples of evidence might include cookie crumbs or dirty handprints. Encourage children to look for the evidence in the poem they are about to read.

Discussion

Read the poem with the class. Then discuss the following questions:

- Why did the girl come out pink?

- What is the evidence in the poem?

- What do you think would have happened if the girl had fallen into blueberry jam?

- Do you like this poem? Why or why not?

She Fell into the Bathtub
by Jack Prelutsky

She fell into the bathtub,
She fell into the sink,
She fell into the raspberry jam,
And

came

out

pink.

188

Art

Making Footprint Pictures Invite children to draw footprint pictures that tell a story. Encourage them to brainstorm different types of feet and situations the feet may get into. For example, you might model the activity by showing a picture of the footprints of a bear that has gotten into a honey jar. Children can display their artwork as they tell their stories.

Shake **My Sillies** Out

Gotta **shake, shake, shake** my sillies out,
Shake, shake, shake my sillies out,
Shake, shake, shake my sillies out,
And **wiggle** my waggles away.

Music by
Raffi

Words by
Bert and Bonnie Simpson

189

Introduce the Literature

Building Background

Display the song and read the title aloud. Talk about what the *sillies* might be. When do children feel the sillies? Children who are familiar with Raffi's work may want to talk about their musical experiences as well.

Interact with Literature

Singing the Song

 Audio Tape for Get the Giggles: *The Lady with the Alligator Purse*

Read the song aloud with the class. You may also want to sing along with the song on the audio tape. Challenge children to create movements to accompany the words.

Instruct and Integrate

Art

Drawing Sillies Children will enjoy drawing sillies.

> **Materials**
> - construction paper
> - crayons or markers

Ask children to describe what *sillies, jiggles,* or *waggles* might look like. Then invite them to draw a picture of one of them. Have them describe their art for the class.

Gotta **jump, jump, jump** my jiggles out,
Jump, jump, jump my jiggles out,
Jump, jump, jump my sillies out,
And **wiggle** my waggles away.

Gotta **shake, shake, shake** my sillies out,
Shake, shake, shake my sillies out,
Shake, shake, shake my sillies out,
And **wiggle** my waggles away.

190

Instruct and Integrate

Vocabulary

Finding Action Words Make a collection of action words. Begin with *shake, jump,* and *wiggle* from the song. Challenge children to add more words, along with pictures that illustrate them.

Shake My Sillies Out

Social Studies

Identifying Emotions Talk about other emotions children feel and the circumstances in which they feel them. Examples might be "angries," "happies," or "grumpies." Emphasize that everybody has feelings. Talk about how to express these emotions. Besides shaking and jumping, children might yell or stomp or skip. Sing the song again, replacing words and getting out the new emotions.

Conquering the KneeWobblies Set the stage for talking about KneeWobblies—scary things—by dimming the lights and sitting in a circle. Talk about things that make your knees wobble. Children may be surprised by how many fears they share. To conclude the activity, children can draw KneeWobblies on one side of a sheet of paper and their plan for conquering the KneeWobblies on the other side.

Theme Assessment Wrap-Up

Time: About 1 hour

Evaluates

1. **Theme Concept:** Some stories make us laugh!

2. **Skills:** Cause and Effect; Sequence

This is a brief, informal performance assessment activity. For a more extended reading-writing performance assessment, see the Integrated Theme Test.

Making a Funny Story

LAB, p. 70

Materials
- construction paper
- markers or crayons

Introducing

Tell children they will make up a story about a character who does something silly. Children should be prepared to discuss the consequences of their character's actions. Help children plan their stories on *Literacy Activity Book* page 70. Use the following questions to guide them:

1. What silly thing does your character do?

2. What happens because the character did that?

3. How does your story end?

Literacy Activity Book, p. 70

Making a Funny Story

Plan a funny story.
Who will be in it?

_____

_____

_____

What will happen? Draw or write about it.

FIRST	NEXT	LAST

Now draw your story.
Check your work.

- ☐ I made up a funny story.
- ☐ My story shows what happened first, next, and last.
- ☐ My story shows why something happened.

70 Get the Giggles

Evaluating

Read aloud the checklist on *Literacy Activity Book* page 70. Then let children share their stories with classmates. You might first ask a classmate to take the three pictures and try to put them in sequence before the author tells about the story. If necessary, ask the author to explain how each event led to the next. Evaluate using the scoring rubric.

Scoring Rubric

Criterion	1	2	3	4
The child produces a funny story.	Child does not produce a story of any kind.	Story has no funny or silly elements.	Story has funny elements but is not very coherent.	Story is both funny and coherent.
The story has a clear sequence of events.	Story has no logical sequence.	Sequence of events is not very clear.	Sequence of two events is clear, but not third event.	Sequence of all three events is clear.
The story involves at least one cause and effect.	Story has no cause-effect relationship.	Cause-effect relationship is not clear.	Cause-effect is clear but child cannot explain it.	Clear cause-effect relationship, good explanation

Portfolio Opportunity

- *Literacy Activity Book* page 70
- Save children's funny stories.

Choices for Assessment

Informal Assessment

Review the Informal Assessment Checklist and observation notes to determine:

- How well did children understand the major theme concept and the comprehension skills taught in this theme?

- How well can children apply the new word skills they have learned?

- Did children's reactions to the reading indicate that they enjoyed the theme?

Formal Assessment

Select formal tests that meet your classroom needs:

- Integrated Theme Test for Get the Giggles as well as The World Outside My Door.

- Theme Skills Test for Get the Giggles

See the *Teacher's Assessment Handbook* for guidelines for administering tests and using answer keys, scoring rubrics, and children's sample papers.

Portfolio Assessment

Evaluating *Literacy Activity Book* Pages

Selected pages from the *Literacy Activity Book* are good to include in children's portfolios, as an indication of children's daily work and as a record of their progress in reading comprehension, vocabulary, and skills.

Saving too many *Literacy Activity Book* pages, however, can quickly create a management problem. The tips can help you keep *Literacy Activity Book* pages under control.

- Plan to save only a few *Literacy Activity Book* pages from each theme. Select pages that show important growth or that reflect areas where a child needs more improvement.

- Don't try to grade every *Literacy Activity Book* page. Ungraded pages are often useful as indicators of particularly good work or as confirmation of results from tests or writing samples.

Managing Assessment
Report Cards

Question: How can I use portfolio information to help with report cards?

Answer: Try these tips at report-card time:

- Review each child's portfolio, ordering work chronologically to note changes over time. Use this evidence to help you complete report cards.

- Use the work samples in the portfolio to evaluate several literacy abilities. For example, journal entries provide information about writing to express ideas, invented spelling, and sound-symbol associations. Some *Literacy Activity Book* pages may provide information about reading comprehension, decoding, and writing.

- Use the Theme Assessment Checklist, running records, and anecdotal notes as confirming evidence for the report card.

- *Literacy Activity Book* pages with the portfolio icon are designed to be evaluated and scored easily.

For more information on this and other topics, see the *Teacher's Assessment Handbook*.

Celebrating the Theme

Choices for Celebrating

Did You Ever See a Lassie (or Laddie)?

- Have children stand in a circle with one child in the middle and sing the traditional song "Did you ever see a Lassie?"

- When they get to the part of the song, "go this way and that way," ask the child in the center to pantomime an action from one of the stories in the theme. Ask the rest of the children to imitate him or her.

- When the song stops, have children in the circle guess which scene they were pantomiming.

The Funniest Story

Have children evaluate what stories in the theme were the funniest. You might do the following:

- Reread the three stories. Record (without children noticing) the number of times children laugh. Ask them which book they think is the funniest, then share your results.

- Survey children as to which book they think is the funniest and graph the results.

- Hold a silent vote on which book was funniest. If possible, compare your results with those of another class.

Class Comics Page

If children created comic strips as suggested in Launching the Theme on page T218, publish them in a newspaper format.

- Have children trace over their drawings with a fine-tip black marker.

- Reduce their comic strips on a photocopier so they will fit on one or two sides of legal-size paper.

Make enough copies for every child and fold the pages like a newspaper.

Home Connection Give each child a class comics page to take home and share with his or her family.

Self-Assessment

Have children meet in small groups to discuss what they learned in the theme. Use the following prompts to foster their discussion:

- Which selection in the theme did you like best? Why?

- How can you tell if a book is going to be funny?

- If you had to choose a silly story or a serious story, which one would you choose? Why?

Acknowledgments

ACKNOWLEDGMENTS

For each of the selections listed below, grateful acknowledgment is made for permission to excerpt and/or reprint original or copyrighted material, as follows:

Selections

Bugs!, by Patricia and Fredrick McKissack. Copyright © 1988 by Regensteiner Publishing Enterprises, Inc. Reprinted by permission of Childrens Press.
"Can You Find the Funny Faces in Funny Places?" from the March, Series III issue of *Your Big Backyard* magazine. Copyright © 1984 by The National Wildlife Federation. Reprinted by permission.
Citybook, written by Shelley Rotner and Ken Kreisler, illustrated by Shelley Rotner. Text copyright © 1994 by Shelley Rotner and Ken Kreisler. Illustrations copyright © 1994 by Shelley Rotner. Reprinted by permission of Orchard Books.
The Foot Book, by Dr. Seuss. Copyright © 1968 by Dr. Seuss. Reprinted by permission of Random House, Inc.
"Knock Knock . . . Who's There?" traditional.
The Lady with the Alligator Purse, by Nadine Bernard Westcott. Copyright © 1988 by Nadine Bernard Westcott. Reprinted by permission of Little, Brown & Company.
Listen to the Desert/Oye al desierto, by Pat Mora, illustrated by Francisco X. Mora. Text copyright © 1994 by Pat Mora. Illustrations copyright © 1994 by Francisco X. Mora. Reprinted by permission of Clarion Books, a division of Houghton Mifflin Company. All rights reserved.
Comic strip from *Yukon Ho! A Calvin & Hobbs Collection*, by Bill Watterson. Copyright © 1987 by Bill Watterson. Reprinted by permission of Universal Press Syndicate.

Poetry

"I Love the World," by Paul Wolner, from *Miracles: Poems by Children of the English-Speaking World*, collected by Richard Lewis. Copyright © 1966 by Richard Lewis. Reprinted by permission of The Touchstone Center, New York.
"The Lost Cat," from *A Light in the Attic*, by Shel Silverstein. Copyright © 1981 by Evil Eye Music, Inc. Reprinted by permission of HarperCollins Children's Books, a division of HarperCollins Publishers.
My Street Begins at My House, by Ella Jenkins. Copyright © 1971 by Ella Jenkins, ASCAP. Reprinted by permission of Ell-Bern Publishing.
"Shake My Sillies Out," music by Raffi, words by Raffi and B. & B. Simpson. Copyright © 1977 by Homeland Publishing, a division of Troubadour Records Ltd. Reprinted by permission.
"She Fell into the Bathtub," public domain.
"Sleeping Outdoors," from *Rhymes About Us*, by Marchette Chute. Copyright © 1974 by Marchette Chute. Reprinted by permission of Elizabeth Roach.
"Snap!" from *A Light in the Attic*, by Shel Silverstein. Copyright © 1981 by Evil Eye Music, Inc. Reprinted by permission of HarperCollins Children's Books, a division of HarperCollins Publishers.

"Sunrise," from *City Sandwich*, by Frank Asch. Copyright © 1978 by Frank Asch. Reprinted by permission of Greenwillow Books, a division of William Morrow & Company, Inc.

Special thanks to the following teachers whose students' compositions appear in the Be a Writer features in this level: Sabreen Akbar, William Blackstone Elementary School, Boston, Massachusetts; Leslie Edwards, Ray Clark Elementary School, Tulsa, Oklahoma; Linda Vaile, John F. Kennedy Elementary School, Green Bay, Wisconsin; Ramona Wright, Navy Point Elementary School, Pensacola, Florida.

CREDITS

Illustration 5, 11–37 Fred Willingham; 6, 42 Shari Halpern; 76 Shaleesha Rice; 77 Sheronda Fulton; 80 Mike Reed; 1, 2 (left center), 7, 90–111 Francisco X. Mora; 8, 120 Katherine Tillotson; 9, 121 John Stadler; 8, 122–151 Theodor S. Geisel (Dr. Seuss); 158 Erik Mitchel Cornelius; 159 Thuy Huynh; 160–161 Shel Silverstein; 9, 162–185 Nadine Bernard Westcott; 187 Bill Watterson.

Assignment Photography 10–11, 38, 76–77, 82 (bottom center); 87 Banta Digital Group; 81 Dan Rest; 88–89, 112 (border), 118–124, 152–155, 162, 164–165, 185–186, 188 Tony Scarpetta; 185 Terry Pommett; 39, 40–43 (background), 2 (top), (right center), 75, 78–79, 82–86, 112, 115, 118–121, 186, 189–190, back cover (insets) Tracey Wheeler.

Photography 2 Sandved Photography (b) 10 Courtesy of the McKissacks 38 Courtesy of Fred Willingham 40 ©Wolfgang Kaehler/Liason International (mr); ©Chromosohm/Sohm MCMXC11/The Stock Market (l); © 1994 Zefa Germany/The Stock Market (m); © 1994 Zefa Germany/The Stock Market (m) 44–45 ©Robert Landau/Westlight 44 Courtesy of Ken Kreisler (t); Jose Ramon Garcia/ Courtesy of Shelley Rotner (b) 76 Courtesy of Shaleesa Rice 77 Courtesy of Sheronda Fulton 88 Courtesy of Pat Mora (tl); Courtesy of Francisco X. Mora 113 ©Wolfgang Kaehler/Liason International; Anthony Banister/Natural History Photographic Agency (tl); ©Thomas D. W. Friedman/Photo Researchers (mr); ©Roy Morsch/The Stock Market (bl) 114 Mark Bahti (t,tm,tr); Emil Muench/ Photo Researchers (b) 116 © Photri/The Stock Market 123 Robert Burroughs/Liason International 156 Lynn Stone (tl) 156 ©Kjell B. Sandved/Sandved Photography (b) 157 ©Kjell B. Sandved/Sandved Photography (tl,bl,br); 157 Larry West (bl) 158 Courtesy of Erik Mitchel Cornelius (mr) 159 Courtesy of Thuy Huynh (ml) 185 Terry Pommett/ Courtesy of Nadine Bernard Westcott (tl) 189 Mario Ruiz/Courtesy of Raffi

191

For each of the selections listed below, grateful acknowledgment is made for permission to excerpt and/or reprint original or copyrighted material, as follows:

My River

Text

1 *My River*, written and illustrated by Shari Halpern. Copyright © 1992 by Shari Halpern. Reprinted by permission of Macmillan Books for Young Readers, Simon & Schuster Children's Publishing Division.

Photography

i Tony Scarpetta. **ii** Courtesy of Shari Halpern. **33** Bequest of William Sturgis Bigelow. Courtesy, The Museum of Fine Arts, Boston. **34** ZEFA/The Stock Market (l); N.Y. Gold/ZEFA/The Stock Market (tr); © John Warden/Tony Stone Images Inc. (br). **35** ZEFA/The Stock Market (t); © 1994 Animals Animals/ James D. Watt (bl); © Animals Animals/Richard Shiell (br). **36** © Willard Clay/Tony Stone Images, Inc. (t); © 1992 Ivan Massar/Positive Images (b). **37** Tony Scarpetta (tr, bl, br); Tracey Wheeler (c). **38** Tony Scarpetta (r); Tracey Wheeler (tl, cl, bl).

On Top of Spaghetti

Text

1 *On Top of Spaghetti.* Public domain. **28** "What's Silly?" from *What's Silly?* by Niki Yektai, illustrated by Susannah Ryan. Text copyright © 1989 by Helene Niki Yektai. Illustrations copyright © 1989 by Susannah Ryan. Reprinted by permission of Clarion Books, a division of Houghton Mifflin Company. All rights reserved.

Illustrations

ii Katherine Tillotson (picture frame). **26** Pat Rossi.

Photography

i Banta Digital Group. **ii** Courtesy of Katherine Tillotson (br); Tony Scarpetta (background). **27** Tracey Wheeler (tr); Banta Digital Group (background, c). **28–29** Susannah Ryan.

Teacher's Handbook

Study Skills

Following Directions

INTERACTIVE LEARNING

Teach/Model

Ask children to think of times when they have had to follow directions, and remind them that following directions is a part of many things they do every day. Discuss the important things to keep in mind when following oral and written directions:

- Listen to or read the directions carefully.

- Think about what should be done.

- Do the steps in the correct order.

Display Transparency H–4. Point out that directions for making things often include pictures to help readers see what to do or how the things should look at different steps. Read the transparency with children, modeling how to follow the directions.

Think Aloud

First, I learn what I need: celery, peanut butter, and raisins.

Next, I see that there are five steps. I know from my own experience that probably I should read and do those things in order, beginning with number 1. Now I will read each step carefully and think about it *before* I do it. . . . If I forget what to do, I can always go back and read the steps again. If I follow all the steps correctly, I'll have a snack called "Ants on a Log."

Practice/Apply

Call for volunteers to take turns rereading each step in the directions for "Ants on a Log" and pantomiming what to do. Point out that in recipe directions, items such as a knife, a plate, and water for washing food are usually not listed. You may wish to provide the ingredients so that children can follow the directions for making the snack.

Have children summarize what they have learned about following directions by asking these questions:

- What do the numbers in front of each step tell you when you are following directions?

- What do pictures in a set of directions tell you?

- Why is it important to read and sometimes reread directions carefully?

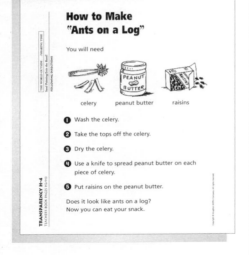

Transparency H–4

How to Make "Ants on a Log"

You will need

celery   peanut butter   raisins

1. Wash the celery.
2. Take the tops off the celery.
3. Dry the celery.
4. Use a knife to spread peanut butter on each piece of celery.
5. Put raisins on the peanut butter.

Does it look like ants on a log?
Now you can eat your snack.

SKILL FINDER Minilesson, p. T203

Study Skills
Parts of a Book

INTERACTIVE LEARNING

Teach/Model

Table of Contents Display any Big Book Plus and ask children where they would find the table of contents. Open the book to that page and ask children to describe what they see. Explain that a table of contents can be found in the front of many books, and that the reader can use it to find different sections inside the book.

Think Aloud

This book looks interesting. To find out what's inside, I'll read the table of contents.... Each entry tells me about a different section of the book. If I want to read *this* section, I look at the number next to the title to find out which page it starts on. Now I'll turn to that page and read the section.

Practice/Apply

Have children turn to the table of contents in their own books, and read the page with them. Reread one of the entries and ask children on what page that section begins. Then invite each child to read the title of a section, name the page where it begins, and turn there to verify the page number. Volunteers may wish to read aloud parts of the sections they choose.

Have children summarize what they have learned about using a table of contents to locate information quickly. Use the following prompts:

- What is a table of contents?
- Where can you find the table of contents in a book?
- What information can you find in there?
- How are tables of contents useful?

SKILL FINDER · Minilesson, p. T227

Shake My Sillies Out

Music by Raffi
Words by Bert and Bonnie Simpson

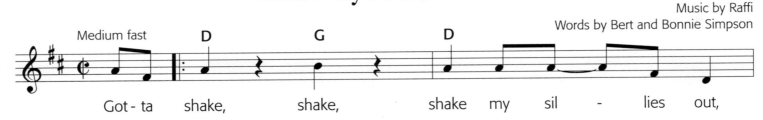

Got - ta   shake,   shake,   shake my   sil   -   lies   out,

Shake,   shake,   shake my   sil   -   lies   out,   Shake,   shake,

shake my   sil   -   lies   out,   And   wig - gle   my   wag - gles   a - way.   2. Got - ta

way.   And   wig - gle   my   wag - gles   a - way.

2. Gotta jump, jump, jump my jiggles out,
   Jump, jump, jump my jiggles out,
   Jump, jump, jump my jiggles out,
   And wiggle my waggles away.

3. Gotta shake, shake, shake my sillies out,
   Shake, shake, shake my sillies out,
   Shake, shake, shake my sillies out,
   And wiggle my waggles away.

On Top of Spaghetti

1. On top of spa - ghet - ti_____ All cov - ered with
(2.) ta - ble_____ And on - to the

cheese,_____ I lost my poor meat - ball_____
floor,_____ And then my poor meat - ball_____

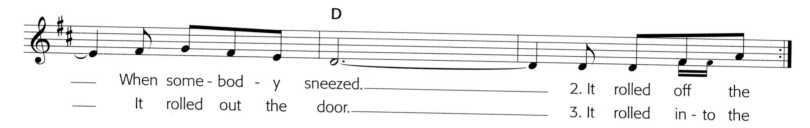

___ When some - bod - y sneezed._____ 2. It rolled off the
___ It rolled out the door._____ 3. It rolled in - to the

3. It rolled into the garden
   And under a bush,
   And then my poor meatball
   Was nothing but mush.

4. And early next summer
   It grew into a tree,
   All covered with meatballs
   As big as could be.

5. So if you eat spaghetti
   All covered with cheese,
   Hold on to your meatball
   And don't ever sneeze!

The Hokey Pokey

Music by Don Fox

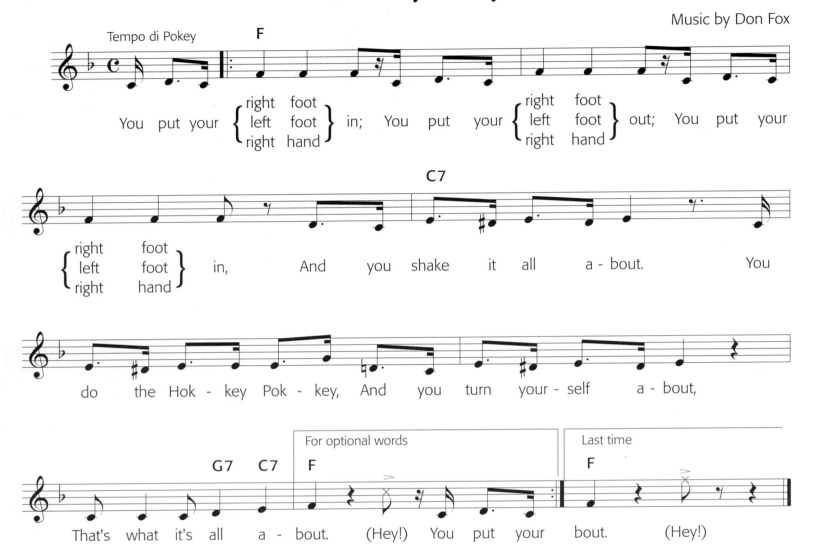

4. Hey, you put your left hand in;
   You put your left hand out;
   You put your left hand in,
   And you shake it all about.
   You do the Hokey-Pokey,
   And you turn yourself about,
   That's what it's all about.

5. Hey, you put your right shoulder in;
   You put your right shoulder out;
   Etc.

6. Hey, you put your left shoulder in;
   You put your left shoulder out;
   Etc.

7. Hey, you put your right hip in;
   You put your right hip out;
   Etc.

8. Hey, you put your left hip in;
   You put your left hip out;
   Etc.

9. Hey, you put your whole self in;
   You put your whole self out;
   Etc.

Miss Lucy Had a Baby

1,2. Miss Lu - cy had a ba - by, She
(3.) drank up all the wa - ter, He

named him Ti - ny Tim. She put him in the
ate up all the soap, He tried to eat the

bath - tub, to see if he could swim. 3. He
bath - tub, But it would - n't go down his throat. 4. Miss

4. Miss Lucy called the Doctor,
   Miss Lucy called the Nurse,
   Miss Lucy called the lady
   With the alligator purse.

5. "Measles," said the Doctor,
   "Mumps," said the Nurse,
   "A virus," said the lady
   With the alligator purse.

6. "Penicillin," said the Doctor,
   "Bed rest," said the Nurse,
   "Pizza," said the lady
   With the alligator purse.

7. "He'll live," said the Doctor,
   "He's all right," said the Nurse,
   "I'm leaving," said the lady
   With the alligator purse.

INFORMAL ASSESSMENT CHECKLIST

Record observations of student progress for those areas important to you.

−　= **Beginning Understanding**
✔　= **Developing Understanding**
✔+ = **Proficient**

Student Names

My River								
Reading								
Responding								
Comprehension: Text Organization and Summarizing								
Phonics and Spelling: Clusters with _r_								
Phonics/Decoding: Think About Words								
Vocabulary: High-Frequency Words								
Listening and Speaking								

Citybook								
Reading								
Responding								
Comprehension: Noting Details								
Phonics and Spelling: Clusters with _l_ and _s_								
Vocabulary: High-Frequency Words								
Listening and Speaking								

Listen to the Desert/Oye al desierto								
Reading								
Responding								
Comprehension: Making Generalizations								
Phonics and Spelling: Review of Clusters								
Vocabulary: High-Frequency Words								
Listening and Speaking								

INFORMAL ASSESSMENT CHECKLIST

Student Names

Record observations of student progress for those areas important to you.

− = **Beginning Understanding**
✔ = **Developing Understanding**
✔+ = **Proficient**

Performance Assessment								

General Observation								
Independent Reading								
Independent Writing								
Work Habits								
Self-Assessment								

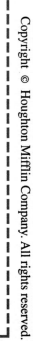

INFORMAL ASSESSMENT CHECKLIST

Record observations of student progress for those areas important to you.

- **–** = **Beginning Understanding**
- **✔** = **Developing Understanding**
- **✔+** = **Proficient**

Student Names

On Top of Spaghetti

Reading									
Responding									
Comprehension: Cause and Effect									
Phonics and Spelling: Digraphs *sh, th*									
Phonics/Decoding: Think About Words									
Vocabulary: High-Frequency Words									
Listening and Speaking									

The Foot Book

Reading									
Responding									
Comprehension: Fantasy and Realism									
Phonics and Spelling: Digraph *ch*									
Vocabulary: High-Frequency Words									
Listening and Speaking									

The Lady with the Alligator Purse

Reading									
Responding									
Comprehension: Sequence									

INFORMAL ASSESSMENT CHECKLIST

Record observations of student progress for those areas important to you.

− = **Beginning Understanding**
✔ = **Developing Understanding**
✔+ = **Proficient**

Student Names

The Lady with the Alligator Purse *(continued)*									
Phonics and Spelling: Review of Digraphs									
Vocabulary: High-Frequency Words									
Listening and Speaking									

Performance Assessment									

General Observation									
Independent Reading									
Independent Writing									
Work Habits									
Self-Assessment									

Audio-Visual Resources

Adventure Productions
3404 Terry Lake Road
Ft. Collins, CO 80524

AIMS Media
9710 DeSoto Avenue
Chatsworth, CA
91311-4409
800-367-2467

Alfred Higgins Productions
6350 Laurel Canyon
Blvd.
N. Hollywood, CA
91606
800-766-5353

American School Publishers/SRA
P.O. Box 543
Blacklick, OH
43004-0543
800-843-8855

Audio Bookshelf
R.R. #1, Box 706
Belfast, ME 04915
800-234-1713

Audio Editions
Box 6930
Auburn, CA 95604-6930
800-231-4261

Audio Partners, Inc.
Box 6930
Auburn, CA 95604-6930
800-231-4261

Bantam Doubleday Dell
1540 Broadway
New York, NY 10036
212-782-9652

Barr Films
12801 Schabarum Ave.
Irwindale, CA 97106
800-234-7878

Bullfrog Films
Box 149
Oley, PA 19547
800-543-3764

Churchill Films
12210 Nebraska Ave.
Los Angeles, CA 90025
800-334-7830

Clearvue/EAV
6465 Avondale Ave.
Chicago, IL 60631
800-253-2788

Coronet/MTI
108 Wilmot Road
Deerfield, IL 60015
800-777-8100

Creative Video Concepts
5758 SW Calusa Loop
Tualatin, OR 97062

Dial Books for Young Readers
375 Hudson St.
New York, NY 10014
800-526-0275

Direct Cinema Ltd.
P.O. Box 10003
Santa Monica, CA 90410
800-525-0000

Disney Educational Production
105 Terry Drive,
Suite 120
Newtown, PA 18940
800-295-5010

Encounter Video
2550 NW Usshur
Portland, OR 97210
800-677-7607

Filmic Archives
The Cinema Center
Botsford, CT 06404
800-366-1920

Films for Humanities and Science
P.O. Box 2053
Princeton, NJ 08543
609-275-1400

Finley-Holiday
12607 E. Philadelphia St.
Whittier, CA 90601

Fulcrum Publishing
350 Indiana St.
Golden, CO 80401

G.K. Hall
Box 500, 100 Front St.
Riverside, NJ 08057

HarperAudio
10 East 53rd Street
New York, NY 10022
212-207-6901

Hi-Tops Video
2730 Wiltshire Blvd.
Suite 500
Santa Monica, CA 90403
213-216-7900

Houghton Mifflin/Clarion
Wayside Road
Burlington, MA 01803
800-225-3362

Idaho Public TV/Echo Films
1455 North Orchard
Boise, ID 83706
800-424-7963

Kidvidz
618 Centre St.
Newton, MA 02158
617-965-3345

L.D.M.I.
P.O. Box 1445
St. Laurent
Quebec, Canada
H4L 4Z1

Let's Create
50 Cherry Hill Rd.
Parsippany, NJ 07054

Listening Library
One Park Avenue
Old Greenwich, CT
06870
800-243-4504

Live Oak Media
P.O. Box 652
Pine Plains, NY 12567
518-398-1010

Mazon Productions
3821 Medford Circle
Northbrook, IL 60062
708-272-2824

Media Basics
Lighthouse Square
705 Boston Post Road
Guildford, CT 06437
800-542-2505

MGM/UA Home Video
1000 W. Washington
Blvd.
Culver City, CA 90232
310-280-6000

Milestone Film and Video
275 W. 96th St.,
Suite 28C
New York, NY 10025

Miramar
200 Second Ave.
Seattle, WA 98119
800-245-6472

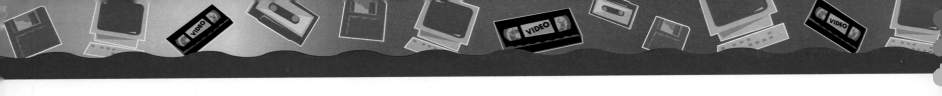

Audio-Visual Resources *(continued)*

National Geographic
Educational Services
Washington, DC 20036
800-548-9797

The Nature Company
P.O. Box 188
Florence, KY 41022
800-227-1114

Philomel
1 Grosset Drive
Kirkwood, NY 13795
800-847-5575

Premiere Home Video
755 N. Highland
Hollywood, CA 90038
213-934-8903

Puffin Books
375 Hudson St.
New York, NY 10014

Rabbit Ears
131 Rowayton Avenue
Rowayton, CT 06853
800-800-3277

Rainbow Educational Media
170 Keyland Court
Bohemia, NY 11716
800-331-4047

Random House Media
400 Hahn Road
Westminster, MD 21157
800-733-3000

Reading Adventure
7030 Huntley Road,
Unit B
Columbus, OH 43229

Recorded Books
270 Skipjack Road
Prince Frederick,
MD 20678
800-638-1304

SelectVideo
7200 E. Dry Creek Rd.
Englewood, CO 80112
800-742-1455

Silo/Alcazar
Box 429, Dept. 318
Waterbury, VT 05676

Spoken Arts
10100 SBF Drive
Pinellas Park, FL 34666
800-126-8090

SRA
P.O. Box 543
Blacklick, OH
43004-0543
800-843-8855

Strand/VCI
3350 Ocean Park Blvd.
Santa Monica, CA 90405
800-922-3827

Taliesin Productions
558 Grove St.
Newton, MA 02162
617-332-7397

Time-Life Education
P.O. Box 85026
Richmond, VA
23285-5026
800-449-2010

Video Project
5332 College Ave.
Oakland, CA 94618
800-475-2638

Warner Home Video
4000 Warner Blvd.
Burbank, CA 91522
818-243-5020

Weston Woods
Weston, CT 06883
800-243-5020

Wilderness Video
P.O. Box 2175
Redondo Beach, CA
90278
310-539-8573

BOOKS AVAILABLE IN SPANISH
Spanish editions of English titles referred to in the Bibliography are available from the following publishers or distributors.

Bilingual Educational Services, Inc.
2514 South Grand Ave.
Los Angeles, CA
90007-9979
800-448-6032

Charlesbridge
85 Main Street
Watertown, MA 02172
617-926-5720

Children's Book Press
6400 Hollis St., Suite 4
Emeryville, CA 94608
510-655-3395

Childrens Press
5440 N. Cumberland
Ave.
Chicago, IL 60656-1469
800-621-1115

Econo-Clad Books
P.O. Box 1777
Topeka, KS 66601
800-628-2410

Farrar, Straus, & Giroux
9 Union Square
New York, NY 10003
212-741-6973

Harcourt Brace
6277 Sea Harbor Drive
Orlando, FL 32887
800-225-5425

HarperCollins
10 E. 53rd Street
New York, NY 10022
717-941-1500

Holiday House
425 Madison Ave.
New York, NY 10017
212-688-0085

Kane/Miller
Box 310529
Brooklyn, NY
11231-0529
718-624-5120

Alfred A. Knopf
201 E. 50th St.
New York, NY 10022
800-638-6460

Lectorum
111 Eighth Ave.
New York, NY 10011
800-345-5946

Santillana
901 W. Walnut St.
Compton, CA 90220
800-245-8584

Simon and Schuster
866 Third Avenue
New York, NY 10022
800-223-2336

Viking
357 Hudson Street
New York, NY 10014
212-366-2000

Index

Boldface page references indicate formal strategy and skill instruction.

Books

for independent reading, T6, T42–
T43, T56, T85, T143, T197,
T212–T213, T255, T307, T319
for shared reading, T43, T213
for teacher read aloud, T43, T195,
T213, T223, T241
See also Paperback Plus books.

Brainstorming, T36, T67, T75, T82,
T84, T95, T99, T139, T141, T143,
T146, T149, T161, T194, T208,
T224, T243, T250, T251, T258,
T277, T297, T305, T308, T312,
T316, T353, T355, T357, T364

C

Categorizing/classifying, T72, T135,
T141, T148, T160, T175, T188,
T189, T195, T205, T223, T225,
T235, T258, T272, **T285,** T291,
T296, T299, T308, T309, T351.
See also Theme 2.

**Cause and effect, T235, T242–T243,
T335.** *See also* Themes 6, 8.

Centers

art, T49, T86, T145, T199, T219,
T254, T310, T362
phonics and word study, T49, T77,
T137, T191, T219, T244, T300
science, T219, T255, T361
social studies, T49, T87, T144
writing and computer, T49, T82,
T187, T194, T219, T241, T297

Character(s)

analyzing, T64, T68, T70, T108,
T130, T133, T155, T156, T187,
T283, T285, T318, T330, T334,
T335, T336, T340, T346, T364
feelings, T134, T156, T278, T340,
T346
traits, T294
understanding, T74

Characters, making inferences about.
See Inferences, making.

Choices for Reading. *See* Reading
modes.

Choral

reading, T5, T54, T55, T75, T80,
T190, T248
speaking, T5, T77, T107, T123, T187

Classifying. *See* Categorizing.

Classroom management, T3, T4, T46,
T49, T85, T97, T143, T159, T197,
T213, T221, T263, T307, T321

Classrooms, multi-age. *See* Multi-age
classrooms.

Cloze reading, T55, T77, T78, T79,
T246, T247, T301, T354

Collaborative learning. *See*
Cooperative learning activities.

Communication activities, T84, T142,
T196, T306. *See also* Listening;
Speaking; Viewing.

Community-school interaction. *See*
*Home/Community Connections
Booklet.*

Compare/contrast, T36, T61, T64,
T68, T84, T133, T150, T172, T184,
T187, T202, T206, T270, T297,
T304, T318, T349

Comparing, T123, T133, T150, T160,
T164, T172, T178, T189, T192,
T199, T249, T255, T265, T278,
T282, T296

Comprehension

assessing, T36, T133, T187, T297,
T349
guided reading, T58, T60, T64,
T68, T70, T108, T114, T120,
T130, T172, T178, T184, T228,
T232, T236, T238, T268, T278,
T284, T290, T294, T324, T330,
T336, T340, T346
interactive learning, T74, T134,
T188

Comprehension skills. *See* Interactive
Learning; Minilessons; Skills,
major; Strategies, reading.

Comprehension strategies. *See*
Strategies, reading.

Computer activities. *See* Technology
resources; Writing skills, word
processor, using.

Concepts of print

book titles, T61
capitalization, T82, T232
ellipsis, T292
exclamation point, T295
poetry, T113, T232

print size, T31, T293
italics, T70
punctuation
exclamation mark, T60
question mark, T59
period, T59
signs, T111, T140, T142, T337
songs, T232
for Spanish-speakers, T60

Conclusions, drawing, T108, T120,
T130, T175, T177, T187, T188, T189,
T227, T232, T238, **T239,** T283,
T294, T298, T329. *See also*
Inferences, making.

Connections

between grammar and writing,
T83, T141, T195, T251, T305,
T357
between reading and writing, T316
between selections, T187, T189,
T208, T349, T370

Consonants

clusters with *l*, **T67, T123, T136,
T138, T181, T190, T191,** T231,
T281
clusters with *r*, **T65, T76, T77, T107,
T181, T190, T191,** T281, **T331**
clusters with *s*, **T67, T123, T137,
T138,** T176, **T181, T190, T191,**
T231, T244, T281, **T331**
digraph *wh*, **T229**
double, T67, T76, T107, T123, T136,
T137, T138, T176, T177, T182,
T190, T191, T231
final, T77, T118, T176, T180, T183,
T185, T244, T249, T279, T301,
T352
initial, T63, T65, T67, T69, T77,
T79, T103, T106, T115, T117,
T118, T121, T125, T137, T170,
T176, T178, T180, T183, T185,
T229, T231, T232, T234, T239,
T244, T278, T279, T286, T287,
T289, T300, T301, T303, T331,
T353
middle, T244, T245

Constructing meaning from text. *See*
Interactive Learning.

Content areas, reading in the
art, T89, T202–T203
language arts, T158–T186

class charts, T133
comparison charts, T150
floor graphs, T223, T308
lists, T82, T99, T140, T141, T161,
T187, T188, T189, T191, T194,
T196, T203, T208, T229, T236
maps, T82, T160, T200
sentence frames, T189, T205,
T354, T356, T357
sentence strips, T55, T75, T78, T80,
T225, T241, T246, T248, T299,
T302, T351
story maps, T83
webs, T181
word webs, T4, T36, T99, T139,
T181, T193, T194, T224, T297,
T355

Guided reading. *See* Reading modes,
guided reading.

High-frequency words, T59, T67, **T80,**
T99, T103, T104, T108, T114,
T125, **T138,** T161, T166, T172,
T174, **T192,** T229, T233, T234,
T236, T238, **T248,** T265, T270,
T275, T277, T278, T281, T284,
T286, T289, T290, T275, T277,
T284, T286, T290, **T302,** T307,
T323, T327, **T354**

High-utility words. *See* Spelling;
Vocabulary, selection.

Home-Community Connections, T93,
T95, T99, T140, T141, T150, T208,
T360, T370

Home Connection, T35, T48, T63,
T116, T131, T140, T186, T222,
T241, T296, T307, T315, T348

Home-school communication. *See*
Home Connection.

Homework. *See* Home Connection.

Homophones, T311

I

Idioms, T104, T110, T311

Illustrating
copied sentences, T233, T241,
T302
ideas, T94, T95, T142, T157, T206,

T360, T361, T366
original writing, T63, T69, T73,
T76, T77, T92, T109, T116,
T133, T136, T141, T194, T224,
T297, T299, T305
prewriting, T147, T161, T186, T191,
T192, T195, T272, T304, T316,
T351, T367
songs, T241
words, T179, T181, T244, T247,
T249, T250, T265, T287, T331,
T353

Illustrators
of Big Book Plus books
Halpern, Shari, T56
Tillotson, Katherine, T226
of Paperback Plus books
Heyman, Ken, T41
of selections in Anthology
Geisel, Theodor Seuss
("Dr. Seuss"), T266
Mora, Francisco X., T163
Westcott, Nadine Bernard,
T347
Willingham, Fred, T34

Independent reading
promoting, T46, T85, T143, T216
student-selected books, T46, T85,
T143, T197, T307
suggestions for, T6, T34, T42–T43,
T56, T85, T143, T197, T212–
T213, T255, T307, T319

Independent reading option. *See*
Reading modes, independent
reading.

Independent writing
promoting, T85, T143, T197
self-selected, T85, T143, T197, T307
suggestions for, T35, T85, T131,
T143, T186, T197, T307

Individual needs, meeting
challenge, T32, T46, T137, T157,
T171, T175, T177, T181, T198,
T213, T234, T236, T240, T241,
T285, T296, T305, T309, T315,
T318, T335, T351, T353, T360
extra support, T5, T25, T46, T55,
T71, T73, T106, T107, T110,
T130, T138, T140, T149, T168,
T174, T180, T189, T200, T213,
T223, T225, T229, T238, T277,

T294, T306, T323, T346
guided reading, T58, T60, T64,
T68, T70, T108, T114, T120,
T130, T172, T178, T184, T228,
T232, T236, T238, T268, T278,
T284, T290, T294, T324, T330,
T336, T340, T346
reteaching, T75, T135, T189, T243,
T299, T351
Students acquiring English, T5,
T27, T46, T61, T72, T83, T99,
T104, T108, T131, T142, T161,
T178, T186, T189, T191, T213,
T223, T230, T233, T235, T251,
T252, T265, T271, T272, T280,
T297, T301, T302, T310, T311,
T323, T334, T345, T348, T349,
T353, T357

Inferences, making
about characters' actions and
feelings, T68, T70, T108, T130,
T133, T134, T155, T156, T278,
T318, T329, T330, T334, T335,
T336, T340, T342, T346, T364
by drawing conclusions, T108,
T120, T130, T175, T177, T187,
T188, T189, T227, T232, T238,
T239, T243, T272, T283, T294,
T298, T318, T329, T364
by drawing on personal experi-
ence, T91, T239, T364
from illustrations, T294, T335,
T342
by predicting, **T17,** T54, T155,
T239, T243, T272, T299, T308.
See also Themes 2, 7, 9.
by understanding cause-effect
relationships, **T235, T242–T243,
T335**

Inflected forms, T127, T332

Informal Assessment Checklist, T47,
T217, H9–H12

Information skills, T48, T53, T58,
T61, T67, T74, T75, T81, T82, T84,
T91, T92, T123, T133, T139, T160,
T191, T198, T234, T255, T309

Integrated Theme Test, T47, T207,
T217

Interactive Learning
building background, **T4, T52, T98,
T160, T222, T264, T322**

comprehension, **T74, T134, T188, T242, T298, T350**

phonics/decoding, **T76, T77, T78, T136, T137, T190, T191, T244, T245, T246, T300, T301, T352, T353**

prior knowledge, **T4, T52, T98, T160, T222, T264, T322**

shared reading and writing, **T54, T224**

study skills, **H2, H3**

theme, launching the, **T48, T218**

Interviewing, T360

Invented spelling, T147, T351

Journal, T26, T62, T105, T130, T179, T228, T232, T236, T268, T272, T295, T307, T324, T342

Knowledge, activating prior. *See* Background, building.

Language and usage

language games, T37, T76, T77, T80, T138, T190, T195, T245, T302, T305, T319, T323, T354

spelling connection, T83, T141, T195, T251, T305, T357

See also Grammar and usage.

Language concepts and skills

alliteration, **T303**

clue words/transition words, T350

colorful language, T196

descriptive language, T161, T180, T181, T193

expressions, T125

idioms, T104, T109

language patterns, T55, T152, T170, T172, T187, T189, T224, T225, T311, T322, T356

nonverbal, T71, T83, T149

onomatopoeia, **T193**

other languages, T17

primary language activities, T17, T72, T83, T119, T161, T189

repeating phrases, T55, T154, T170, T225, T322

rhyming words, T275, T278, T279, T297, T306, T319, T322, T330, T354

sensory words, T170, **T193,** T194, T195

similarities between English and other languages, T17

Spanish words, T166, T168, T170, T172, T177

synonyms, T150, T182, T278, T286, T335

Language mechanics. *See* Mechanics, language.

Learning styles, activities employing alternate modalities to meet individual, T4–T5, T8, T35–T37, T73, T98–T99, T102, T132–T133, T160–T161, T164, T186–T187, T222–T223, T228, T240–T241, T264–T265, T268, T296–T297, T322–T323, T324, T348–T349. *See also* Individual needs, meeting; Reteaching.

Limited English proficient students. *See* Students acquiring English.

Linking literature

to health and safety, T109, T239, T326, T333, T337

to language arts, T166, T172, T177

to math, T64, T282, T291, T341, T343

to multicultural studies, T17, T112, T119, T166, T168, T170, T223, T315, T333, T341

to music, T114

to science, T61, T64, T68, T110, T115, T120, T126, T167, T168, T173, T175, T235, T270, T283, T291

to social studies, T60, T123

to technology, T67, T117, T128

to visual literacy, T31, T70, T71, T105, T111, T116, T155, T167, T179, T182, T184, T279, T334

Listening activities

content

to an audio tape, T43, T55, T84, T142, T195, T196, T225, T251, T306, T365

to book reports, T75

to directions, T80, T182, T200,

T203, T250, T258, T302, T310, T362

to discussion, T4, T8, T9, T11, T17, T19, T31, T33, T53, T66, T69, T71, T79, T89, T90, T93, T94, T98, T112, T139, T142, T149, T151, T160, T204, T241, T243, T244, T245, T255, T257, T258, T265, T268, T281, T283, T285, T306, T309, T311, T326, T350, T355, T360, T361, T366, T367

to dramatics, T73, T74, T84, T142, T200, T257, T304, T348, T363

to introductions, T357

to jump-rope chants, T362

to listening walk, T188

to literature discussion, T58, T61, T73, T75, T92, T93, T130, T133, T146, T148, T150, T152, T170, T186, T187, T191, T224, T225, T232, T238, T241, T268, T270, T283, T297, T299, T318, T322, T329, T340, T349, T363, T365

to oral presentations, T84, T94, T206, T208

to oral reading, T4, T9, T11, T17, T54, T68, T70, T71, T76, T78, T102, T108, T154, T161, T176, T220, T227, T229, T243, T245, T246, T257, T259, T264, T274, T294, T295, T314, T316, T322, T332, T351, T352, T356. *See also* Rereading.

to oral stories, T53, T192, T241, T299

to retelling, T240

to riddles, T190

to singing, T52, T190, T223, T224, T228, T246, T256, T264, T310, T365, T367, T370

to summaries, T33, T69, T72, T108, T340

to teacher modeling, T8, T9, T11, T17, T19, T31, T32, T33, T54, T64, T77, T78, T79, T99, T107, T125, T136, T137,

responding to. *See* Responding to literature.

Little Big Book Plus books
My River by Shari Halpern, T50–T72, T85
On Top of Spaghetti illustrated by Katherine Tillotson, T220–T229

Locating information, T48, T53, T227, H3

M

Main idea and supporting details, identifying, T74, T75, T109, T143, T340

Maps
making, T83, T157, T200
using, T91, T160, T200

Mathematics activities. *See* Cross-curricular activities.

Meaning, constructing from text.
See Interactive Learning; Skills, major; Strategies, reading.

Measuring, T308

Mechanics, language
capitalization
first word in a line, T290
lines of poetry, T113
proper nouns, T83, T356, T357
punctuation
apostrophe, T81, T355
exclamation mark, T60
period, T59, T113, T351
question marks, T59, T314

Media. *See* Cross-curricular activities, media literacy.

Metacognition. *See* Skills, major; Strategies, reading; Think Aloud.

Minilessons
comprehension, **T61, T69, T71, T109, T125, T175, T177, T235, T237, T239, T283, T285, T329, T333, T335.** *See also* Themes 1, 6, 7, 8, 10.
decoding, **T65, T67, T79, T107, T123, T127, T181, T229, T233, T247, T287, T289, T327, T331**
language and writing, **T82, T140, T194, T250, T304, T356**

reading strategies, **T9, T11, T17, T19, T31, T33**
study skills, **T203, T227**
vocabulary
expansion, **T81, T139, T193, T249, T303, T355**
skill, **T81, T139, T193, T249, T303, T355**

Modeling
student, T70, T181, T190, T195, T203, T306, T331
student writing, T73, T82, T133, T141, T146–T147, T189
teacher, T8, T9, T11, T17, T19, T31, T33, T54, T58, T61, T62, T64, T67, T69, T71, T74, T78, T79, T81, T107, T109, T127, T139, T175, T177, T181, T188, T227, T228, T230, T233, T235, T239, T246, T247, T283, T285, T287, T289, T298, T300, T301, T327, T329, T333, T335, T355, T357, T360, T364

Monitoring comprehension option.
See Strategies, reading.

Morphemes. *See* Decoding skills.

Movement, T154, T187, T190, T200, T218, T223, T250, T261, T264, T306, T362, T365, T367, T370

Multi-age classrooms, T71, T130, T238, T294, T346

Multicultural activities/information
bilingual literature, T158–T186
careers, T333
Chinese language, T119
faces, T315
food from different countries and times, T112, T124, T341
Navajo sand painting, T202–T203
words in other languages, T17, T119, T166, T168, T170, T172, T177

Multigenerational activities, T116

N

Narrative text, T2–T35, T50–T72, T93–T94, T102–T131

Newsletter. *See* Home Connection.

Nonfiction, T56–T72, T75, T93–T94, T146–T147, T201

Nouns
names for animals, T69, T70, T79, T160, T174
names for bodies of water, **T81,** T89
names for people, T356, T357
names for places, **T82, T140**
names for sounds, T160, T161, T168, T170, T175, T178, T181, T184, T188, T189, **T193,** T312
names for things in a city, **T139**

Numbers
counting, T291, T296
equal parts, T360
games, T5, T37
practicing, T5, T25, T343
recognizing, T64, T225, T291, T308
sentences, T64

O

Oral
composition. *See* Speaking activities.
language development, T83, T141, T195, T251, T305, T357
presentation, T84, T94, T142, T206, T208
reading, T4, T9, T11, T17, T20, T24, T54, T66, T68, T70, T71, T75, T78, T80, T102, T108, T160, T165, T200, T227, T229, T243, T274, T286, T303, T332, T351. *See also* Rereading.
sentences, T9, T36, T52, T53, T54, T59, T67, T69, T74, T103, T104, T107, T108, T114, T120, T125, T136, T137, T138, T139, T166, T172, T174, T195, T229, T233, T234, T236, T238, T244, T245, T248, T279, T281, T297, T302, T310, T312, T355
stories, T53, T192, T299, T364
summary, T33, T62, T108, T240, T340

types
about what students have learned, T186
addresses, T140
adventure, T143
advertisement, T143
antipollution publicity, T95
books, T73, T307
captions, T186, T191, T192, T197
class letter, T132
class poem, T187, T189
class song, T224
class story, T297
comic strips, T363
complete the story, T65
completing sentences, T81, T188, T354, T357
description of hands, T307
drawing with captions, T85
hometown book, T133
ideas, T272
journal. *See* Journal.
labels, T52, T53, T135, T149, T161, T191, T192, T249, T250, T255, T265, T296
letters, T157, T205
lists, T105
knock-knock jokes, T312
make-believe story, T299
map with labels, T143, T157
messages, T356
mural with rhyming words, T307

names for a scene, T75
new verse, T224, T349
opinions, T141
pet story, T116
phone messages, T356
picture essay with labels, T157
plan for conquering the knee-wobblies, T367
poems, T205, T318, T353
post card, T197
poster, T85, T149
publishing, T186
purpose-setting questions, T269
quick-write, T161
report, T85
riddles, T352
sentences, T36, T73, T79, T92, T109, T136, T161, T190, T342, T351
signs, T149
silly sentences, T229
sound book, T197
song lyrics, T256
speech balloons, T74, T160, T251
stories, T53, T136, T189, T351, T356
super stretched-out sentence, T192
verse, adding another, T187

Writing as a process. *See* Reading-Writing Workshop (process writing).

Writing conferences, T85, T147, T307, T316, T317

Writing skills
copying, T140, T233, T241, T248, T302, T331, T354
describe a person, animal, or thing, **T304–T305**
describe places, **T194–T195**
details, using, T147, T197
drafting, T55, T147, T224, T317
names for bodies of water, **T81**
names for people, **T356–T357**
names for places, **T82, T140**
planning and prewriting, T54, T85, T143, T146, T186, T224, T316
preparing envelopes for mailing letters, T157
process, T85. *See also* Reading Writing Workshop.
publishing, T54, T147, T224, T241, T249, T297, T302, T305, T370
rehearsal. T143
revising, T147, T317
topic, chosing, T146, T316
to tell where, **T250**
word processor, using, T3, T46, T83, T147, T216, T305, T357
See also Language and usage.